Sylvain Mayer

The Law of Agricultural Holdings

comprising the Agricultural Holdings Act, 1893 and County Court rules

Sylvain Mayer

The Law of Agricultural Holdings
comprising the Agricultural Holdings Act, 1893 and County Court rules

ISBN/EAN: 9783337080402

Printed in Europe, USA, Canada, Australia, Japan

Cover: Foto ©ninafisch / pixelio.de

More available books at **www.hansebooks.com**

THE LAW
OF
AGRICULTURAL HOLDINGS

COMPRISING

THE AGRICULTURAL HOLDINGS ACT, 1893, AND COUNTY COURT RULES;

THE LAW OF DISTRESS AMENDMENT ACTS, 1888 & 1895;

THE TENANTS COMPENSATION ACT, 1890; and

THE MARKET GARDENERS' COMPENSATION ACT, 1895.

ALL FULLY ANNOTATED TOGETHER WITH

Two Chapters on the Principles of the Agricultural Holdings Act, 1883, and the Procedure for the Recovery of Compensation.

ALSO AN

APPENDIX OF FORMS AND PRECEDENTS OF AGREEMENTS AND NOTICES.

(*Being in part a third edition and extension of Jeudwine's Agricultural Holdings Act, 1883.*)

BY

SYLVAIN MAYER, B.A. (Lond.), PH. D.

(*Of the Middle Temple, Barrister-at-Law*).

AUTHOR OF "A CODE OF THE LAW OF RATING AND PROCEDURE ON APPEAL, THE FRENCH CODE OF COMMERCE," ETC.

London:
WATERLOW AND SONS LIMITED, LONDON WALL, E.C.
1898.

PREFACE.

ALTHOUGH a portion of this work is offered as a third edition of Mr. Jeudwine's book on the Agricultural Holdings Act 1883, it is, in view of the fact that the second edition of that book was published before the Agricultural Holdings Act 1883 came into force, to all intents and purposes a new work.

The author has endeavoured to incorporate and discuss the numerous decisions that have been given on the law of Agricultural Holdings, and has added the "Law of Distress Amendment Acts 1888 and 1895," the "Tenants Compensation Act 1890," and the "Market Gardeners' Compensation Act 1895," all of which must be read as part and parcel of the Law of Agricultural Holdings.

The County Court Rules applicable to the Agricultural Holdings Act 1883, and the new rules under the Law of Distress Amendment Acts are also included.

There are two introductory chapters, one devoted to the "Principles" of the Agricultural Holdings Act 1883, and the other to the "Procedure" for the recovery of compensation.

In the Appendix the author has retained Mr. Jeudwine's Precedents and Forms with such alterations and modifications as alterations in the law and rules of procedure have rendered necessary. It is hoped that these agreements and clauses will be of assistance to the legal profession in drafting contracts of tenancy.

The author takes this opportunity of thanking Mr. J. S. Henderson, of the Middle Temple, for kindly revising the references to the various cases.

SYLVAIN MAYER.

1, Garden Court, Temple, E.C.
July 1, 1898.

CONTENTS.

	PAGE
Preface	iii.
Table of Cases	vii.

Chapter I.—
    The Principles of the Agricultural Holdings Act, 1883   1

Chapter II.—
    Procedure for the Recovery of Compensation   23

The Agricultural Holdings Act, 1883 (*46 & 47 Vict. c. 61*) 41-99
    Part I.—Improvements .   41
    Part II.—Distress .   84
    Part III.—General Provisions   91
    Schedules .   98

The County Court Rules 1889, Order XL. and Forms 100-106

Law of Distress Amendment Act, 1888 (*51 & 52 Vict. c. 21*) 107-110

Law of Distress Amendment Act, 1895 (*58 & 59 Vict. c. 24*) 111-112

Rules made pursuant to Law of Distress Amendment Acts 1888 and 1895 . . 113-118

CONTENTS.

	PAGE
Tenants Compensation Act, 1890 (*53 & 54 Vict. c. 57*)	119-120
Market Gardeners' Compensation Act, 1895 (*58 and 59 Vict. c. 27*)	121-124
Appendix I.	125-134
FIRST PRECEDENT—AGREEMENT FOR A LEASE	125
SECOND PRECEDENT—DITTO (SHORT FORM)	133
Appendix II.—	
NOTICES TO QUIT AND MISCELLANEOUS FORMS	135-136
Appendix III.—	
FORMS UNDER THE COMPENSATION CLAUSES	136-144
Appendix IV.—	
COUNTY COURT FORMS	145-149
Appendix V.—	
FORMS UNDER DISTRESS CLAUSES	149-150
Index	151

TABLE OF CASES CITED.

A

	PAGE
ASTBURY, *ex parte*, (1869), L.R. 4 Ch. 630 ; 38 L.J. Banky. 9 ; 20 L.T. 997	76

B

BAILY *v.* DE CRESPIGNY, (1869), L.R. 4 Q.B. 180 ; 38 L.J.Q.B. 98 ; 19 L.T. 681 ; 17 W.R. 494 71

BARLOW *v.* TEAL, (1885), 15 Q.B.D. 501 ; 54 L.J.Q.B. 564 ; 54 L.T. 63 ; 34 W.R. 54 ; 50 J.P. 100 . . . . . 3, 74

BEW, *in re, ex parte* BULL. *See* BULL *ex parte, in re* BEW.

BLACK *v.* CLAY, (1894), A.C. 368 ; 71 L.T. 446 ; 6 R. 362 . 53

BRADBURN *v.* FOLEY, (1878), 3 C.P.D. 129 ; 47 L.J.C.P. 331 ; 38 L.T. 421 ; 26 W.R. 423 92

BULL, *ex parte, in re* BEW, (1887), 18 Q.B.D. 642 ; 56 L.J.Q.B. 270 ; 56 L.T. 571 ; 35 W.R. 455 ; 51 J.P. 710 . . . 6, 85

C

COODE *v.* JOHNS, (1886), 17 Q.B.D. 714 ; 55 L.J.Q.B. 475 ; 55 L.T. 290 ; 35 W.R. 47 ; 51 J.P. 21 114

CORNFORTH *v.* GEER, (1715), 2 Vern. 705 . . 63

D

DAVENPORT *v.* REG., (1877), 3 App. Cas. 115 ; 47 L.J.P.C. 8 ; 37 L.T. 727 43

DAVISON *v.* GENT, (1857), 1 H. & N. 744 ; 26 L.J. Ex. 122 ; 3 Jur. N.S. 342 42

	PAGE
DAY, *in re, ex parte* YOUNG, (1879), 41 L.T. 40; 27 W.R. 942	43
DOE *v.* ARCHER, (1811), 14 East. 245	82
DOE *v.* BANCKS, (1821), 4 B. & Ald. 401	43
DOE *v.* COX, (1846), 15 L.J.Q.B. 317; 4 D. & L. 75; 11 Jur. 991	63

E

EAST AND WEST INDIA DOCK CO. *v.* HILL, (1882), 22 Ch. D. 14; 52 L.J. Ch. 44; 47 L.T. 270; 31 W.R. 55	43
EDMUNDS *v.* WALLINGFORD, (1884), 14 Q.B.D. 811; 54 L.J.Q.B. 305; 32 L.T. 720; 33 W.R. 647; 49 J.P. 549	51
ELWES *v.* MAWE, (1802), 2 Smith, L.C. (10 ed.) 183; 3 East. 38; 6 R.R. 523	76
ERNE (Earl of) *v.* ARMSTRONG, (1872), 20 W.R. 370; 6 Ir. R., C.L. 379	42

F

FARQUHARSON *v.* MORGAN, (1894), 1 Q.B. 552; 63 L.J.Q.B. 474; 70 L.T. 152; 42 W.R. 306; 58 J.P. 495	65
FAVELL *v.* GASKOIN, (1852), 7 Ex. 273; 21 L.J. Ex. 85	92
FOULDS, *in re, ex parte* LEAROYD, (1878), 10 Ch.D. 3; 48 L.J. Bank.y. 17; 39 L.T. 525; 27 W.R. 277	89

G

GASLIGHT AND COKE CO. *v.* HOLLOWAY, (1885), 52 L.T. 434; 49 J.P. 344	55
GOUGH *v.* GOUGH, (1891), 2 Q.B. 665; 60 L.J.Q.B. 726; 65 L.T. 110; 39 W.R. 593; 55 J.P. 807	69, 96
GRIFFENHOOFE *v.* DAUBUZ, (1854), 4 E. & B. 230; 24 L.J.Q.B. 20; affirmed at 5 E. & B. 746	51
GRIFFITHS AND MORRIS, *in re*, (1895), 1 Q.B. 866; 64 L.J.Q.B. 386; 72 L.T. 290; 43 W.R. 652; 59 J.P. 134; 15 R. 301	30, 56, 57, 61, 103

H

HANMER v. KING, (1887), 57 L.T. 367 ; 51 J.P. 804 . . 89
HARNETT v. MAITLAND, (1847), 16 M. & W. 257; 16 L.J.Ex.
   134 ; 4 D. & L. 545 51
HART-DYKE, ex parte, in re MORRISH, (1882), 22 C.D. 410 ; 52
   L.J.Ch. 570 ; 48 L.T. 303 . . . . 43, 77
HELLAWELL v. EASTWOOD, (1851), 6 Ex. 295 ; 20 L.J. Ex. 154   76
HIGHAM, in re, (1840), 9 Dowl. 203 59
HOGARTH v. JENNINGS, (1892), 1 Q.B. 907 ; 61 L.J.Q.B. 601 ;
   66 L.T. 821 ; 40 W.R. 517 ; 56 J.P. 485 109
HOLLAND v. HODGSON, (1872), L.R. 7 C.P. 328 ; 41 L.J.C.P.
   146 ; 26 L.T. 709 ; 20 W.R. 990 76
HOLME v. BRUNSKILL, (1878), 3 Q.B.D. 495 ; 47 L.J.C.P. 610 ;
   38 L.T. 838 42
HOLMES AND FORMBY, in re, (1895), 1 Q.B. 174 ; 64 L.J.Q.B.
   391 ; 71 L.T. 842 ; 43 W.R. 205 ; 15 R. 114 . . 51, 54, 64
HUTTON v. WARREN, (1836), 1 M. & W. 466 ; 5 L.J.Ex. 234 ;
   1 T. & G. 646 51

I

INCHIQUIN v. LYONS, (1887), 20 Ir. L.R. 474 .   42

J

JOHNSON v. GOLDSWAINE, (1817), 3 Anstr. 749 . . . 51
JONES v. PHIPPS, (1868), L.R. 3 Q.B. 567 ; 37 L.J.Q.B. 198 ;
   18 LT. 813 ; 16 W.R. 1018 ; 9 B. & S. 761 . . 42

K

KING v. EVERSFIELD, (1897), 2 Q.B. 475 ; 66 L.J.Q.B. 809 ;
   77 L.T. 195 ; 46 W.R. 51 ; 61 J.P. 740 . . 3, 74, 96, 123

L

LATHAM, in re, (1881), 19 Ch.D. 7 ; 51 L.J.Ch. 367 ; 45 L.T.
   484 ; 30 W.R. 144 77

TABLE OF CASES CITED.

                                                                   PAGE

LAVIES, *in re, ex parte* STEPHENS, (1877), 7 Ch.D. 127 ; 47 L.J. Banky. 22 ; 37 L.T. 613 ; 26 W.R. 136 77

LEAROYD, *ex parte, in re* FOULDS. *See* FOULDS, *in re*.

LEVY, *in re, ex parte* WALTON, (1881), 17 Ch.D. 746 ; 50 L.J. Ch. 657 ; 45 L.T. 1 ; 30 W.R. 395 43

LONDON AND YORKSHIRE BANK *v.* BELTON, (1885), 15 Q.B.D. 457 ; 54 L.J.Q.B. 568 ; 34 W.R. 31 ; 50 J.P. 86 . 86

LONGBOTTOM *v.* BERRY, (1869), L.R. 5 Q.B. 123 ; 39 L.J.Q.B. 37 ; 22 L.T. 385 ; 10 B. & S. 852 76

LYON *v.* REED, (1844), 13 M. & W. 285 ; 13 L.J. Ex. 377 ; 8 Jur. 762 42

M

MASTERS *v.* GREEN, (1888), 20 Q.B.D. 807 ; 59 L.T. 476 ; 36 W.R. 591 ; 52 J.P. 597 87

MATHER *v.* FRASER, (1856), 25 L.J. Ch. 361 ; 2 K. & J. 536 ; 2 Jur. N.S. 900 76

MELLOR *v.* WATKINS, (1874), L.R. 9 Q.B. 400 ; 23 W.R. 55 . 42

MEUX *v.* COBLEY, (1892), 2 Ch. 253 ; 61 L.J. Ch. 449 ; 66 L.T. 86 . . . . 51, 77, 122

MILES *v.* FURBER, (1873), L.R. 8 Q.B. 77 ; 42 L.J.Q.B. 41 ; 27 L.T. 756 ; 21 W.R. 262 88

MORDUE *v.* PALMER, (1870), L.R. 6 Ch. 22 ; 40 L.J. Ch. 8 ; 23 L.T. 752 ; 19 W.R. 86 58

MORGAN *v.* DAVIES, (1878), 3 C.P.D. 260 ; 26 W.R. 816 . 74

MORLEY *v.* CARTER, (1898), 1 Q.B. 8 ; 77 L.T. 337 ; 46 W.R. 77 53

MORRISH, *in re, ex parte* HART-DYKE. *See* HART-DYKE, *ex parte*.

N

NICKELL *v.* ATHERSTONE, (1847), 10 Q.B. 944 ; 16 L.J.Q.B. 371 42

O

OASTLER *v.* HENDERSON, (1877), 2 Q.B.D. 575 ; 46 L.J.Q.B. 607 ; 37 L.T. 22 42

P

	PAGE
PAUL, *in re, ex parte* EARL OF PORTARLINGTON, (1890), 24 Q.B.D. 247; 59 L.J.Q.B. 30; 61 L.T. 835; 54 J.P. 644 .	52
PHENÉ *v.* POPPLEWELL, (1862), 12 C.B.N.S. 334; 31 L.J.C.P. 235; 6 L.T. 247; 10 W.R. 523; 8 Jur. N.S. 1104 . .	42
PHILLIPS *v.* REES, (1890), 24 Q.B.D. 17; 59 L.J.Q.B. 1; 38 W.R. 53	114
PORTARLINGTON (Earl of), *ex parte, in re* PAUL. *See* PAUL *in re*.	
PRATT *v.* BRETT (1817), 2 Madd. 62	51

R

REG. *v.* LEE, (1866), L.R. 1 Q.B. 241; 35 L.J.M.C. 105; 7 B. & S. 188; 13 L.T. 704; 14 W.R. 311; 12 Jur. N.S. 225	76

S

SCHOFIELD *v.* HINCKS, (1889), 58 L.J.Q.B. 147; 60 L.T. 573; 37 W.R. 157 . . . . 43, 46,	52
SCOTTISH WIDOWS' FUND *v.* CRAIG, (1882), 20 Ch.D. 208; 51 L.J.Ch. 363; 30 W.R. 463	69
SHRUBB *v.* LEE, (1888), 59 L.T. 376; 53 J.P. 54 . .	60
SIMMONS *v.* NORTON, (1831), 7 Bing. 640; 5 M. & P. 645 .	51
SMITH *v.* ACOCK, (1885), 53 L.T. 230 . . . 41, 49, 54,	97
SMITH *v.* RICHMOND, (1898), 1 Q.B. 683; 67 L.J.Q.B. 439; 78 L.T. 174; 46 W.R. 401 77,	122
STEPHENS, *ex parte, in re* LAVIES. *See* LAVIES, *in re*.	
SWIRE *v.* LEACH, (1865), 18 C.B.N.S. 479; 34 L.J.C.P. 150; 11 L.T. 680; 13 W.R. 385; 11 Jur. N.S. 179 . .	88

T

TANHAM *v.* NICHOLSON, (1872), L.R. 5 H.L. 561 . .	42
TAYLEUR *v.* WILDIN, (1868), L.R. 3 Ex. 303; 37 L.J. Ex. 173; 18 L.T. 655; 16 W.R. 1018	42

V

	PAGE
VIVIAN *v.* MOAT, (1881), 16 Ch.D. 730; 50 L.J. Ch. 331; 44 L.T. 210; 29 W.R. 504	43

W

WALLIS *v.* HANDS, (1893), 2 Ch. 75; 62 L.J. Ch. 586; 68 L.T. 428; 41 W.R. 471; 3 R. 351 42
WALTON, *ex parte, in re* LEVY. *See* LEVY, *in re.*
WATHERELL *v.* HOWELLS, (1808), 1 Camp. 227 . . . 51
WILKINSON *v.* CALVERT, (1878), 3 C.P.D. 360; 47 L.J.C.P. 679; 38 L.T. 813; 26 W.R. 829 74
WRIGHTSON *v.* BYWATER, (1838), 3 M. & W. 199; 7 L.J. Ex. 83 63

Y

YOUNG, *ex parte, in re* DAY. *See* DAY, *in re.*

THE LAW
OF
AGRICULTURAL HOLDINGS.

CHAPTER I.

THE PRINCIPLES OF THE AGRICULTURAL HOLDINGS ACT, 1883.

THE Agricultural Holdings Act, 1883, applies only to those holdings which are "either wholly agricultural or wholly pastoral, or in part agricultural and as to the residue pastoral, or in whole or in part cultivated as a market garden," and it does not apply to any holding let to the tenant during his continuance in any office, appointment or employment of the landlord.

To what holdings the Act applies. S. 54 (a).

It applies only to leases and yearly tenancies (b).

The Law of Distress Amendment Act, 1888, the Law of Distress Amendment Act, 1895, and the Market Gardeners' Compensation Act, 1895 (bb), must also be read and construed as part of this Act. Under the last-named statute if a holding is to be let or treated as a market garden, the parties must so agree in writing.

(a) *Post* p. 91.
(b) See definition of "contract of tenancy" in section 61 of the Agricultural Holdings Act, 1883, *post* p. 94.
(bb) *Post* p. 121.

With the exception of the clauses relating to compensation for *unexhausted improvements*, in respect of which it is professedly compulsory, the Act is permissive. Sect. 55 makes void all contracts, agreements, or covenants, whereby a tenant deprives himself of his right to claim compensation under this Act. Great facilities are, however, given for contracting out of the Act by means of agreements to be substituted for compensation under the Act. If it is desired to exclude it altogether, such clauses as those suggested below (*c*) may be inserted in the agreement, or penal rents may be imposed on the execution of improvements. This course, however, is not advisable, as it would probably result in litigation.

<small>Permissive nature of Act.</small>

<small>S. 55 (*c*).</small>

<small>Ss. 2, 3, 4, 5, 8 (*d*).</small>

<small>Matters dealt with by the Act.</small>

The Act alters the law on the following points:—

(1.) The length of notices to quit.

(2.) The right of a Tenant to fixtures and buildings erected by him.

(3.) The Law and Procedure under a distress.

(4.) The right of a Tenant to have compensation for the unexhausted value of capital laid out upon his holding, called in the Act "com-"pensation for improvements."

Notices to Quit.

<small>Notice to quit under yearly tenancy. Ss. 33, 61 (*f*).</small>

Before the Act where no agreement or custom regulated the length of notice to be given under a

---

(*c*) *Post* p. 91.
(*d*) *Post* pp. 45-49, 54.
(*e*) *Post* p. 18.
(*f*) *Post* pp. 73, 94.

yearly tenancy, *a half-year's notice expiring with a year of the tenancy*, was *by law* necessary to determine it. The Act now makes "*a year's notice so expiring*" Forms 2, 3 (*g*). necessary, and permits a landlord and tenant who wish to exclude this section to do so by writing under their hands. But sect. 33 does not apply where a half- Current tenancies. year's notice or any other notice is expressly stipulated for (*gg*). It has also been decided by the Court of Appeal that a tenancy which provides for three calendar months' notice to quit on any day of the year may nevertheless be a tenancy from year to year (*h*). In what degree the section affects current tenancies is fully considered in the notes to sect. 33. The section is not to apply to a case where the tenant is bankrupt, or has filed a petition for a composition or for arrangement with his creditors.

The Act also makes provision for the landlord Resumption for improvements. taking possession of part of the holding for certain S. 41 (*hh*). purposes (specified in sect. 41). In such a case the landlord gives the tenant notice to quit the part that Form 4 (*i*). he requires, stating the purpose for which he requires it. The tenant may within 28 days after such notice, Form 5 (*k*). if he please, give notice to the landlord that he accepts the landlord's notice as notice to quit the entire holding.

If the tenant, however, accepts the landlord's notice for part of the holding, he will be entitled to a

---

(*g*) Appendix II., *post* p. 135.
(*gg*) *Barlow* v. *Teal*, (1885), 15 Q.B.D. 501 ; 54 L.J.Q.B. 504 ; 54 L.T. 63 ; 34 W.R. 54 ; 50 J.P. 100. *Post* p. 74.
(*h*) *King* v. *Eversfield*, (1897), 2 Q.B. 475 : 66 L.J.Q.B. 809 ; 77 L.T. 195 ; 46 W.R. 51 ; 51 J.P. 740. *Post* pp. 74, 96, 123.
(*hh*) *Post* p. 80.
(*i*) Appendix II., *post* p. 135.
(*k*) Appendix II., *post* p. 135.

proportionate reduction of rent, both in respect of the land comprised in the notice, and in respect of the depreciation in value caused to his holding by the withdrawal of such land from the holding, and he will also be entitled to compensation in respect of any improvements made on such land.

Appendix I, Clause 28 (*l*).

It will probably be found always more convenient to insert in every agreement clause 28 of Appendix I., giving the landlord power to resume without any notice being necessary.

Fixtures.

Fixtures, S. 34 (*m*).

The Act allows the tenant to remove a fixture, machinery or building, erected after the commencement of the Act, to which he would not be entitled to compensation under the first part of the first schedule to the Act.

Form 15 (*n*).

Form 16 (*o*).

Before he does so he must give a month's notice in writing of his intention to remove it. The landlord may then elect to purchase it, and if the parties cannot agree as to its value, disputes will be settled by reference as in case of compensation, but without appeal.

The circumstances under which a tenant may remove fixtures are detailed in sect. 34 of the Act. This section is mainly a re-enactment of sect. 53 of the Agricultural Holdings (England) Act, 1875.

(*l*) *Post* p. 66.
(*m*) *Post* p. 75.
(*n*) Appendix III., *post* p. 139.
(*o*) Appendix III., *post* p. 139.

By sect. 3 of the Market Gardeners' Compensation Act, 1895 (*p*), the provisions of sect. 34 are made to extend to every fixture or building affixed or erected by the tenant to or upon his holding for the purposes of his trade or business of a market gardener.

Distress.

The Law and Procedure under a distress were materially altered by sects. 44-52 of the Act. Sects. 49-52 are repealed by the Law of Distress Amendment Act, 1888, (*q*) and re-enacted with certain additions and modifications. The application of the provisions of the new Act is more general. Besides important modifications in the law and practice of making distress, sect. 46 provides a new method of procedure for the decision of the many vexatious little questions which often arise under a distress; namely, a summary trial either in the County Court or before justices with an appeal to Quarter Sessions. This mode is not compulsory, and the tenant may still, if he pleases, replevy or bring his action in the High Court. Clauses 29 and 13A, *infra*, if inserted in a farming agreement, may save a costly action in the High Court for illegal distress.

<small>Distress.</small>

<small>S. 46 (*r*).</small>

<small>Procedure permissive.</small>

<small>Appendix I, Clauses 29, 13A (*s*).</small>

Sect. 44 limits the landlord's right of distress to one year's rent, but modifies this limitation by a proviso as to rent collected after it becomes legally due.

<small>S. 44 (*t*).</small>

(*p*) *Post* p. 121.
(*q*) 51 & 52 Vict. c. 21, *post* p. 107.
(*r*) *Post* p. 88.
(*s*) *Post* pp. 132, 134.
(*t*) *Post* p. 84.

6   *Principles of the Agricultural Holdings Act*, 1883.

A landlord may distrain for rent legally due, but not payable according to the course of dealing, and also for rent which has become legally due more than a year previously, but had become payable according to the custom of dealing less than a year previously, even although the total amount distrained for exceeds one year's rent (*u*).

<small>Appendix 1, Clause 7 (*x*).</small>

Clause 7 of Appendix I. enabling the landlord to distrain in advance will probably be more often resorted to, and if more than one year's credit is required, the landlord may take a bill of sale over his tenant's effects. This course, however, should not be adopted if it can be avoided.

<small>S. 45 (*y*). Privilege from distress.</small>

Sect. 45 gives a conditional privilege from distress to live stock (defined by sect. 61) which are upon the premises by way of agisting, and absolutely protects machinery, and live stock taken in solely for breeding purposes, and which are on the premises under a *bonâ fide* agreement for hire, and are the *bonâ fide* property of a third person.

<small>S. 47 (*z*). Set-off against rent in arrear.</small>

Sect. 47 provides for a set-off, as against rent in arrear, of compensation ascertained, not only "under the Act," but under "any custom or contract." Other changes made by sects. 5, 6, 7, and 8 of the Law of Distress Amendment Act, 1888 (*a*), are the abolition of appraisement, except in cases where the tenant or owner of the goods and chattels by writing requires

---

(*u*) *Ex parte Bull, in re Bew*, (1887), 18 Q.B.D. 642 ; 56 L.J.Q.B. 270; 56 L.T. 571 ; 35 W.R. 455; 51 J.P. 710.   *Post* p. 85.

(*x*) *Post* p. 126.

(*y*) *Post* p. 85.

(*z*) *Post* p. 90.

(*a*) 51 & 52 Vict. c. 21.   *Post* pp. 107-110.

such appraisement to be made ; extension of time for replevy ; distress to be levied by certified bailiffs, appointed by certificate in writing from the County Court Judge ; and a fresh scale of charges under the rules made pursuant to sect. 8 (*b*).

Compensation.

The main object of the Act, more important than all the matters above mentioned, is *to provide compensation for the tenant*, if he be forced to leave his farm before improvements effected by the capital which he has invested in it have been exhausted. The principle on which the tenant's right to compensation is based "is precisely similar to his right to emblements, which right rests on the principle that a farmer is entitled to reap or be paid for the crop which he has sown, but which he is compelled to leave before it grows ripe." Compensation for improvements. Ss. 1-6 (*c*).

The Act provides a special mode of procedure for the assessment of compensation by referees, with an appeal to the County Court, which will be found set out in the Chapter on Procedure (*d*). Procedure to assess compensation.

The Act only applies to improvements executed before January 1st, 1884 : (1) as to improvements mentioned in the third part of the first schedule (*f*), when they have been executed within ten years previous to that date, (2) as to improvements mentioned in the first or second part of the first Improvements executed before Jan. 1st, 1884. S. 2 (*e*).

(*b*) *Post* p. 110.
(*c*) *Post* pp. 41-51.
(*d*) *Post* p. 23.
(*e*) *Post* p. 45.
(*f*) *Post* p. 99.

schedule (*g*), when they have been executed within ten years previous to that date and the landlord has consented, in writing, to the making of them within one year after that date. In either case only when the tenant is not entitled under any contract, custom, or the Agricultural Holdings Act, 1875, to compensation in respect of them.

Improvements executed after Jan. 1st, 1884, under tenancies current at that date. S. 5 (h).

The Act does not interfere with contracts of tenancy current on January 1st, 1884, where, under any agreement in writing, or custom, or the Agricultural Holdings Act, 1875, "specific compensation" is payable in respect of improvements executed after that date. Compensation will continue to be payable under such agreement, custom, or Act, until the contract of tenancy becomes one beginning after the Act, pursuant to sect. 61 (*i*). Where no such specific compensation is provided, the landlord can exclude the Act, as to the improvements in Part III. of the First Schedule (*k*), by executing a particular agreement with his tenant, providing "fair and reasonable compensation."

Improvements executed under tenancies beginning after 1st Jan., 1884. S. 61 (i).

Current tenancies from year to year soon become tenancies beginning after the commencement of the Act, but the provisions above-mentioned will continue to apply to leases.

S. 1 (l).

(*When right to compensation arises.*)

The "quitting tenant."

The right to compensation only arises on the tenant "quitting his holding on the determination of a

---

(*g*) *Post* pp. 98, 99.
(*h*) *Post* p. 48.
(*i*) *Post* p. 94.
(*k*) Sect. 5, *post* p. 48.
(*l*) *Post* p. 94.

tenancy." No attempt is made to provide for the contingency of the rent being raised upon the tenant's own improvements. Every change of tenancy involves expense and loss to the landlord; the rent could only be raised either with the consent of the tenant, or by serving him with a notice to quit, and if a notice to quit were given by either party the landlord might be liable for compensation; so he is hardly likely to rack-rent the tenant on his own improvements.

Sect. 58 (*m*) provides for compensation for improvements made during a former tenancy, where the tenant continues in his holding during a change of tenancy, as, for instance, where a lessee increases his holding during the currency of a lease. Compensation on change of tenancy.

Where trustees are authorised to lease at the best rent obtainable they need not, in renewing leases, raise the rent on the tenant's improvements. Leases of Trust and Charity lands. S. 43 (*n*).

(*Matters in respect of which compensation may be claimed.*)

The matters in respect of which compensation can be claimed are set out in the three parts of the First Schedule to the Act.

So far as the improvements in Part I. are concerned, matters are left very much as they were before the Act. The *consent of the landlord in writing* must be obtained before they can be executed, and they are generally of a permanent nature and involve a large outlay of capital. The landlord may give his consent upon any terms he pleases, and, in fact, arrange with his tenant as before. Schedule I. Part I. (*o*).

(*m*) *Post* p. 93.
(*n*) *Post* p. 83.
(*o*) *Post* p. 98.

10 *Principles of the Agricultural Holdings Act*, 1883.

Schedule 1, Part 2 (*p*). Drainage.
S. 4 (*q*).
Form 8 (*r*).

Part II. contains only one improvement, namely, Drainage.

Sect. 4 relating to drainage, provides that before drainage can be executed, the tenant must give not more than three and not less than two months' notice in writing of his intention to do the drainage (stating the manner in which he intends to do the work), to the landlord. The Act then provides three alternative modes :—The landlord may do the drainage himself and charge the tenant interest at £5 per cent. on the outlay for any length of time, or such a sum as will repay principal and interest at £3 per cent. in a term not exceeding twenty-five years ; or, the landlord may stand by and see the tenant do the drainage at his own risk ; or the landlord and tenant may agree upon the terms "as to compensation or otherwise on which the improvement is to be executed by the tenant."

Charge of drainage on holding. S. 29 (*s*).

If the landlord do the drainage himself he may charge the cost of it upon the holding.

Drainage by tenant in default.

If the landlord undertakes to drain and does not comply with his undertaking within a reasonable time, the tenant may execute the draining and claim compensation.

Schedule 1, Part 3 (*t*).

Part III. contains some improvements of a durable nature, such as chalking, liming, and so on, and others, the effects of which are very quickly exhausted, such as the application of artificial manures and consumption of feeding stuffs.

(*p*) *Post* p. 99.
(*q*) *Post* p. 46.
(*r*) Appendix III., *post* p. 136.
(*s*) *Post* p. 67.
(*t*) *Post* p. 99.

No consent or notice is necessary before these improvements in Part III. are executed, though notice of claim must be given (*u*).

By sect. 3, sub-sect. (3) of the Market Gardeners' Compensation Act, 1895 (*x*), certain other improvements there mentioned are to be deemed to be comprised in Part III. of Schedule I. of the Agricultural Holdings Act, 1883, where it has been agreed between the parties that the holding shall be let or treated as a market garden.

<small>Market Garden Improvements.</small>

(*Specific and fair and reasonable compensation.*)

The landlord and tenant may exclude the Act, as to the improvements in Part III., by "a particular agreement in writing, providing fair and reasonable compensation."

<small>S. 5 (*y*).</small>

In considering what constitutes such fair and reasonable compensation as would oust compensation under the Act, regard is to be had to the "circumstances existing at the time of making such agreement." Thus a sudden increase in prices, or in the value of the land, will not affect the fairness or reasonableness of an agreement. If this provision is construed liberally, as it ought to be, and the state of things existing at the time of executing the agreement fairly weighed and considered, it ought not to be a difficult matter to draft an agreement providing fair and reasonable compensation. The provisions of the Act itself, taken with the customs of each particular district, will form a fair test of what is fair and reasonable compensation.

(*u*) Appendix III., form 11, *post* p. 137.
(*x*) 58 & 59 Vict. c. 27, *post* p. 121.
(*y*) *Post* p. 48.

How ascertained.
S. 17 (z).
Procedure for reference applies to substituted compensation.

The Act does not provide any means for ascertaining whether compensation by agreement is specific or fair and reasonable. The procedure for reference provided by sect. 17 applies to such substituted compensation only so far as to give the referees power, if compensation is claimed under the Act, to award compensation for improvements provided for by such agreements, "if and so far as the same can, consistently with the terms of the agreement, if any, be ascertained by the referees or umpire" and the award is, when necessary, to distinguish such improvements and the amount awarded in respect thereof.

The effect of the section would, at first sight, appear to be that a tenant might claim compensation under the Act for matters contained in his agreement, and also for matters not covered by the agreement but included in the schedule to the Act, and that he could then obtain compensation for all such matters before a referee. But it must be remembered that the compensation provided by sects. 3, 4, and 5, is to be deemed to be substituted for compensation under this Act; the object of the section is only to give the tenant the option of having the compensation due under his agreement assessed by referees as if it were compensation due under the Act, and it does not give the referee any power of ascertaining the validity and meaning of an agreement; any tenant questioning the agreement on the ground that the compensation is not specific or fair or reasonable, must still seek the assistance of a court of law. It will, however, be very difficult for a tenant to upset the agreement, as

---

(z) *Post* p. 59.

the Court will not give him any assistance unless it is quite clear that the Act has been evaded.

On the other hand, under any agreement providing *substituted compensation* the tenant can always force his landlord to a reference with an appeal to the County Court, unless a provision like clauses 29 or 13*a* of Appendix I. (*b*) is inserted in such an agreement, and, it may be, even in spite of such an agreement. If the tenant claims more than £100 under the Act, and less than £100 is awarded to him, either party may appeal under sect. 23, the test of the right to appeal being whether the sum *claimed* exceeds £100. It will, however, always be worth while, notwithstanding the ambiguous terms of sect. 17, to contract out of the Act, and to provide a mode of assessing compensation. _{Compulsory reference—appeal. Ss. 17, 23 (*a*).}

There is nothing in the Act to prevent a landlord from imposing terms upon his tenant as to what improvements should be executed, or prohibiting him from executing certain improvements without the landlord's consent. Sect. 55 (*c*) only avoids an agreement depriving a tenant of his right to compensation for improvements already executed. If the agreement specifies certain improvements and gives specific compensation for them, stating it to be in substitution for compensation under the Act, such an agreement, even if it contains terms prohibiting improvements or regulating their execution, would hardly be considered by a court of law as unfair or unreasonable. Where an agreement provides for a reduction of rent as _{Landlord may impose terms.}

(*a*) *Post* pp. 59, 62.
(*b*) Appendix I., *post* pp. 132, 134.
(*c*) *Post* p. 91.

compensation in consideration of the tenant executing improvements the fact should be distinctly stated.

(*Basis on which compensation is calculated.*)

S. 1 (*d*).

The basis upon which compensation is to be calculated is to be the "value of the improvement to an incoming tenant," and not as in the Act of 1875 the unexhausted value of the "outlay." The criterion of the value to an incoming tenant will no doubt be in most cases the rental value, and part of this may be due to a general rise in the value of land, or causes other than the making of the improvement. This test of value is, however, limited as follows :—

Restrictions and limitations on compensation.
S. 1 (*d*).

(1.) The valuers are not, in estimating, to take into account what is justly due to the inherent capabilities of the soil.

S. 6 (*e*).

(2.) The landlord may set-off against the tenant's claim arrears of rent, rates, taxes, tithes, waste, damages for breach of covenant, and benefits and allowances made in consideration of the improvements. Notice must be given as pro-

S. 7 (*f*).

vided by sect. 7.

S. 59 (*g*).

(3.) With the exception of the improvements numbered 22 and 23 (*h*), no compensation can be claimed for improvements begun after the following times :—

If the tenant is a yearly tenant, and entitled to a year's notice—within one year before he quits

---

(*d*) *Post* p. 41.
(*e*) *Post* p. 49.
(*f*) *Post* p. 52.
(*g*) *Post* p. 93.
(*h*) *Post* p. 99.

his holding, or after he has given or received notice resulting in his quitting ;—

If he is a yearly tenant, and entitled to six months' notice only—within one year before he quits, if *he* gives notice resulting in his quitting; if he has begun within the year and *his landlord* gives him notice, he may go on and claim ;—

If he is a lessee—within one year before the expiration of his lease.

If the tenant previous to beginning the improvement has given notice of his intention to the landlord, and the landlord has assented, or has failed to object for a month after receipt of notice, the tenant can claim compensation.   Form 10 (*i*).   Consent of landlord.

(4.) Before the tenant can obtain compensation he must have given the notices required by sect. 7.   S. 7 (*k*).

On the other hand, the tenant may add to his claim any sum due in respect of a breach of covenant or other agreement connected with a contract of tenancy and committed by the landlord.   Additions to claim for compensation. S. 6 (*l*).

The "inherent capabilities of the soil" (if it means anything, and was not inserted *ex majori cautelâ*) forms a field for speculation and dispute, as what such capabilities are must rest solely on the diverse decisions of valuers (*m*).   The inherent capabilities.

The provision for set-off does not provide for one very common case. In most leases and agreements   Set-off. What is a benefit. S. 6 (*l*).

(*i*) Appendix III., *post* p. 137.
(*k*) *Post* p. 52.
(*l*) *Post* p. 49.
(*m*) See notes to section 1, *post* p. 41.

the tenant covenants to bring and spread upon the farm yearly so much manure : *i.e.*, without compensation. By the same instrument the rent of the farm is fixed. Now, however (unless the valuers decide that good husbandry only ought not to entitle the tenant to compensation, and that the artificial manure brought on was only sufficient to keep the farm in good condition), the tenant, although he has contracted to incur expenditure without compensation, will be entitled to compensation for keeping his farm in good condition, and the rent fixed can hardly be considered a " benefit " within the section.

Improvements after notice to quit. S. 59 (*n*).

The restriction on the execution of improvements, after notice to quit, will afford no protection to landlords, unless a year's notice to quit is required. If six months' notice has been agreed for, and the tenant begins his improvement before he receive notice, he may finish it after notice, and then claim compensation. This, at any rate, seems to be the meaning of the first proviso of sect. 59.

(*Notice of claim by tenant.*)

Notice of claim.

The tenant intending to claim compensation under the Act must be most careful to give the necessary notices (*o*). Under the Agricultural Holdings Act of 1875, many claims were lost for want of the proper notices. If the tenant give no notice, or give notice too late, he cannot claim under the Act, and must make the best he can of any agreement or custom. It may sometimes, in such a county as Lincolnshire,

---

(*n*) *Post* p. 93.
(*o*) Chapter on Procedure, *post* p. 23.

be of more advantage for tenants to remain under agreement or custom than to give notice under the Act.

On notice being given by the tenant, the landlord and tenant may agree as to the amount, mode, and time of payment of the compensation. *S. 8 (p).*

If they do not agree as to the amount, the landlord may give the tenant a counter-notice of claim, under sect. 7 (*q*), in respect of any waste or breach of covenant or other agreement. If the tenant does not proceed with his claim, there is nothing to prevent the landlord from going on with his counter-claim and obtaining compensation. *Landlord's counterclaim-notice.*

This section will have the effect of preventing an outgoing tenant, whose rent is in arrear, and who leaves his farm in bad condition, claiming compensation from his landlord in the hope of forcing him to a reference, as he may be immediately met by such a counter-claim.

The parties will then proceed to a reference in the manner mentioned in sect. 9, *et seq.* (*r*).

See as to the bankruptcy of the tenant, notes to sect. 1 (*s*).

When the landlord has paid compensation to the tenant, or when he has expended money in doing drainage after notice (*t*), he may obtain from the County Court a charge upon the holding for the amount paid or expended. *Charge on holding, payment and recovery of compensation.*

(*p*) *Post* p. 54. See also Form 13, *post* p. 138.
(*q*) *Post* p. 52.
(*r*) *Post* pp. 55-61.
(*s*) *Post* p. 41.
(*t*) *Ante* p. 10; *post* p. 67.

If the landlord is a trustee he can obtain such a charge before payment (*u*).

The tenant may also in some cases obtain a charge (*x*).

The provisions as to the charge of compensation on the holdings, the payment, and recovery of compensation will be found set out in the Chapter on Procedure (*y*).

(*Precedents of Agreements.*)

Evading the Act. There is no clause in the Precedents in Appendix I. providing for evading the Act; but the Act could possibly be evaded by inserting, as a rent for the last year of the tenancy, a sum roughly calculated to recoup compensation, and then, providing that if the tenant shall not in the last year of the tenancy execute any improvement upon the farm in respect of which he might claim compensation under the Act, or shall not put on the land certain specified artificial manures without first obtaining his landlord's consent in writing, the landlord should accept rent for the last year at the same rate as for the other years; or, providing that the tenant should, on quitting, accept a sum equal in amount to the increase in the last year's rent as compensation for every matter in respect of which he is entitled to compensation.

The second Precedent (*z*) is intended for use when a form is required in haste, or where it is not necessary to reduce all the terms to writing.

(*u*) Section 31, *post* p. 71.
(*x*) Sections 30, 31, *post* p. 71.
(*y*) Chapter II., *post* p. 23.
(*z*) Appendix I., *post* p. 133.

A few remarks may here be made about the clauses and objects of the first Precedent (a).

Clause 2 excludes sect. 33 of the Act, providing for one year's notice to quit. It may be questionable, however, whether it is expedient to exclude this section, having regard to the provisions of sect. 59. *Notice to quit.*

The clauses will necessarily be modified according to the customs, and the different relations of landlord and tenant in the different counties. The rents and penalties in clause 5 (b) will not by any means be universally applicable. Tenants in some counties are allowed great liberty as to rotation of crops, and as to the crops to be put upon the land, and at the present day it is inexpedient to press a tenant too closely. *Rents and penalties.*

The same remark applies to clause 7 (c). In some counties no tenant would accept such a clause. In others it is frequent; in others it is only the last half-year's rent which is made payable in advance. Its effect is that, if the landlord is compelled to distrain, he can distrain for one year and a half's rent " accrued due." *Rent payable in advance.*

The agreement for compensation (d) referring to the second schedule of the agreement, clause 12 (e) providing for payment of compensation by the incoming to the outgoing tenant, and the second schedule itself, only extend to the matters in Part III. of the First Schedule to the Act (f). In practice the *Compensation.*

(a) Appendix I., *post* p. 125.
(b) Appendix I., *post* p. 126.
(c) Appendix I., *post* p. 126.
(d) Clause 10 of First Precedent, Appendix I., *post* p. 127.
(e) Appendix I., *post* p. 128.
(f) *Post* p. 99.

compensation for the permanent and durable improvements will be paid by the landlord, but for the transient improvements such as manures and feeding stuffs by the incoming tenant just as he now pays for seeds and tillages. The incoming tenant may leave himself before the value of a durable improvement is exhausted.

By whom paid.

If the landlord and tenant come to any agreement as to the execution of matters in Part I., they will probably do so by a separate agreement.

Drainage.

Clauses 9 (*g*) and 18 (*h*) provide an agreement for drainage. Independently of such an agreement there is no clause in the Act giving the landlord any power to drain and charge the holding in the first instance where he has an obstinate tenant who refuses to drain. He must either give his tenant notice to quit, or do it himself under clause 3 (*i*) at his own expense, and charge the holding under section 29 (*k*) of the Act with the amount.

Cultivation.

As above mentioned the clauses as to cultivation may be dispensed with or greatly modified according to the variety of soils and climates in the country. Those in the Precedent are applicable in the four course system only, as being the most general system in the country.

Selling off crops.

Clause 15 (*l*) relating to selling off produce will, in many cases, require considerable modification in form

---

(*g*) Appendix I., *post* p. 127.
(*h*) Appendix I., *post* p. 129.
(*i*) Appendix I., *post* p. 125.
(*k*) *Post* p. 67.
(*l*) Appendix I., *post* p. 128.

or in practice. In many counties tenants are allowed to sell off produce for the first two or three years.

Clause 16 (*m*) relating to samples of artificial manures may be sometimes found impracticable owing to the amount of labour which it would entail on the landlord, but where practicable it would be decidedly useful by giving the landlord control over the quality of the manure put upon the soil, and it would enable him to ascertain the value of the manures in the event of a reference, as otherwise the valuer on estimating the amount of compensation has nothing to guide him but the tenant's vouchers. Such a clause would not be within the provisions of sect. 55 (*n*), nor would it render an agreement unfair or unreasonable. *Artificial manures.*

Manufactured manures and feeding stuffs are matters in which farmers are very liable to be imposed upon, some of them are hardly worth the cost of carriage.

The clauses relating to the last year of the tenancy and quitting vary greatly. Those which are most general have been inserted, and it is believed that the general valuation clause 24 (*o*) will be found in most cases to include the tenant right by custom not touched by the Act. *Last year, and quitting.*

It may very likely be objected that the procedure under the Act is not sufficiently satisfactory for general purposes of valuation, but it has been thought better to make use of it to avoid two different kinds of valuation at the termination of a tenancy, one *Arbitration clause.*

(*m*) Appendix I., *post* p. 128.
(*n*) *Post* p. 91.
(*o*) Appendix I., *post* p. 130.

under the Act, and one under custom, especially in view of sect. 17 (*p*). It will be observed that the procedure has been modified so as to avoid the most objectionable features. The procedure before Justices relating to a distress is also incorporated in clause 29 (*q*).

(*p*) *Post* p. 59.
(*q*) Appendix I., *post* p. 132.

CHAPTER II.

PROCEDURE.

THE procedure under the Act is of three kinds :—

(1.) PROCEEDINGS BEFORE A REFEREE, REFEREES, OR UMPIRE— *Procedure on reference— (1) Before referees.*

    (*a.*) To obtain compensation for unexhausted improvements.

    (*b.*) To assess the value of a fixture claimed by the tenant.

(2.) PROCEEDINGS IN THE COUNTY COURT—

    (*a.*) To appoint a referee or umpire. *(2) In the County Court.*

    (*b.*) To extend the time for delivering the award.

    (*c.*) On appeal from a reference.

    (*d.*) To appoint a guardian or next friend.

    (*e.*) To tax costs.

(3.) SUMMARY PROCEEDINGS IN THE COUNTY COURT, OR BEFORE JUSTICES— *Procedure under Distress clauses.*

    (*a.*) To decide matters arising under the sections relating to distress.

The two first will be treated together, as they both apply to the same matters, the County Court being a Court of Assistance as well as a Court of Appeal from the reference.

The forms for use in the proceedings will be found in Appendices II. to V. (*a*).

(*a*) *Post* pp. 135-150.

Parties to proceedings.

Landlord and tenant are the parties contemplated by the Act as taking these proceedings; but other persons may, under sect. 46 (*b*), become parties to the proceedings under the distress clauses, and there is nothing in the Act to prevent mortgagees, remaindermen, and others, from attending the reference or County Court proceedings to see after their interests, though there is no provision in the Act for allowance of their costs if they do so. The costs of the reference are in the discretion of the referees or umpire, and the costs of County Court proceedings and proceedings before the Justices are in the discretion of the Court.

Costs. ss. 26, 27, 46 (c).

Appointment of guardian. s. 25 (d).

By sect. 25, where a landlord or a tenant is an infant without a guardian, or is of unsound mind not so found by inquisition, the County Court, on the application of any person interested, may appoint a guardian for the purposes of this Act, and may change the guardian if and as occasion requires.

Married women. s. 25 (e).

The County Court may also appoint a person to act as the next friend of a married woman for the purposes of this Act, and may remove or change that next friend if and as occasion requires.

Forms 34, 36 (f).

No special mode of procedure is provided for such applications, and they may be made by summons.

Service of notices, &c. s. 28 (g).

Any notice, request, demand, or other instrument may be served on any person under this Act—

(1.) Personally.

(*b*) *Post* p. 88.
(*c*) *Post* pp. 61, 66, 88.
(*d*) *Post* p. 65.
(*e*) *Post* p. 66.
(*f*) Appendix IV., *post* pp. 145, 146.
(*g*) *Post* p. 66.

(2.) By leaving it at his last known place of abode in England.

(3.) By sending it through the post in a registered letter addressed to him there.

Under the compensation clauses all appointments, notices, and requests must be in writing (with the exception perhaps of the notice in sect. 14 (*h*) by the referees to the parties), and it will always be well to send notices in writing in any case.

PROCEDURE ON REFERENCE.

Procedure on reference.

Giving Notice.

Where a tenant has executed any improvement in the Schedule to the Act, and he has agreed with his landlord for substituted compensation under any of the sects. 2—5, he need not give notice of his intention to claim compensation in respect of such improvements, unless he desires to have the compensation under the agreement assessed by reference under the Act, as provided in sect. 17 (*k*). Otherwise the compensation is payable in pursuance of the agreement, and the agreement must be set aside in a court of law before either party can claim under the Act. *Of the notices necessary before reference.*

Compensation by agreement. Ss. 2—5 (i).

Where, however, the tenant has made no agreement with his landlord, and he wishes to get compensation for unexhausted improvements under the compulsory clauses of the Act, or where he wishes to have the compensation payable under his agreement assessed *Compensation under the Act.*

Notice of Claim. S. 7 (l).

(*h*) *Post* p. 58.
(*i*) *Post* pp. 45-49.
(*k*) *Post* p. 59.
(*l*) *See* notes and cases to sect. 7, *post* p. 52.

by reference under the Act, he must be most careful not to neglect giving to his landlord notice in writing *at least two months before the determination of his tenancy* of his intention to claim compensation.

If he neglect to give this notice or give it a day too late, his claim to all compensation under the Act is gone, and he must recover what compensation he can by custom or in any other manner allowed by sect. 57 (*n*).

On receipt of such notice the landlord may, on his part, *before, or within fourteen days after, the determination of the tenancy*, give a counter-notice in writing that he claims to set-off against the tenant's claim a claim for compensation in respect of the matters mentioned in sect. 6.

It must be noticed that the landlord cannot give notice to a tenant in the first place. The power of beginning proceedings for compensation lies with the tenant. When the tenant has once begun, the landlord may go on with his counter-claim, even if the tenant's claim is withdrawn.

When under sect. 34 the tenant intends to remove a fixture or building put up by him upon his holding, after January 1st, 1884, he must give *one month's previous notice* in writing of his intention to remove it, and satisfy all the obligations which by that section are conditions precedent to its removal.

(*m*) Appendix III., *post* p. 137.
(*n*) *Post* p. 92.
(*o*) *Post* pp. 49-54.
(*p*) Appendix III., *post* p. 137.
(*q*) *Post* p. 75.
(*r*) Appendix III., *post* p. 139.

The month's notice ought to be given before the determination of the tenancy, as it is only a *tenant* who can give the notice ; but it need not necessarily have expired before the tenancy has determined.

The landlord may at any time before the expiration of the notice of removal give notice in writing that he elects to purchase the fixture.

<small>Counter notice by landlord.

Form 16 (s).</small>

Agreement as to Compensation or Value of Fixture.

The landlord and tenant may then by agreement between themselves settle the question of compensation for unexhausted improvements, or the value of the fixture.

<small>Agreement as to compensation or value. S. 8 (t).</small>

They may agree as to the "amount, mode, and time of payment of compensation" for improvements, or as to the value of the fixture. If they differ, the difference is to be settled by a reference in manner provided by the Act.

<small>Form 13 (u).</small>

Appointment of a Referee.

A referee may be appointed—

(1.) By the parties jointly by agreement.
(2.) By each party separately.
(3.) By the County Court.
(4.) By the Land Commissioners for England.

<small>The referee. Ss. 9—14 (x).</small>

The parties may agree in writing in appointing a single referee.

<small>Appointment by agreement of a single referee. S. 9. Sub-s. 1, 2 (y).</small>

(s) Appendix III., *post* p. 139.
(t) *Post* p. 54.
(u) Appendix III., *post* p. 138.
(x) *Post* pp. 55-58.
(y) *Post* p. 55.

Form 17 (z).	If before award the referee die, or become incapable, or if he fail to act after seven days' notice in writing requiring him to act from either of the parties, they may agree and appoint a fresh referee, or they may appoint separate referees as below.
Revocation of submission. S. 12 (a).	The delivery will be a submission to reference by the parties delivering it. Neither party can revoke a submission or the appointment of a referee without the consent of the other.
Forms 20, 21 (b).	
	The single referee will then consider the matters referred, and make his award.
Where parties do not agree. S. 9. Sub-s. 3 (c). Sub-s. 4 (d).	Where the parties do not agree, each shall appoint a referee in writing.
	If either of these referees before award die, or become incapable of acting, or if either fail to act after seven days' notice in writing from either of the parties requiring him to act, the party appointing him shall appoint a fresh referee.
Forms 17, 19 (e).	
Notice of appointment. S. 9. Sub-ss. 5, 6 (f).	On each appointment the appointing party must give notice in writing to the other party stating the fact of the appointment, and requiring the other party, if he has not already done so, to appoint a referee.
Form 18 (g).	
S. 10 (h). Form 24 (i).	Either party may also by such notice require that the umpire shall be appointed by the Land Commissioners or by the County Court.

(z) Appendix III., *post* p. 139.
(a) *Post* p. 57.
(b) Appendix III., *post* p. 140.
(c) *Post* p. 55.
(d) *Post* p. 55.
(e) Appendix III., *post* pp. 139, 140.
(f) *Post* p. 55.
(g) Appendix III., *post* p. 140.
(h) *Post* p. 56.
(i) Appendix III., *post* p. 141.

When the two referees are appointed, they shall, before they enter on the reference, appoint, in writing, an umpire (where one has not been previously appointed by the County Court or by the Land Commissioners). If before award the umpire die, or become incapable of acting, they shall appoint another umpire. Appointment of umpire. S. 9. Sub-s. 7 (k). Form 27 (l). Sub-s. (m).

When the referees cannot agree they must give notice to the umpire of the reference to him. When referees cannot agree. S. 18 (n). Form 28 (o).

When the parties fail to appoint referees or umpires, and in certain other events, powers of appointment are given to the County Court and the Land Commissioners. They are as follows:— When parties fail to appoint. S. 9, Sub-s. 6, and S. 10 (p).

(1.) Where any party fails to appoint a referee for fourteen days after receiving a notice from the other party requiring him to do so, the Judge of the County Court, or by consent of the parties the Registrar, may on the application (by summons in chambers) of the party giving notice, appoint a referee. Appointment of referee by County Court. S. 9. Sub-ss. 4, 6 (q). Forms 32, 33 (r).

(2.) Either party, if he has appointed a referee, may give notice in writing to the other party that he requires that the umpire shall be appointed by the Land Commissioners. Appointment of umpire by Land Commissioners. S. 10. Sub-s. 1 (s). Forms 24, 25 (t).

(k) *Post* p. 56.
(l) Appendix III., *post* p. 142.
(m) *Post* p. 56.
(n) *Post* p. 59.
(o) Appendix III., *post* p. 142.
(p) *Post* p. 56.
(q) *Post* p. 55.
(r) Appendix IV., *post* p. 145.
(s) *Post* p. 56.
(t) Appendix III., *post* p. 141.

The Land Commissioners will then, on the application of either party to them, appoint an umpire or a fresh umpire.

Appointment of umpire by County Court on application.
S. 10.
Sub-s. 2, s. 11 (u).

(3.) Either party may, if he has appointed a referee, give notice that he requires that the umpire shall be appointed by the County Court. If the other party do not dissent, the Judge of the County Court (or by consent of the parties the Registrar) may, on the application of either party, by summons in chambers, appoint an umpire or a fresh umpire. The other party may, however, dissent in writing from this. If he do so, the Land Commissioners will, on the application of either party, appoint an umpire or a fresh umpire.

Forms 25, 26, 32, 33 (x).

Appointment of umpire by County Court in default.
S. 9.
Sub-s. 9, s. 11 (y).

(4.) Where the referee for seven days after request from either party fail to appoint an umpire or a fresh umpire, the County Court shall in like manner, on the application of either party within fourteen days appoint an umpire.

The procedure on application for appointment of a referee or umpire by the County Court is regulated by the County Court Rules, 1889, Order XL., Rule 7A (z). The appointment must be made by the County Court Judge unless the parties consent to the jurisdiction being exercised by the Registrar (a).

(u) *Post* p. 57.
(x) Appendix III., *post* p. 141; Appendix IV., *post* p. 145.
(y) *Post* pp. 56, 57.
(z) *Post* p. 102. See also *In re Griffiths and Morris*. (1895), 1 Q. B. 866; 64 L J.Q.B. 386; 72 L.T. 290; 43 W.R. 652; 59 J.P. 134; 15 R. 301.
(a) County Court Rules, 1889, Order XL., rule 7A (2), *post* p. 102.

The costs of proceedings in the County Court are in the discretion of the Court. _{Costs. S. 27 (b).}

The referee, referees or umpire will then proceed to consider the matters referred. _{The hearing.}

They may proceed in the absence of parties after giving notice. _{S. 14 (c). Form 29 (d).}

They may call for the production of "any sample or voucher, or other document, or other evidence which is in the possession or power of either party, or which either party can produce, and which," to them, "seems necessary for the determination of the matter referred," and they may examine the witnesses on oath. There is no provision in the Act enabling referees, in the event of persons disobeying their orders, to enforce production of documents or samples, or imposing a penalty on non-production. It must be noticed, too, that they can only call for the production of evidence "in the possession or power of either party, or which either party can produce." _{Evidence. S. 13 (e). Form 30 (f).}

As a referee could disallow any claim which could only be supported by evidence which is not produced, and make the offending party pay the costs, the section will probably work in practice, notwithstanding the absence of means of enforcing the referee's orders.

A referee must obtain evidence on all the points which must be specified in his award. If any such _{S. 10 (g). Form 31 (h).}

(b) *Post* p. 66.
(c) *Post* p. 58.
(d) Appendix III., *post* p. 142.
(e) *Post* p. 57.
(f) Appendix III., *post* p. 142.
(g) *Post* p. 60.
(h) Appendix III., *post* p. 143.

evidence is wanting, he cannot award any compensation in respect of the matters covered by it.

<small>Costs of reference. S. 22 (*i*). Form 31 (*k*).</small> The costs of and attending the reference, including the remuneration of the referees or umpire, and "other proper expenses," are in their discretion. Such costs are subject to taxation by the Registrar of the County Court, on the application of either party, in chambers, in the same way as in an ordinary action in the County Court, and the taxation is subject to review by the Judge of the County Court.

<small>Time for delivery of award. By referee. S. 16 (*l*).</small> The times for delivering the award are as follows :—

(1.) For a single referee, twenty-eight days after appointment.

<small>Form 22 (*m*).</small> (2.) For two referees, twenty-eight days after the appointment of the last appointed of them, or—

(3.) The two referees may, from time to time, jointly fix a further time by writing under their hands, not exceeding, in the whole, forty-nine days after the appointment of the last appointed of them.

<small>Form 28 (*n*).</small> If the two referees fail to deliver their award within such time, the matters stand referred to the umpire.

<small>By umpire. S. 18 (*o*). Form 28.</small> (4.) For the umpire, twenty-eight days after notice in writing, given to him by either party, or by the referees of the reference to him, *unless*—

(*i*) *Post* p. 61.
(*k*) Appendix III., *post* p. 143.
(*l*) *Post* p. 58.
(*m*) Appendix III., *post* p. 141.
(*n*) Appendix III., *post* p. 142.
(*o*) *Post* p. 59.

(5.) The Registrar of the County Court, from time to time, appoints an extended time, on the application of the umpire, or of either party, made before the twenty-eight days, or time or times already extended by the Registrar, have expired. *Extension of time by Registrar of County Court. S. 18.*

Forms 35, 36 (p).

The Registrar may make what extension of time he pleases, as no limit is placed upon his discretion.

The award must be in writing, signed by the referee or referees, or umpire. *What the award must contain. S. 19 (q).*

It must specify, "so far as possible,"

(a.) The several improvements, acts, and things, in respect whereof compensation is awarded. *Form 31 (r).*

(b.) The time at which each improvement, act, or thing, was executed, done, or permitted.

(c.) The sum awarded in respect of each improvement, act, or thing.

Where the landlord desires to charge his estate with the amount of the compensation found due to the tenant—

(d.) The time at which, for the purposes of such charge, each improvement, act, or thing, in respect of which compensation is awarded, is to be exhausted.

Also—

(e.) In what proportion the costs of the reference are to be borne by the parties, or by whom they are to be borne. *s. 20 (s).*

(p) Appendix IV., post pp. 145, 146.
(q) Post p. 60.
(r) Appendix III., post p. 143.
(s) Post p. 61.

(*f.*) A direction for payment of costs.

S. 21 (*t*).

(*g.*) A time, not sooner than one month after the delivery of the award, for the payment of money awarded for compensation, costs, or otherwise.

Award when final.

When the sum "claimed for compensation" (which means, it is submitted, the sum claimed by either party, and not the aggregate of the sums claimed by both parties) is less than £100, the award is final.

Either party may then apply to tax the costs of the reference.

Appeal from award. S. 23 (*u*).

If the sum claimed exceeds £100, either party may appeal to the Judge of the County Court; on such appeal the decision of the Judge is final, except on questions of law, on which he must state a case for the High Court, at the request of either party.

The decision of the High Court, not only on the case, but on costs, and any other matter connected therewith, is final, and must be enforced as if it were a judgment of the County Court.

The award cannot be questioned except by appeal. S. 22 (*x*).

The submission, or award, cannot be made a rule of Court, or be removable by process into any Court, and an award cannot be questioned in any other way than by appeal to the County Court as above.

Time for appeal. S. 23 (*y*).

If either party intend to appeal he must do so *within seven days after the delivery of the award* to him, and if no appeal is brought within such time the award is final.

(*t*) *Post* p. 61.
(*u*) *Post* p. 62.
(*x*) *Post* p. 61.
(*y*) *Post* p. 62.

The appeal may be made on all or any of the grounds set out in sect. 23. *Grounds of appeal. S. 23.*

The Procedure on Appeal is regulated by the County Court Rules, 1889, Order XL., rules 1—6 (z).

The Judge shall hear and determine the appeal, and may in his discretion remit the case to be re-heard, as to the whole, or any part thereof, by the referee, or referees, or umpire, with such directions as he may think fit. *Procedure appeal.*

Recovery of sums agreed, awarded, or ordered, to be paid.

When the parties have agreed under sect. 8 (b), as to the moneys to be paid—or where a sum has been awarded—or where an order has been made on appeal for a sum to be paid—for compensation, costs, or otherwise; then, if the money is not paid within fourteen days after the "time when it is agreed, or awarded, or ordered to be paid," it is recoverable in the County Court as if it were money ordered to be paid by the County Court under its ordinary jurisdiction. *Compensation, how recovered. Ss. 24, 31 (a). Form 39 (c). S. 24.*

Sect. 31 provides that, where the landlord is a trustee or person entitled to the rents in any character otherwise than for his own benefit, the amount shall not be recoverable from him personally, but he may charge it on the holding, either before or after it has been paid to the tenant, or in default of payment by the landlord the tenant may charge it, within one month after he has quitted his holding. *Trustee or mortgagee, s. 31.*

(z) *Post* pp. 100, 101.
(a) *Post* pp. 63, 71.
(b) *Post* p. 54. See also notes to sect. 24. *post* p. 63.
(c) *Post* p. 147.

Charge of Compensation.

Obtaining a charge.
Ss. 29-32 (d).

A landlord, on paying the amount due to the tenant for compensation, or on draining, under sect. 4, after notice to drain given by the tenant, may obtain from the County Court a charge on the holding to the amount of the sum so paid or expended in draining.

The case of a trustee, or person having no beneficial interest, is dealt with by section 31 (e).

Evidence required.
S. 29 (f).

The Court will require from a beneficial owner,

(1.) Proof of the payment, or expenditure, of the sum sought to be charged ;
and it will also, in any case, require to be satisfied of—
(2.) The observance, in good faith, by the parties of the conditions imposed by this Act.

Order of charge.

The Court must then make an order, charging the holding with the amount paid with such interest and by such instalments and with such directions for giving effect to the charge as the Court thinks fit.

Ss. 27, 30 (g).

The instalments and interest will be charged in favour of the landlord, his executors, administrators, and assigns upon the landlord's interest in the land, and " for all interest therein subsequent to that of the landlord." Where, however, the landlord is himself a tenant who pays compensation to an underlessee he can only charge the land for the interests of himself and his representatives. Where the landlord is a limited owner only, the instalments and interest will

Underleases.

Limited Owners.

(d) *Post* pp. 67-73.
(e) *Post* p. 71.
(f) *Post* p. 67.
(g) *Post* pp. 67-71.

be spread over a smaller number of years, regard being had to the time when the improvement is taken to have been exhausted according to the declaration of the award, or if no award has been made, according to the opinion of the Court.

Incumbents of benefices cannot give consent to improvements, or charge compensation on the glebe, without the approval in writing of the patron, or the Governors of Queen Anne's Bounty, who may then pay the compensation, and take a charge on the holding. *Incumbent benefices. S. 39 (h).*

The landlord may assign the charge to a Land Company, and the Land Company may assign it to any person or persons whomsoever. *Assignment of charge. S. 32 (i).*

No special rules of procedure have been made under these sections 29-32 of the Act, [*which are nearly identical with ss. 42-44 of the Agricultural Holdings Act, 1875*]. *Procedure to obtain charge.*

Proceedings may therefore be taken either by petition or plaint. Petition would appear to be the more convenient form. It could be served, if necessary, on any parties interested, such as remaindermen or mortgagees. There is no special provision for the costs of interested parties appearing, but the costs are in the discretion of the Court. *Petition. Form 40 (k).*

Summary Procedure before Justices and at Quarter Sessions.

Disputes as to the ownership of goods distrained, the fairness of price for agisting and other matters set *Procedure under the distress clauses. S. 46 (l).*

(h) *Post* p. 80.
(i) *Post* p. 73.
(k) Appendix IV., *post* p. 148.
(l) *Post* p. 88.

out in the notes to sect. 46 relating to a distress upon the holding, may (but the section is not compulsory) be decided either by the County Court, or by a Court of Summary Jurisdiction [consisting of two or more Justices of the Peace, *Summ. Jurisd. Act, 1879, S. 20, Subs. 9.*], with an appeal to Quarter Sessions.

In County Court. The observations above, as to the proceedings to obtain a charge, will apply to the proceedings in the County Court. In this case it would be more convenient to begin them by plaint, and to frame the plaint as far as possible according to the ordinary forms of action in the County Court for damages, illegal or excessive distress, detinue, and so on.

Before Justices. The disputes under these clauses are to be deemed

" An order on complaint." to be matters "in which a Court of Summary Jurisdiction has authority by law to make an order on complaint in pursuance of the Summary Jurisdiction Acts."

By sect. 6 of the Summary Jurisdiction Act, 1879, sums recoverable by a summary order on complaint are deemed to be civil debts and are recoverable as such.

The proceedings will therefore be initiated by summons on complaint, and the subsequent forms will be those provided for the recovery of civil debts, that is to say :—

The particulars of the claim will be annexed to or embodied in the summons.

Order for payment of money. On the summons an order may be made for payment of the sum adjudged as damages, or as the price of live stock or things unlawfully distrained, or otherwise, and for costs.

S. J. A., 1879. S. 7. The Court may allow time for payment of the sum adjudged ; may direct payment by instalments, or may direct an undertaking with security to be given for its payment.

In default of payment a distress warrant, to levy *Default of payment.* distress on the defendant's goods, may be obtained.

In default of distress, a judgment summons must *Default of distress. S. J. A., 1879. S. 35.* be taken out, and the applicant must prove to the Court that the defendant has means to pay. If he do so, an order will be made for payment, or for commitment in the alternative.

The forms for the recovery of money under such *Forms.* procedure may be obtained from the clerk to the magistrate, or from any law stationer.

In addition, however, to the power of making *Order for restoration of chattel. S. 46 (m).* orders for the payment of money, the Court may under the 46th section of the Act, "*make an order for restoration,*" and may make declarations as to the property in goods. The form of order in such a case *Form 43.* differs from the forms mentioned above, and the procedure subsequent to the order is different.

By sect. 34 of the S. J. Act, 1879, where a power "is *S. J. A., 1879. S. 34.* "given by any future Act to a Court of Summary "Jurisdiction, of requiring any person to do, or "abstain from doing, any act or thing other than the "payment of money, or of requiring any act or thing "to be done, or left undone, other than the payment "of money, and no mode is prescribed of enforcing "such requisition, the Court may exercise such power "by an order or orders," with or without conditions, "and may suspend or rescind the order, on such "undertaking being given, or condition being per-"formed, as the Court may think just, and generally "may make such arrangement for carrying into effect "such power as to the Court seems meet."

"A person making default in complying with an *Disobedience to Order.* "order may, in the discretion of the Court, be ordered "to pay a sum [to be enforced as a civil debt,

---

(*m*) *Post* p. 88.

"recoverable summarily under this Act] not exceeding £1 for every day during which he is in default,"
and not exceeding, in the aggregate, £20, "*or* to be
"imprisoned until he has remedied his default," such
imprisonment not to exceed two months.

It should be noticed that the punishment in default
is in the alternative, and that the justices could send
to prison in the first instance, without imposing a
fine.

Any 'person aggrieved" by the decision of the
Court may appeal to Quarter Sessions. He must
appeal to the next practicable court having jurisdiction in the county, borough, or place, for which
the said Court of Summary Jurisdiction acted, and
holden not less than fifteen days after the day on
which the decision was given, upon which the conviction or order was founded.

He must give notice of appeal within seven days
after the day on which the decision was given, by
serving on the other party, and on the Clerk of the
Court of Summary Jurisdiction, notice in writing of
his intention to appeal, and of the general grounds of
such appeal.

He must enter into a recognizance within three
days after the day on which he gave notice of appeal,
or, if the Court think fit, give security.

The proceedings on appeal will be found set out in
sect. 31 of the Summary Jurisdiction Act, 1879.

(*n*) Appendix V., *post* p. 149.
(*o*) *Post* p. 88.
(*p*) Appendix V., *post* p. 150.

THE AGRICULTURAL HOLDINGS (ENGLAND) ACT, 1883.
[46 & 47 VICT. c. 61.]

N.B.— Words which, by sect. 61, have a special meaning are throughout printed in italics.

PART I.

IMPROVEMENTS.

Compensation for Improvements.

1. Subject as in this Act mentioned, where a *tenant* has made on his *holding* any improvement comprised in the First Schedule hereto, he shall, on and after the commencement of this Act, be entitled on quitting his *holding* at the *determination of a tenancy* to obtain from the *landlord* as compensation under this Act for such improvement such sum as fairly represents the value of the improvement to an incoming *tenant*: Provided always, that in estimating the value of any improvement in the First Schedule hereto there shall not be taken into account as part of the improvement made by the *tenant* what is justly due to the inherent capabilities of the soil.

General right of tenant to compensation.

Subject as in this Act mentioned—See sects. 2 to 5 and see sect. 7 as to notice (*a*).
On his holding—See sect. 54 (*b*).
On and after the commencement of this Act—January 1st, 1884 (*c*). Where a claim is made under the Agricultural Holdings Act, 1875, the procedure to be adopted is the procedure provided by this Act (*d*).
On quitting his holding at the determination of a tenancy—Except as provided by sect. 58 (*e*) a tenant who remains in his holding at the

---
(*a*) *Post* pp. 45-49.
(*b*) *Post* p. 91.
(*c*) Sect. 53, *post* p. 91.
(*d*) *Smith* v. *Acock*, (1885), 53 L.T. 230, *post* pp. 49, 54
(*e*) *Post* p. 93.

46 & 47 VICT.
c. 61.

determination of a tenancy must make the best bargain that he can with his landlord. He has always the threat of quitting, to be followed by compensation, as a weapon in his hands to bring his landlord to terms. By the provisions of sect. 58, a tenant who remains in his holding during a change or changes of tenancy is not deprived of his right to claim compensation on quitting, so that a tenant who has given notice to quit to his landlord, when the rent has been raised on his improvements, if he afterwards agree with his landlord to withdraw his notice and stay, can claim for his improvements made before notice was given.

Determination of tenancy defined.

By sect. 61 (*f*) "determination of a tenancy" means the cesser of "a contract of tenancy" (which is also there defined) "by reason of effluxion of time or from any other cause."

How a tenancy may be determined.

A tenancy may be determined by the expiration of the term granted, or on the happening of any event on which it is made determinable (such as, in the case of a lease for lives, the death of the *cestui que vie*) or by merger of the term and the reversion in the same right.

Notice to quit.

A tenancy may also be determined by notice to quit. By such notice a tenancy from year to year is determined on the expiration of the current year, and a waiver of the notice creates a new tenancy, taking effect on the expiration of the old one (*g*). The notice to quit may be given on behalf of the landlord either by himself or by his agent, and the agent may give the notice in his own name where the agency is a general agency to manage the property (*h*.) The notice may be delivered to the servant of the tenant or to some person whose duty it would be to deliver it to the tenant (*i*).

Surrender.

A tenancy may also be determined by surrender of the term granted. This may be either express, in which case it must be by deed (29 Car. II. c. 3, sect. 3, and 8 9 Vict. c. 106, sect. 3), or by operation of law. Surrender by operation of law takes place where the tenant has been party to some act, the validity of which he is by law afterwards estopped from disputing, and which would not be valid if his tenancy had continued to exist (*k*). Such is, for instance, the grant of a new lease of the same premises to another with the tenant's consent (*l*). An agreement between the parties, followed by a virtual taking of possession on the part of the landlord, makes a surrender by operation of law (*m*). A surrender of part of the premises and a proportionate reduction of rent does not create a new tenancy (*n*).

Rights of an under-lessee on surrender.

An under-lessee's rights cannot be put an end to by a voluntary surrender of his lessor's interest (*o*), nor can his liabilities be

---

(*f*) *Post* p. 74. See notes and decisions thereunder.
(*g*) *Tayleur* v. *Wilding*, (1868), L.R., 3 Ex. 303; 37 L.J. Ex. 173; 18 L.T. 655; 16 W.R. 1013; but see also *Holme* v. *Brunskill*, (1878). 3 Q.B.D. 495; 47 L.J C.P. 610; 38 L.T. 838; and *Inchiquin* v. *Lyons*, (1887), 20 Ir. L.R. 474.
(*h*) *Jones* v. *Phipps*, (1868), L.R. 3 Q.B. 567; 37 L.J. Q.B. 198; 18 L.T. 813; 16 W.R. 1018; 9 B. & S. 761. *Erne (Earl of)* v. *Armstrong*, (1872), 20 W.R. 370; 6 Ir. R.C.L. 279.
(*i*) *Tanham* v. *Nicholson*, (1872), L.R. 5 H.L. 561.
(*k*) *Lyon* v. *Reed*, (1844), 13 M. & W. 285; 13 L.J. Ex. 377; 8 Jur. 762. *Nichell* v. *Atherstone*, (1847), 10 Q.B. 944; 16 L.J. Q.B. 371. *Wallis* v. *Hands*, (1893), 2 Ch. 75; 62 L.J. Ch. 586; 68 L.T. 428; 41 W.R. 471; 3 R. 351.
(*l*) *Davison* v. *Gent*, (1857), 1 H. & N. 744; 26 L.J. Ex. 122; 5 W.R. 229; 3 Jur. N.S. 342. *Wallis* v. *Hands, supra* (*k*).
(*m*) *Phené* v. *Popplewell*, (1862), 12 C.B.N.S. 334; 31 L.J.C.P. 235; 6 L.T. 247; 10 W.R. 523; 8 Jur. N.S. 1104. *Oastler* v. *Henderson*, (1877), 2 Q.B.D. 575; 46 L.J Q.B. 607; 37 L.T. 22.
(*n*) *Holme* v. *Brunskill*, note (*g*), *supra*.
(*o*) *Mellor* v. *Watkins*, (1874), L.R. 9 Q.B. 400; 23 W.R. 55.

affected (*p*). In the disclaimer by the trustee in bankruptcy of the lessee's interest, the landlord may distrain on the underlessee for the original rents and sue him on the covenants as if he were lessee, but he cannot eject him from the property (*q*); and if the underlease is made at a rent less than the rent reserved by the original lease, the underlessee is, after the disclaimer, entitled to prove in the bankruptcy for the value of the difference between the two rents (*q*). The landlord would then, it is submitted, be liable to pay the sub-lessee compensation for his improvements. 46 & 47 VICT. c. 61.

A trustee in bankruptcy, who has disclaimed, cannot claim compensation for improvements under this Act (*r*). Bankruptcy of lessee.

It has been held that there is no right of set-off where the creditor becomes a debtor to the bankrupt's estate after the bankruptcy, as would be the case as to compensation " on quitting the holding " (*s*). In the case of *In re Morrish, exparte Hart Dyke* (*t*), it was held that in respect of breaches of covenant committed by the tenant during his occupation, the remedy of the landlord was to prove for damages in the liquidation, and that he had no right of set-off as against moneys due by him to the trustees for severed crops.

The tenancy may also be determined by forfeiture of the tenant's interest. Any acts or defaults which give rise to a forfeiture only render the lease voidable at the option of the lessor, and do not give the lessee power to avoid the lease, and if the lessor choose he may waive the forfeiture (*u*). Forfeiture.

A disclaimer in writing of the landlord's title by the tenant operates as a forfeiture, and the landlord will be entitled to eject the tenant without any notice to quit (*x*). Disclaimer of title.

A tenant's interest may also be forfeited for non-payment of rent, or for breaches of covenant in a lease. Sect. 14 of the Conveyancing Act, 1881 (*y*), prohibits the right of entry on forfeiture for a breach of any covenant or condition in a lease other than (as provided by subsection 6) on the breach of a covenant against assigning or underletting, or of a condition for forfeiture on bankruptcy or taking in execution of the lessee's interest, or for a breach of certain conditions in mining leases, until notice has been served on the lessee specifying the breach and requiring that it shall be remedied, and requiring the lessee to make compensation in money for the breach, and the lessee has failed to comply with these demands. Non-payment of rent or breach of covenant.

By sect. 2, sub-section (2) of The Conveyancing Act, 1892 (*z*) subsect. 6 of sect. 14 of The Conveyancing Act, 1881, is to apply to a condition for forfeiture on bankruptcy of the lessee, or on taking in execution of the lessee's interest only after the expiration of one year from the date of the bankruptcy, or taking in execution, and provided the lessee's interest be not sold within such one year, but in case the

---

(*p*) 8 & 9 Vict., c. 106, sect 9.
(*q*) In re *Levy, Ex parte Walton*, (1881), 17 Ch. D. 746; 50 L.J. Ch. 657; 45 L.T. 1; 30 W.R. 305. *East and West India Dock Co. v. Hill*, (1882), 22 Ch.D. 14; 52 L.J. Ch. 44; 47 L.T. 270; 31 W.R. 55.
(*r*) *Schofield* v. *Hincks*, (1888), 58 L.J. Q.B. 147; 60 L.T. 573; 37 W.R. 157.
(*s*) *In re Day, exparte Young*, (1879), 41 L.T., 40; 27 W.R. 942.
(*t*) (1882), 22 Ch. D. 410; 52 L.J. Ch. 570; 48 L.T. 303.
(*u*) *Doe v. Banks*, (1821), 4 B. & A. 401. *Davenport v. Rees*. (1377), 3 A.C. 115; 47 L.J. P.C. 8; 37 L.T. 727.
(*x*) *Vivian* v. *Moat*, (1881), 16 Ch. D. 730; 50 L.J. Ch. 331; 44 L.T. 210; 29 W.R. 504.
(*y*) 44 & 45 Vict., c. 41.
(*z*) 55 & 56 Vict., c. 13.

44   *Agricultural Holdings (England) Act, 1883.*

46 & 47 Vict. c. 61.

lessee's interest be sold within such one year, sub-sect. 6 shall cease to be applicable thereto. Sub-sect. (2), however, is not to apply to any lease of agricultural or pastoral land, and it therefore does not apply to leases under the Agricultural Holdings Act.

Basis on which compensation is calculated.

The value of the improvement to an incoming tenant.—It is submitted that where an improvement is due to good farming only, it ought not to be matter for compensation, and that valuers ought to construe this sect. so as not to give compensation to a tenant who has merely farmed, as he was bound to do according to the rules of good husbandry, but only when he has done something over and above that.

Fair and reasonable compensation. S. 5.

According to the limits laid down by the Agricultural Holdings Act, 1875, which were calculated by outlay, the improvements in Parts 1 and 2 of the First Schedule of this Act would be deemed to be exhausted at the end of twenty years from the year in which the outlay was made (except Nos. 2 and 14, which were not included in the Schedule to that Act); the improvements in Part 3, Nos. 16-21, at the end of seven years, and those numbered 22 and 23 at the end of two years. It will be useful to bear this in mind, in dealing with the provisions of sect. 5. as the Act of 1875 may prove a useful guide to fair and reasonable agreements; and looking to the difficulties raised by the provisions of sect. 17 (*a*) it will always be well for a landlord to frame his agreement according to some standard which a valuer cannot quarrel with.

Inherent capabilities.

The "inherent capabilities of the soil" may mean anything or nothing. If a railway comes near a farm and doubles the rental value, is this due to the "inherent capabilities," or is the tenant to be compensated for his good fortune? Beyond evidence of outlay, rental is practically the only means of arriving at a conclusion as to value, and rental might be very much affected by such a matter. This proviso will probably lead to considerable litigation.

Valuations for mortgage or purchase.

Valuations for mortgage or purchase will be conducted under some difficulty, as it will not be to the interest of either landlord or tenant to give any information as to the compensation due, and it will not be possible by enquiry to find what claims may have to be met.

Compensation to tenants when mortgagee in possession.

By the *Tenants' Compensation Act, 1890* (*b*), an occupier of mortgaged land is entitled as against the mortgagee to any compensation which is or would, but for the mortgagee taking possession, be due to the occupier from the mortgagor with respect to crops, improvements, tillages, or other matters connected with the land. Any sum ascertained to be due to the occupier for such compensation or for any costs connected therewith, may be set-off against any rent or other sum due from him in respect of the land and recovered as compensation, but unless so set-off shall, as against the mortgagee, be charged and recovered in accordance with sect. 31 of the Agricultural Holdings Act. 1883 (*c*).

An occupier is also entitled to six months' notice in writing from the mortgagee, of the latter's intention to deprive him of possession; and if he is deprived of possession he is entitled to compensation for any expenditure upon the land which he has made in the expectation of holding the land for the full term of his contract of tenancy, in so far as any improvement resulting therefrom is not exhausted at the time of his being deprived of possession (*d*).

(*a*) *Ante* p. 12.
(*b*) 53 & 54 Vict., c. 57, *post* p. 119.
(*c*) *Post* p. 71.
(*d*) 53 & 54 Vict., c. 57, sect. 2, sub-sect. (2), *post* p. 120.

As to Improvements executed before the Commencement of Act.

46 & 47 VICT. c. 61.

2. Compensation under this Act shall not be payable in respect of improvements executed before the commencement of this Act, with the exceptions following, that— *Restriction as to improvements before Act.*

(1.) Where a *tenant* has within ten years before the commencement of this Act made an improvement mentioned in the third part of the First Schedule hereto, and he is not entitled under any contract, or custom, or under the Agricultural Holdings (England) Act, 1875, to compensation in respect of such improvement ; or

(2.) Where a *tenant* has executed an improvement mentioned in the first or second part of the said First Schedule within ten years previous to the commencement of this Act, and he is not entitled under any contract, or custom, or under the Agricultural Holdings (England) Act, 1875, to compensation in respect of such improvement, and the *landlord* within one year after the commencement of the Act declares in writing his consent to the making of such improvement, then such *tenant* on quitting his *holding* at the *determination of a tenancy* after the commencement of this Act, may claim compensation under this Act in respect of such improvement in the same manner as if this Act had been in force at the time of the execution of such improvement. *Form 6 (e).*

Within ten years, &c. This limitation acts in two ways, it prevents the tenant from taking the benefit of an improvement in part 3, such as clay burning which lasts for a long time, and then claiming for it, and it operates to give tenants compensation for improvements in parts 1 and 2 which do not take immediate effect, such as the laying down of permanent pasture which may not bring in a return until after the time of quitting the holding. *Improvements not taking immediate effect.*

(e) Appendix III., *post* p. 136.

46 *Agricultural Holdings (England) Act,* 1883.

46 & 47 Vict.
c. 61.

The Agricultural Holdings Act, 1875 (*f*), is repealed by sect. 62 of this Act.

Determination of a Tenancy after the commencement of this Act— The effect of these words, coupled with the definition of " determination of a tenancy" in sect. 61, is that a yearly tenant, whose tenancy determines after January 1st. 1884, whether the notice to quit was given before or after that date, is entitled to compensation (*g*).

As to Improvements executed after the Commencement of Act.

Consent of landlord as to improvement in First Schedule, Part I.

Form 6 (*h*).

3. Compensation under this Act shall not be payable in respect of any improvement mentioned in the first part of the First Schedule hereto, and executed after the commencement of this Act, unless the *landlord,* or his agent duly authorised in that behalf, has, previously to the execution of the improvement and after the passing of this Act, consented in writing to the making of such improvement, and any such consent may be given by the *landlord* unconditionally, or upon such terms as to compensation, or otherwise, as may be agreed upon between the *landlord* and the *tenant,* and in the event of any agreement being made between the *landlord* and the *tenant,* any compensation payable thereunder shall be deemed to be substituted for compensation under this Act.

This clause practically leaves parties much upon the same footing as they were before the Act.

It is always desirable that the authority to the agent should be in writing, although this section does not render writing necessary. The tenant must obtain the consent of the landlord in writing previous to the execution of an improvement. Failure to obtain this is an absolute bar to compensation (*i*).

Notice to landlord as to improvement in First Schedule, Part II.

4. Compensation under this Act shall not be payable in respect of any improvement mentioned in the second part of the First Schedule hereto, and executed after the commencement of this Act, unless the *tenant* has, not more than three months and not less than two months before beginning to execute such

---

(*f*) 38 & 39 Vict., c. 92.
(*g*) *See* notes to sects. 1 and 33.
(*h*) Appendix III., *post* p. 136.
(*i*) *Schofield* v. *Hincks* (1888), 58 L.J.Q.B. 147 ; 60 L.T. 573 ; 37 W.R. 157 ; *post* p. 52.

improvement given to the *landlord*, or his agent duly authorised in that behalf, notice in writing of his intention so to do, and of the manner in which he proposes to do the intended work, and upon such notice being given, the *landlord* and *tenant* may agree on the terms as to compensation or otherwise on which the improvement is to be executed, and in the event of any such agreement being made, any compensation payable thereunder shall be deemed to be substituted for compensation under this Act, or the *landlord* may, unless the notice of the *tenant* is previously withdrawn, undertake to execute the improvement himself, and may execute the same in any reasonable and proper manner which he thinks fit, and charge the *tenant* with a sum not exceeding five pounds per centum per annum on the outlay incurred in executing the improvement, or not exceeding such annual sum payable for a period of twenty-five years as will repay such outlay in the said period, with interest at the rate of three per centum per annum, such annual sum to be recoverable as rent. In default of any such agreement or undertaking, and also in the event of the *landlord* failing to comply with his undertaking within a reasonable time, the *tenant* may execute the improvement himself, and shall in respect thereof be entitled to compensation under this Act.

46 & 47 Vict. c. 61.
Form 8 (k).
Form 7 (l).
Form 9 (m).

The *landlord* and *tenant* may, if they think fit, dispense with any notice under this section, and come to an agreement in a lease or otherwise between themselves in the same manner and of the same validity as if such notice had been given.

Form 7 (n).

Second part of the Schedule hereto. This deals only with drainage. Drainage is not defined. It may be difficult sometimes to say whether cleaning out and renewing old drains, where the tenant is not under covenant to repair, may be called drainage. Strictly speaking, the Act only contemplates the making of new drains.

Drainage.

Notice in writing.—The notice need not specify anything more than the rough particulars of the work to be done. The tenant is not bound to estimate the cost, and he had better not do so.

Notice.

(k) Appendix III., *post* p. 136.
(l) Appendix III., *post* p. 136.
(m) Appendix III., *post* p. 137.
(n) Appendix III., *post* p. 136.

Unless the notice of the tenant—These words are only inserted to prevent the tenant being absolutely bound by his notice, if the landlord elects to do the work. If, after notice, the landlord elects to drain, he will not be bound by the notice, but may improve on the particulars contained in it, and charge a percentage on the whole amount.

The improvement is to be executed—The Act means "executed by the tenant" as the section provides, as an alternative, that the landlord may execute the improvement himself, and regulates the terms on which he may do so. If the landlord wish to do the drainage himself he must either exclude the Act by agreement under the last paragraph or charge the percentage allowed by the section.

Reservation as to existing and future contracts of tenancy.

5. Where, in a case of tenancy under a *contract of tenancy* current at the commencement of this Act, any agreement in writing or custom, or the Agricultural Holdings (England) Act, 1875, provides specific compensation for any improvement comprised in the First Schedule hereto, compensation in respect of such improvement, although executed after the commencement of this Act, shall be payable in pursuance of such agreement, custom, or Act of Parliament, and shall be deemed to be substituted for compensation under this Act.

Tenancies after this Act. Fair and reasonable compensation by agreement.

Where in the case of a tenancy under a *contract of tenancy* beginning after the commencement of this Act, any particular agreement in writing secures to the *tenant* for any improvement mentioned in the third part of the First Schedule hereto, and executed after the commencement of this Act, fair and reasonable compensation, having regard to the circumstances existing at the time of making such agreement, then in such case the compensation in respect of such improvement shall be payable in pursuance of the particular agreement, and shall be deemed to be substituted for compensation under this Act.

Clause 10 (*o*).

The last preceding provision of this section relating to a particular agreement shall apply in the case of a tenancy under a *contract of tenancy* current at the commencement of this Act in respect of an improvement mentioned in the third part of the First Schedule hereto, specific compensation for which is not provided by any agreement in writing, or custom, or the Agricultural Holdings Act, 1875.

(*o*) Appendix I., *post* p. 127.

Current at the commencement of the Act—A notice by a tenant in occupation of a tenancy current at the commencement of this Act, of a claim for compensation for improvements executed after the commencement of the Act is good if given under the Agricultural Holdings Act, 1883, though the compensation is to be based upon the principles of the Agricultural Holdings Act, 1875 (*p*).

46 & 47 VICT.
c. 61.

Specific compensation—The Act does not necessarily mean that the compensation must be ascertained beforehand, but that it must be capable of ascertainment. A reduction of rent, or leave to commit breaches of the covenant or waste, made or given in consideration of the execution of an improvement, and clearly referring to the improvement, would be probably held to be "specific compensation" within the section, but not such reduction or leave not referring to the improvement.

Specific compensation, what is.

This substituted compensation is payable "in pursuance of such agreement, custom, or Act," and is therefore prima facie to be ascertained and recovered in a Court of Law. By sect. 17, the provisions of the Act as to reference are so far extended to such agreements as to give the tenant the option of having compensation assessed by the referee.

How ascertained.

Particular agreement in writing—These words exclude custom after the commencement of the Act. "Particular" probably only means that if the Act is excluded, it must be excluded expressly and not by implication.

Fair and reasonable—It is impossible to define a "fair and reasonable agreement," or to suggest any tests beyond those mentioned in Chapter I. (*q*). In those counties where the custom provides specific compensation this will probably be held to be fair and reasonable. Where no such compensation is provided, some such clause as No. 10 of Form 1, of Appendix I. (*r*), and the 2nd Schedule to that appendix (*s*), or No. 12a. of Form 2 (*t*), may be used. The same Court which decides whether or not compensation is fair and reasonable will also decide what is included in "circumstances existing" at the time of executing the agreement. These may be very various, and in some cases involve a mass of evidence, as, for instance, if it is contended that a new branch line of railway has increased the value of the holding since the date of the agreement.

"Fair and reasonable."

"Circumstances existing."

Where the sum claimed for compensation exceeds £100, either party may appeal (*u*).

Regulations as to Compensation for Improvements.

6. In the ascertainment of the amount of the compensation under this Act payable to the *tenant* in respect of any improvement there shall be taken into account in reduction thereof:

Deductions from compensation for improvements.

(*a*.) Any benefit which the *landlord* has given or allowed to the *tenant* in consideration of the *tenant* executing the improvement; and

---

(*p*) *Smith* v. *Acock*, (1885), 53 L.T. 230, *post* p. 54.
(*q*) *Ante* p. 11.
(*r*) *Post* p. 127.
(*s*) *Post* p. 132.
(*t*) Appendix I., *post* p. 134.
(*u*) Sect. 23, *post* p. 62.

46 & 47 Vict.
c. 61.

(*b.*) In the case of compensation for *manures* the value of the *manure* that would have been produced by the consumption on the *holding* of any hay, straw, roots, or green crops sold off or removed from the *holding* within the last two years of the tenancy or other less time for which the tenancy has endured, except as far as a proper return of *manure* to the *holding* has been made in respect of such produce so sold off or removed therefrom ; and

(*c.*) Any sums due to the *landlord* in respect of rent or in respect of any waste committed or permitted by the *tenant*, or in respect of any breach of covenant or other agreement connected with the *contract of tenancy* committed by the *tenant*, also any taxes, rates, and tithe rent-charge due or becoming due in respect of the *holding* to which the *tenant* is liable as between him and the *landlord*.

Augmentation of compensation for improvements.

There shall be taken into account in augmentation of the *tenant's* compensation :

(*d*) Any sum due to the *tenant* for compensation in respect of a breach of covenant or other agreement connected with a *contract of tenancy* and committed by the *landlord*.

Nothing in this section shall enable a *landlord* to obtain under this Act compensation in respect of waste by the *tenant* or of breach by the *tenant* committed or permitted in relation to a matter of husbandry more than four years before the *determination of the tenancy*.

What is a "benefit."

Any benefit—Such as a reduction of rent, a nominal rent on reclamation of waste land, leave to farm arable out of rotation, doing repairs and so on.
It should be noted that the benefit must be " in consideration of the tenant executing the improvement," and must clearly refer to it.

The value of the manure that would have been produced . . a proper return of manure to the holding— Without such incessant overlooking of the farm, as no tenant would stand, and no landlord would be inclined to try, the landlord cannot tell how much hay and straw the tenant has sold off the holding, or how little manure he has brought on. What is "a proper return" to the holding will always be a troublesome question, and this sub-section will hardly be of much value to the landlord. The limitation as to two years is in keeping with the usage on a great many large estates, where the tenant is allowed to sell off anything except in the last years of his tenancy. {46 & 47 VICT. c. 61.}

In respect of any waste— It is not waste at common law, either wilful or permissive, to leave the land uncultivated (*x*), or to carry off straw and manure from the land (*y*). {What is waste.}

The most common acts of waste "in relation to matters of husbandry" are: ploughing or breaking up ancient meadows (*z*), ploughing up strawberry beds (*a*), sowing land with mustard seed, flax, or other pernicious crop (*b*), ploughing up meadow ground (*c*). Other acts of waste are cutting timber trees (*d*), opening gravel pits or mines, or digging for lime, clay, or stone (*e*), draining ponds, not repairing banks against rivers (*f*), and pulling down buildings (*g*). {In relation to matters of husbandry.}

There is also permissive waste, such as allowing buildings to fall out of repair. A tenant at will is not liable for permissive waste, and it is questionable if a tenant from year to year is so outside the term of his tenancy (*h*). {Permissive waste.}

In a recent case it was said that the Agricultural Holdings Act, 1883, goes a long way towards getting rid of some of the old common law doctrines of waste (*i*).

Tithe rent-charge—The remedy for tithe rent-charge is against the land. No person is personally liable for it (*k*). {No personal liability for tithe rent-charge.}

Where a greater amount is awarded to the landlord in respect of waste and breaches of covenant than is awarded to the tenant as compensation for improvements, the landlord cannot recover the balance under the procedure given by the Act (*l*). {Award to landlord in excess of tenant's claim.}

More than four years—The Act only limits the right to compensation for waste "*under this Act*," so that it leaves the landlord free to commence an action in the High Court, if he pleases, concurrently with his remedies under this Act. A landlord will probably find it more to his advantage to overlook his farm once every three years from the time when the tenant entered. Then if the tenant is unsatisfactory, he can give him notice to quit, and set-off the full amount of any waste in relation to a matter of husbandry. {Concurrent remedies in the High Court.}

(*x*) *Per* Parke, B., in *Hutton* v. *Warren*, (1836), 1 M. & W. 466; 5 L.J. Ex. 234; 1 T. & G. 646.
(*y*) *Johnson* v. *Goldswaine*, (1817), 3 Anst. 749.
(*z*) Co. Litt., 53a.
(*a*) *Watherell* v. *Howells*, (1808), 1 Camp. 227.
(*b*) *Pratt* v. *Brett*, (1817), 2 Madd. 62.
(*c*) *Simmons* v. *Norton*, (1831), 7 Bing. 640; 5 M. & P. 645.
(*d*) Co. Litt. 53a.
(*e*) Co. Litt. 53b.
(*f*) Co. Litt. 53b.
(*g*) Co. Litt. 53a.
(*h*) *Harnett* v. *Maitland*, (1847), 16 M. & W. 257; 16 L.J. Ex. 134; 4 D. & L. 545.
(*i*) *Per* Kekewich, J., in *Meux* v. *Cobley*, (1892), 2 Ch. 253; 61 L.J. Ch. 449; 66 L.T. 86.
(*k*) *Griffenhoofe* v. *Daubuz*, (1859), 4 E. & B. 230; 24 L.J.Q.B. 20. Affirmed in Ex. Chamber, 5 E. & B. 746. Explained in *Edmunds* v. *Wallingford*, (1884), 14 Q.B.D. 811; 54 L.J.Q.B. 305; 52 L.T. 720; 33 W.R. 647; 49 J.P. 549.
(*l*) *In re Holmes and Formby*, (1895), 1 Q.B. 174; 64 L.J.Q.B. 391; 71 L.T. 842; 43 W.R. 205; 15 R. 114.

Procedure.

46 & 47 Vict.
c. 61.

Notice of intended claim.

Form 11 (*m*).

Form 12 (*n*).

7. A *tenant* claiming compensation under this Act shall, two months at least before the *determination of the tenancy*, give notice in writing to the *landlord* of his intention to make such claim.

Where a *tenant* gives such notice, the *landlord* may, before the *determination of the tenancy*, or within fourteen days thereafter, give a counter-notice in writing to the *tenant* of his intention to make a claim in respect of any waste or any breach of covenant or other agreement.

Every such notice and counter-notice shall state, as far as reasonably may be, the particulars and amount of the intended claim.

Claim under custom, &c.

Failure to give notice.

Holding over by custom of country.

Compensation under this Act—A tenant is not entitled to claim compensation by custom or otherwise, except in the manner authorised by this Act, in respect of any improvement for which he is entitled to compensation under this Act. Where, however, he is not entitled to compensation under or in pursuance of this Act, he may recover compensation under any other Act of Parliament, or any agreement or custom in the same manner as if this Act had not been passed (*o*).

Although this Act does not make the failure to give notice in writing a bar to the recovery of compensation, this seems to have been the opinion of Lord Coleridge, C.J., and Manisty, J. (*p*). It should be observed that the word "shall" and not "may" is used.

Where a tenant of a farm was entitled, under the custom of the country, to hold over a portion of the land for four months after the expiration of his notice to quit the farm, it was held that the "determination of the tenancy" took place when the tenant's holding under the custom of the country ended; and therefore that a notice of his claim for compensation, given two months before that time, was good (*q*). Lord Coleridge, C.J., after referring to the right of the tenant to hold over part of the farm in accordance with the custom of the country, said: "I entertain no doubt that the words 'determination of the tenancy' there mean the end of the tenant's holding, and not the time at which by the terms of the contract between the landlord and tenant the tenancy is expressed to come to an end. That, I think, is the fair construction of the clause, because if the words 'determination of the tenancy' meant the time specified in the contract for the tenancy to determine, the landlord could not claim against the tenant in respect of waste or breach of covenant or agreement committed whilst the tenant was holding over part of the farm under the custom of the country."

(*m*) Appendix III., *post* p. 137.
(*n*) Appendix III., *post* p. 137.
(*o*) Sect. 57, *post* p. 92.
(*p*) *Schofield* v. *Hincks*, (1885), 58 L.J.Q.B. 147; 60 L.T. 573; 37 W.R. 157.
(*q*) *In re Paul, Ex parte Earl of Portarlington*, (1889), 24 Q.B.D. 247; 59 L.J.Q.B. 30; 61 L.T. 835; 54 J.P. 644.

Since this decision a similar point came before the House of Lords in a Scotch case. It was there held (r) that where a lease is to run for a definite period from the entry of the tenant, which entry took place, as to the houses, grass, and fallow land, on May 26, 1860; as to the arable land in corn crop, at the separation of the crop of the same year from the ground; and as to the barns and barn yard and two cot-houses, at Whitsunday, 1861, a notice of claim for compensation for unexhausted improvements, in order to comply with sect. 7 of the Agricultural Holdings (Scotland) Act, 1883 (which requires that a tenant must give notice to his landlord, in writing, of his intention to make a claim *four months* at least before the termination of the tenancy) must be given four months prior to the separation of the crop (*i.e.* Martinmas) in the year in which the lease terminates. This case decides that where there are three terms of removal in regard to different portions of the subject-matter of the lease, a notice four months [*in England two would be sufficient*] before the separation of the crop (or its equivalent term, Martinmas) is sufficient. The tenant must be in possession of a tenancy within sect. 35 of the Scotch Act [which is identical with sect. 54 of the English Act] when he gives the notice.

Lord Watson said: "The respondent's holding, in so far as it consisted of lands in crop after Whitsunday, 1892, was agricultural, and that is, in my opinion, sufficient for the disposal of this appeal. But I entertain serious doubts whether, after his removal in the autumn of 1892, the respondent remained in possession of any holding within the meaning of the Act. I do not think that the bare possession of a barn, barn-yard, and two cot-houses, unconnected with any land either pastoral or agricultural, is possession of a holding recognised by the Act."

In a more recent case (s), where a tenant on a farm on a yearly tenancy was by the terms of his lease to hold the land from February 2, and the buildings from May 1, it was held that the tenancy determined, within the meaning of the Agricultural Holdings Act, 1883, on February 2, and not on May 1, and that a notice of claim given on February 26, claiming compensation for unexhausted improvements, was too late.

Wright, J., said: "I think with the assistance of the opinion expressed in *Black* v. *Clay* (*t*) we can have little doubt as to how this case ought to be decided. Sect. 1 gives a tenant a general right to compensation, 'on quitting his holding at the determination of the tenancy.' Then by sect. 54 the Act is not to apply 'to a holding that is not either wholly agricultural or wholly pastoral, or in part agricultural, and as to the residue pastoral'; and by sect. 61 'holding' means any parcel of land held by a tenant. Therefore the Act contemplates compensation being given only on the determination of the tenancy of a holding that is either agricultural or pastoral, or partly one and partly the other. Here after February 2 there was no tenancy by the appellant of any holding of such a description. It was, therefore, too late for him then to claim compensation under the Act."

A notice by a tenant in occupation of a tenancy current at the commencement of the Agricultural Holdings Act, 1883, of a claim for compensation for improvements executed after the commencement of

46 & 47 VICT. c. 61.

Notice required where there are three terms of removal.

Notice necessary where there are two terms, one for land, another for buildings.

Notice where compensation based on Agricultural Holdings Act, 1875.

(r) *Black* v. *Clay*, (1894) A.C. 368; 71 L.T. 446; 6 R. 362.
(s) *Morley* v. *Carter*, (1898), 1 Q.B. 8; 66 L.J.Q.B. 843; 77 L.T. 337; 46 W.R. 77.
(t) *Supra.*

54   *Agricultural Holdings (England) Act,* 1883.

46 & 47 VICT.
c. 61.

the Act is good if given under the Agricultural Holdings Act, 1883, though the compensation is to be based upon the principles of the Agricultural Holdings Act, 1875 (*u*). This was decided by Field, J., who said : " Therefore the question is, whether or no, looking at sect. 62 of this Act, the proceedings to be taken by a tenant for compensation in a case like the present, where it is an improvement to which the Agricultural Holdings Act of 1875 applies, the remedy is under the Act of 1883, or under the Act of 1875. I have come to the conclusion that the proceeding is really and truly under the Act of 1883. And the reason why I do say so is this, on account of the language of sect 62 ; because sect. 62 carefully avoids saying anything about a right under the Act. All it says is a right to compensation, not 'under the Act,' which it might have done, but a right 'to compensation in respect of any improvement to which that Act applies.' The words are really descriptive of the improvement; that is, any improvement to which that Act applies. It means the compensation under the first, second, and third class in sect. 5. It therefore seems to me that the Legislature did not intend to keep the Act of 1875 alive for the purposes of procedure under it, but intended that the parties should proceed under this Act, and under this Act should be entitled to compensation in respect to improvements to which that Act applied."

Set-off and counter-claim.

The landlord may . . . *make a claim*—The landlord can by sect. 6 set-off against the tenant's claim any benefit allowed to the tenant in consideration of the improvement, the value of manures produced by crops sold off, arrears of rent, rates, and taxes, and so on ; but under this section he may make a claim for waste, or a breach of covenant or agreement.

Where a greater amount is awarded to the landlord in respect of waste and breaches of covenant committed by the tenant than is awarded as compensation for improvements, the landlord cannot recover the balance under the procedure given by this Act (*x*).

As far as reasonably may be . . —These words ought not to prevent an increase of the claim afterwards, if the claimant finds that he has estimated it too low, but they will be sufficient to prevent a party from setting up an entirely fresh claim before the referee in respect of other matters.

A sum must be specified.

The party claiming must, it should be noticed, claim a specific sum in respect of compensation. No right of appeal is given unless the "sum claimed" exceeds £100 (*y*); this refers to each party's original claim, and not to the sum total of the claims both of landlord and tenant.

The limitation "as far as reasonably may be" should make parties careful to prevent all kinds of bolstered up claims by means of an ambiguous notice, and in support of which there is no evidence.

Compensation agreed or settled by reference.
Form 13

8. The *landlord* and the *tenant* may agree on the amount and mode and time of payment of compensation to be paid under this Act. If in any case they do not so agree, the difference shall be settled by a reference.

(*u*) *Smith* v. *Acock,* (1885), 53 L.T. 230.
(*x*) *In re Holmes and Formby,* (1895), 1 Q.B. 174 ; 64 L.J.Q.B. 391 ; 71 L.T. 342 ; 43 W.R. 205 ; 15 R. 114.
(*y*) Sect. 23; *post* p. 62.
(*z*) Appendix III., *post* p. 138.

A claim for compensation by a tenant, if disputed, must be referred to arbitration, and cannot form the subject of a counter-claim in an action for rent brought by the landlord (*a*). Manisty, J., said: "The Legislature has thought right that these new claims for compensation in respect of agricultural improvements should be matters for reference, and not submitted to the decision of a jury. To allow this counter-claim to remain on the record would be a violation of the Act of Parliament, and it is one which is beyond the jurisdiction of the High Court to entertain."

46 & 47 Vict. c. 61.

Reference compulsory.

9. Where there is a reference under this Act, a referee, or two referees and an umpire, shall be appointed as follows:—

Appointment of referee or referees and umpire.

(1.) If the parties concur, there may be a single referee appointed by them jointly: Form 17 (*b*).

(2.) If before award the single referee dies or becomes incapable of acting, or for seven days after notice from the parties, or either of them, requiring him to act, fails to act, the proceedings shall begin afresh, as if no referee had been appointed: Forms 17, 19 (*c*).

(3.) If the parties do not concur in the appointment of a single referee, each of them shall appoint a referee: Form 17 (*b*).

(4.) If before award one of two referees dies or becomes incapable of acting, or for seven days after notice from either party requiring him to act, fails to act, the party appointing him shall appoint another referee: Forms 17, 19 (*c*).

(5.) Notice of every appointment of a referee by either party shall be given to the other party: Form 18 (*d*).

(6) If for fourteen days after notice by one party to the other to appoint a referee, or another referee, the other party fails to do so, then, on the application of the party giving notice, the *county court* shall within fourteen days appoint a competent and impartial person to be a referee: Form 18. Forms 32, 33 (*e*).

(*a*) *Gaslight and Coke Company v. Holloway* (1883). 5= L.T. 434 ; 49 J.P. 344.
(*b*) Appendix III., *post* p. 139.
(*c*) Appendix III., *post* pp. 139, 140.
(*d*) Appendix III., *post* p. 140.
(*e*) Appendix IV., *post* p. 145.

46 & 17 Vict.
c. 61.

Form 27 (*f*).

Form 27.

Form 23 (*g*).

Forms 32, 33.

(7.) Where two referees are appointed, then (subject to the provisions of this Act) they shall before they enter on the reference appoint an umpire :

(8.) If before award an umpire dies or becomes incapable of acting, the referees shall appoint another umpire :

(9.) If for seven days after request from either party the referees fail to appoint an umpire, or another umpire, then, on the application of either party, the *county court* shall within fourteen days appoint a competent and impartial person to be the umpire :

(10.) Every appointment, notice, and request under this section shall be in writing.

Single referee.

Application to County Court for appointment of referee or umpire.

Sub-sect. (1)—The single referee will proceed to the reference without anything further being done under this section.
The procedure on application for appointment of referee or umpire under this sub-section, and under sub-sect. 9 of this section is now regulated by Order XL., Rule 7A, of the County Court Rules, 1889 (*h*). The application is heard by the judge unless the parties consent to its being heard by the registrar (*i*).

Sub-sect. (7)—" Subject to the provisions of this Act." See sect. 10 (*k*).

Sub-sect. (8)—It will be noticed that the Act does not provide for the contingency of the umpire failing to Act.

Sub-sect. (9)—See note to sub-sect (6).

Requisition for appointment of umpire by Land Commissioners, &c.

Forms 24, 25, 26 (*l*).

10. Provided that, where two referees are appointed, an umpire may be appointed as follows :

(1.) If either party, on appointing a referee, requires, by notice in writing to the other, that the umpire shall be appointed by the Land Commissioners for England, then the umpire, and any successor to him, shall be appointed, on the application of either party, by those Commissioners.

(*f*) Appendix III., *post* p. 14*.
(*g*) Appendix III., *post* p. 141.
(*h*) *Post* p. 102.
(*i*) *In re Griffiths and Morris*, (1895), 1 Q.B. 865 ; 64 L.J.Q.B. 186 ; 72 L.T. 270 ; 43 W.R. 652 ; 59 J.P. 134 ; 15 R. 301. County Court Rules, 1889, Order XI... rule 7A, (2) & (3). *Post* p. 102.
(*k*) *Infra*.
(*l*) Appendix III., *post* p. 141.

(2.) In every other case, if either party on appointing a referee requires, by notice in writing to the other, that the umpire shall be appointed by the *county court*, then, unless the other party dissents by notice in writing therefrom, the umpire, and any successor to him, shall on the application of either party be so appointed, and in case of such dissent the umpire, and any successor to him, shall be appointed on the application of either party, by the Land Commissioners for England. 46 & 47 Vict. c. 61.

Sub-sect. (1) *on appointing a referee*—The appointment of a referee is a condition precedent to such a requisition, and notice can only be given on such appointment.
Sub-sect. (2)—There is no date for the dissent. He must be allowed a reasonable time.

11. The powers of the *county court* under this Act relative to the appointment of a referee or umpire shall be exerciseable by the judge of the court having jurisdiction, whether he is without or within his district, and may, by consent of the parties, be exercised by the registrar of the court. Exercise of powers of County Court.

By consent—The power to appoint a referee or umpire under this Act is exercisable by the judge unless the parties consent to its exercise by the registrar (*n*.)

12. The delivery to a referee of his appointment shall be deemed a submission to a reference by the party delivering it; and neither party shall have power to revoke a submission, or the appointment of a referee, without the consent of the other. Mode of submission to reference. Forms 20, 21 (*n*).

13. The referee or referees or umpire may call for the production of any sample, or voucher, or other document, or other evidence which is in the possession or power of either party, or which either party can produce, and which to the referee or referees or umpire seems necessary for determination of the Power for referee, &c., to require production of documents, administer oaths, &c. Form 30 (*o*).

(*m*) *In re Griffiths and Morris*, (1895), 1 Q.B. 866 ; 64 L.J.Q.B. 386 ; 72 L.T. 290 ; 43 W.R. 652 ; 59 J.P. 134 ; 15 R. 301.
(*n*) Appendix III., *post* p. 140.
(*o*) Appendix III., *post* p. 142.

46 & 47 VICT.
c. 61.

matters referred, and may take the examination of the parties and witnesses on oath, and may administer oaths and take affirmations ; and if any person so sworn or affirming wilfully and corruptly gives false evidence he shall be guilty of perjury.

Which is in the possession or power—This limitation considerably narrows the value of this section, as, unless samples, vouchers, and documents, are kept by the parties, the referee may call in vain for the production of them (*p*).

Power to proceed in absence.

Form 29 (*q*).

14. The referee or referees or umpire may proceed in the absence of either party where the same appears to him or them expedient, after notice given to the parties.

Form of award.

Form 31 (*r*).

15. The award shall be in writing, signed by the referee or referees or umpire.

The referee should be very careful in making his award, as a mistake once made cannot be altered when the award is executed (*s*).
The only remedy in such a case is by appeal to the County Court to impeach the award as invalid, and this can only be done when the sum claimed is over £100. The Court will then amend the award, or remit it to be reheard as to whole or part (*t*).
The award must be stamped at the rate of 3d. for every £5 up to £200 ; under £500, 15s. ; under £750, £1 ; under £1,000, £1 5s. ; and above £1,000, £1 15s.

Time for award of referee or referees.

Form 22 (*u*).

16. A single referee shall make his award ready for delivery within twenty-eight days after his appointment.

Two referees shall make their award ready for delivery within twenty-eight days after the appointment of the last appointed of them, or within such extended time (if any) as they from time to time jointly fix by writing under their hands, so that they make their award ready for delivery within a time not exceeding in the whole forty-nine days after the appointment of the last appointed of them.

(*p*) See Appendix I., clauses 16 and 8a, *post* pp. 128, 134.
(*q*) Appendix III., *post* p. 142.
(*r*) Appendix III., *post* p. 143.
(*s*) *Mordue* v. *Palmer*, (1870), L.R. 6 Ch. 22 ; 40 L.J. Ch. 8 ; 23 L.T. 752 19 W.R. 86.
(*t*) Sect. 23, *post* p. 62.
(*u*) Appendix III., *post* p. 141.

17. In any case provided for by sections 3, 4, or 5, if compensation is claimed under this Act, such compensation as under any of those sections is to be deemed to be substituted for compensation under this Act, if and so far as the same can, consistently with the terms of the agreement, if any, be ascertained by the referees or the umpire, shall be awarded in respect of any improvements thereby provided for, and the award shall, when necessary, distinguish such improvements and the amount awarded in respect thereof; and an award given under this section shall be subject to the appeal provided by the Act.

46 & 47 Vict. c. 61.

Award in respect of compensation under ss. 3, 4, 5.

If and so far as the same can—This section is by no means clear. The most reasonable construction would be that the section would only apply when the substituted agreement provides no *mode of assessing* compensation, such as clauses 29 and 13a (*x*). But where there is an agreement providing compensation and a mode of assessing it, there seems to be nothing to prevent the tenant from claiming under the Act, or the referee from making an award, and in doing so deciding on the fairness of the compensation agreed upon, or upon the application of the Act to the holding.

18. Where two referees are appointed and act, if they fail to make their award ready for delivery within the time aforesaid, then, on the expiration of that time, their authority shall cease, and thereupon the matters referred to them shall stand referred to the umpire.

Reference to and award by umpire.

The umpire shall make his award ready for delivery within twenty-eight days after notice in writing given to him by either party or referee of the reference to him, or within such extended time (if any) as the registrar of the *county court* from time to time appoints, on the application of the umpire or of either party, made before the expiration of the time appointed by or extended under this section.

Form 28 (*y*).

Forms 35, 36 (*z*).

Twenty-eight days after—Exclusive of the day on which matters were referred (*a*).

Application of the umpire, etc.—The application must be by summons in chambers. The Act does not fix any limit to extension of time by the Registrar.

(*x*) Appendix I., *post* pp. 130, 134.
(*y*) Appendix III., p. 142.
(*z*) Appendix IV., pp. 145, 146.
(*a*) *In re Higham*, (1840). 9 Dowl. 203.

45 & 47 Vict. c. 61.

Award to give particulars.

Form 31 (b).

19. The award shall not award a sum generally for compensation, but shall, so far as possible specify—

(*a.*) The several improvements, acts, and things in respect whereof compensation is awarded, and the several matters and things taken into account under the provisions of this Act in reduction or augmentation of such compensation ;

(*b.*) The time at which each improvement, act, or thing was executed, done, committed, or permitted ;

(*c.*) The sum awarded in respect of each improvement, act, matter, and thing ; and

(*d.*) Where the *landlord* desires to charge his estate with the amount of compensation found due to the *tenant*, the time at which, for the purposes of such charge, each improvement, act, or thing in respect of which compensation is awarded is to be deemed to be exhausted.

Common law reference including matters within the Agricultural Holdings Act.

A common law reference may include matters within the Agricultural Holdings Act. In *Shrubb* v. *Lee* (*c*), a tenant gave notice of claim for compensation under the Act, and the landlord gave notice to the tenant of a counter-claim for dilapidations and breaches of covenant. The parties not agreeing as to the amounts payable under their respective claims, the landlord gave the tenant notice, under the Act, appointing D. to act on his behalf. The tenant acted in the matter as his own arbitrator. The arbitrators did not appoint an umpire before entering upon the reference, but, differences having arisen, they appointed W. to act as umpire. The appointment of the umpire was in the following form : " We, the undersigned, hereby appoint you our umpire to settle all differences that have arisen between us in this valuation, which relate to compensation for unexhausted lime, manures, and feeding stuffs, and counter-claims for dilapidations and breaches of covenant on both sides, under a lease, dated July 20, 1880, and under the Agricultural Holdings Acts, 1875 and 1883, and we agree to abide by your decision in writing as final and binding on all parties." This was signed by both arbitrators. The umpire made his award in writing, as follows : " I do award that the sum of £96 11s. is payable by the said Charles Shrubb to the said William Lee, balance in full satisfaction of all claims made by either party." The landlord appealed against the award upon the grounds (1) that it was obligatory that the award should have been made under the Agricultural Holdings Act. 1883 : (2) that the award was invalid, because it awarded a sum generally in respect of claims under the Agricultural Holdings Acts, 1875 and 1883, and of claims arising outside those Acts, without distinguishing between the

(*b*) Appendix III., *post* p. 14;.
(*c*) (1888), 59 L.T. 376 ; 53 J.P. 54.

two sets of claims ; (3) that the award was bad, as it awarded a sum 46 & 47 Vict,
generally for compensation, and did not, as required by sect. 19 of the c. 61.
Act, specify (a) the several improvements in respect of which compensation was awarded ; (b) the time at which each improvement was
executed ; (c) the sum awarded in respect of each improvement.

The Court (Lord Coleridge, C.J., and Mathew, J.) held that the
reference was a common law reference, and that the award was outside
the Agricultural Holdings Act, and none the less so because it may
have included some matters which were within the Act ; and that the
award was final and conclusive between the parties.

20. The costs of and attending the reference, Costs of reference.
including the remuneration of the referee or referees
and umpire, where the umpire has been required to
act, and including other proper expenses, shall be
borne and paid by the parties in such proportion as
to the referee or referees or umpire appears just,
regard being had to the reasonableness or unreason-
ableness of the claim of either party in respect of
amount or otherwise, and to all the circumstances of
the case.

The award may direct the payment of the whole Form 31 (d).
or any part of the costs aforesaid by the one party to
the other.

The costs aforesaid shall be subject to taxation by
the registrar of the county court, on the application
of either party, but that taxation shall be subject to
review by the judge of the county court.

A referee or umpire making an award under this Act cannot award Costs.
costs to be paid as between solicitor and client (e).

21. The award shall fix a day, not sooner than one Day for
month after the delivery of the award, for the pay- payment.
ment of money awarded for compensation, costs or Form 31 (d).
otherwise.

22. A submission or award shall not be made a Submission not
rule of any court, or be removable by any process &c.
into any court, and an award shall not be questioned
otherwise than as provided by this Act.

The question of appeal is dealt with in the next section.

(d) Appendix III., post p. 143.
(e) *In re Griffiths & Morris*, (1805). 1 Q.B. 866 ; 64 L.J.Q.B. 386 ; 72 L.T.
290 ; 43 W.R. 652 ; 59 J.P. 134 ; 15 R. 301.

46 & 47 VICT.
c. 61.

Appeal to county court.

23. Where the sum claimed for compensation exceeds £100, either party may, within seven days after delivery of the award, appeal against it to the judge of the *county court* on all or any of the following grounds :

(1.) That the award is invalid ;

Form 37 (*f*).

(2.) That the award proceeds wholly or in part upon an improper application of or upon the omission properly to apply the special provisions of sects. 3, 4, or 5 of this Act ;

Forms 38 (a) (b) 39 (*g*).

(3.) That compensation has been awarded for improvements, acts, or things, breaches of covenants or agreements, or for committing or permitting waste, in respect of which the party claiming was not entitled to compensation ;

(4.) That compensation has not been awarded for improvements, acts, or things, breaches of covenants or agreements, or for committing or permitting waste, in respect of which the party claiming was entitled to compensation ;

and the judge shall hear and determine the appeal, and may, in his discretion, remit the case to be reheard as to the whole or any part thereof by the referee or referees or umpire, with such directions as he may think fit.

If no appeal is so brought, the award shall be final.

Appeal to High Court on point of law.

The decision of the judge of the *county court* on appeal shall be final, save that the judge shall, at the request of either party, state a special case on a question of law for the judgment of the High Court of Justice, and the decision of the High Court on the case, and respecting costs and any other matter connected therewith, shall be final, and the judge of the *county court* shall act thereon.

The "sum claimed."

Sum claimed for compensation exceeds £100.—If the claim comes anywhere near this sum it will probably be increased so as to reserve the right of appeal. The appellant has, however, only seven days in which to consider about appealing. By sect. 7, the amount claimed must be stated in the notice. It is submitted that the "sum claimed"

(*f*) Appendix IV., *post* p. 146.
(*g*) Appendix IV., *post* p. 146, 147.

means the sum claimed by either party in the first instance, and not the aggregate of all sums claimed by both parties or the sum claimed by the tenant only.

Either party may appeal.—This section (with the exception of subsect. 2), is a re-enactment of sect. 36 of the Agricultural Holdings (England) Act, 1875. It was, with other sections of the Act of 1875, originally incorporated in the present Act merely by reference to the Act of 1875; but in deference to a generally expressed opinion in committee that such a course would be objectionable, the Government re-numbered the sections and embodied the whole in one Act. Order XL., rules 1—6 of the County Court Rules, 1889 (*h*), provide for the procedure on appeal under this section.

It is contrary to all precedent to allow an appeal against an award made by arbitrators chosen by the parties, but under this section the parties, even if they have agreed upon their umpire, can appeal.

To the Judge of the County Court.—This would seem to exclude the right to call for a jury.

An improper application.—Having regard to sect. 17 (*i*), it will be a matter entirely in the discretion of the referee whether he awards compensation under a substituted agreement, or whether he refuses to make an award on the ground that he cannot ascertain compensation consistently with the terms of the agreement. Where there is any specific compensation provided by the agreement, and any arbitration clause, this latter would appear to be the proper course for the referee to take. If there is no arbitration clause, he will assess the compensation due under the agreement by his award, in the manner provided by the Act.

That the award is invalid.—The award, generally speaking, will be invalid, if it goes beyond the submission; if it does not decide all the points submitted (unless the terms of the submission shew that the parties did not intend every point to be decided by the referee (*k*)), that is to say, if it is not a complete determination of all the matters submitted by the parties to the referee or umpire, but is uncertain, or not final or impossible; if the amount is uncertain, as, for instance, if the referee ordered the payment of arrears of rent without saying how much the arrears were; if the award upon the face of it shews a plain mistake (*l*).

If the award is bad in part and good in part, and the parts can be separated, the good part may be enforced (*m*).

Shall hear and determine . . and may . . remit.—The Court must hear the case and determine the points in dispute. It may then, if it thinks fit, remit the case to the referees or umpire to make a further award. But the Court may also make an award itself on the hearing instead of remitting to the referees.

46 & 47 Vict. c. 61.

Practice on appeal to the county court.

When award invalid.

24. Where any money agreed or awarded or ordered on appeal to be paid for compensation, costs, or otherwise, is not paid within fourteen days after

Recovery of compensation.

(*h*) *Post* pp. 100, 101.
(*i*) *Ante* p. 59.
(*k*) *Wrightson* v. *Bywater*, (1838), 3 M. & W. 199; 7 L.J.Ex. 83.
(*l*) *Cornforth* v. *Geer*, (1715), 2 Vern. 705.
(*m*) *Doe* v. *Cox*, (1846), 15 L.J.Q.B. 317; 4 D. & L. 75; 11 Jur. 991.

64   *Agricultural Holdings (England) Act*, 1883.

46 & 47 VICT. c. 61.

Form 39 (*n*).

the time when it is agreed or awarded or ordered to be paid, it shall be recoverable, upon order made by the judge of the *county court*, as money ordered by a *county court* under its ordinary jurisdiction to be paid is recoverable.

Within fourteen days.—The fourteen days will run from the date of the agreement between the parties under sect. 8, or from the date when the award is delivered to the party sought to be charged. "After the time when it is awarded," can hardly mean from the date of the award, as hardship might occur if the referee did not notify the award to the parties charged. The time limited for payment is very short, and if the incoming tenant pays the valuation, the provisions of the section may lead to some inconvenience.

As money ordered by a county court, etc.—See, however, the provisions of sect. 31 (*o*).

Proceedings under this section.

Money ordered by a county court under its ordinary jurisdiction to be paid is recoverable by (1) execution against the goods of the debtor, by (2) commitment under a judgment summons, and by (3) attachment of debts under a garnishee order.

A summons would in most cases appear to be necessary under this section for an order on which to ground the execution, as the section says that the sum shall be recoverable only "upon order made by the judge of the county court."

The ordinary form of summons on a plaint for a liquidated sum will, therefore, be applicable to every such case, except the case where the money is ordered to be paid on appeal. In this latter case, the warrant of execution will be grounded on the order of the court.

Application by a person not a party.

When the application is made by some person not a party to the action, an order must be obtained upon summons for payment. The leave of the registrar must then be obtained before the execution can issue.

Award to landlord in excess of tenant's claim.

It has been held (*p*) that where a greater amount is awarded to the landlord in respect of waste and breaches of covenant committed by the tenant than is awarded to the tenant as compensation for improvements, the landlord cannot recover the balance under the procedure given by the Act. Grantham J. said: "The Act was intended to give them (*i.e.* the tenants) compensation for unexhausted improvements, which, it was supposed, they could not otherwise get, and to provide a procedure for the ascertainment and recovery of such compensation. While the matter was in course of debate it was urged that it would be a hardship upon a landlord, having a good claim against his tenant, and being saddled perhaps with the payment of a considerable sum for unexhausted improvements, if the tenant were able to put the money in his pocket and go off, leaving the landlord unable to get payment of what was due to him. Two provisions were therefore inserted in the Act. First, the landlord, on paying compensation to a tenant under the Act, was entitled to obtain from the county court a charge on the holding to the amount of the compensation paid ; and, secondly, if he

---

(*n*) Appendix IV., *post* p. 147.
(*o*) *Post* p. 71.
(*p*) *In re Holmes and Formby*, (1895) 1 Q.B. 174 ; 64 L.J.Q.B. 391 ; 71 L T. 842 ; 43 W.R. 205 ; 15 R. 114.

had any claim against the tenant less than or equivalent to the tenant's claim against him, he could set-off his claim against that of the tenant. I feel confident that if, as has been contended, the Legislature had intended to give the landlord power to claim as fully as the tenant the Act would have been very different."

46 & 47 VICT. c. 61.

A County Court Judge cannot make an order to enforce an award by execution under this section where the umpire has allowed compensation in respect of matters which are not the subject of compensation under the Agricultural Holdings Act, 1883. It has been decided that where a County Court Judge has exceeded his jurisdiction in this way, a writ of prohibition ought to issue with respect to so much of the award as deals with matters outside the Agricultural Holdings Act, and this notwithstanding that the lease provides that compensation in respect of matters outside the Act shall be ascertained upon the basis provided by that Act (*q*). Lord Halsbury, L.C., in giving judgment, said : "It has been long settled that where an objection to the jurisdiction of an inferior court appears on the face of the proceedings, it is immaterial by what means, and by whom the court is informed of such objection. The Court must protect the prerogative of the Crown and the due course of the administration of justice by prohibiting the inferior court from proceeding in matters as to which it is apparent that it has no jurisdiction. The objection to the jurisdiction does not in such a case depend on some matter of fact as to which the inferior court may have been deceived or misled, or which it may have unconsciously neglected to observe, and the judge of such court, therefore, must or ought to have known that he was acting beyond his jurisdiction. I find no authority justifying the withholding of a writ of prohibition in such a case. Looking to what appears on the face of the award in this case, and applying to that the provisions of the Agricultural Holdings Act and the power of enforcing awards given by that Act, I think it is impossible to doubt that there is that on the face of the proceedings which shows that the judge in granting execution under the provisions of that Act was acting beyond his jurisdiction. The Act specifies the matters which are to be the subject of compensation under it; and it appears on the face of the award that there are matters included in the compensation awarded which are outside the provisions of the Act. Sect. 24 of the Act provides in substance that a sum awarded as compensation under the Act may be recovered on the order of the County Court Judge as money recovered by an ordinary county court judgment. It is apparent that, in applying that section to subject-matters which are not included in the provisions of the Act, the county court was exceeding its jurisdiction. Under these circumstances, reluctant as I am to aid the appellant in this case, I am unable to resist the conclusion that the writ ought to issue."

County Court Judge cannot order execution in respect of award outside Agricultural Holdings Act, 1883 — prohibition.

25. Where a *landlord* or *tenant* is an infant without a guardian, or is of unsound mind, not so found by inquisition, the *county court*, on the application of any *person* interested, may appoint a guardian of the

Appointment of guardian.

Forms 34, 36 (r).

(*q*) *Farquharson* v. *Morgan*, (1894), 1 Q.B. 552; 63 L.J.Q.B. 474; 70 L.T. 152; 42 W.R. 306; 58 J.P. 495.
(*r*) Appendix IV., *post* pp. 145, 146.

46 & 47 Vict.
c. 61.

infant or *person* of unsound mind for the purposes of this Act, and may change the guardian if and as occasion requires.

Costs.

On the application of any person interested—No provision is made for the costs of the person applying. They should be asked for at the hearing of the summons, under sect. 27 (*s*).

Provisions respecting married women.

26. Where the appointment of a *person* to act as the next friend of a married woman is required for the purposes of this Act, the *county court* may make such appointment, and may remove or change that next friend if and as occasion requires.

A woman married before the commencement of the Married Women's Property Act, 1882, entitled for her separate use to land, her title to which accrued before such commencement as aforesaid, and not restrained from anticipation, shall, for the purposes of this Act, be in respect of land as if she was unmarried.

Where any other woman married before the commencement of the Married Women's Property Act, 1882, is desirous of doing any act under this Act in respect of land, her title to which accrued before such commencement as aforesaid, her husband's concurrence shall be requisite, and she shall be examined apart from him by the *county court*, or by the judge of the *county court* for the place where she for the time being is, touching her knowledge of the nature and effect of the intended act, and it shall be ascertained that she is acting freely and voluntarily.

Costs in county court.

27. The costs of proceedings in the *county court* under this Act shall be in the discretion of the court.

The Lord Chancellor may from time to time prescribe a scale of costs for those proceedings, and of costs to be taxed by the registrar of the court.

All costs not otherwise specially provided for, are, by sect. 113 of the County Courts Act, 1888, in the discretion of the court.

Service of notice, &c.

28. Any notice, request, demand, or other instrument under this Act may be served on the *person* to

(*s*) *Infra.*

whom it is to be given, either personally or by leaving it for him at his last known place of abode in England, or by sending it through the post in a registered letter addressed to him there; and if so sent by post it shall be deemed to have been served at the time when the letter containing it would be delivered in ordinary course; and in order to prove service by letter it shall be sufficient to prove that the letter was properly addressed and posted, and that it contained the notice, request, demand, or other instrument to be served. 46 & 47 VICT. c. 61.

Charge of Tenant's Compensation.

29. A *landlord*, on paying to the *tenant* the amount due to him in respect of compensation under this Act, or in respect of compensation authorised by this Act to be substituted for compensation under this Act, or on expending such amount as may be necessary to execute an improvement under the second part of the First Schedule hereto, after notice given by the *tenant* of his intention to execute such improvement in accordance with this Act, shall be entitled to obtain from the *county court* a charge on the *holding*, or any part thereof, to the amount of the sum so paid or expended. Power for landlord on paying compensation to obtain charge. Form 40(*t*).

The court shall, on proof of the payment or expenditure, and on being satisfied of the observance in good faith by the parties of the conditions imposed by this Act, make an order charging the *holding*, or any part thereof, with repayment of the amount paid or expended, with such interest, and by such instalments, and with such direction for giving effect to the charge, as the court thinks fit.

But, where the *landlord* obtaining the charge is not absolute owner of the *holding* for his own benefit, no instalment or interest shall be made payable after the time when the improvement in respect whereof compensation is paid will, where an award has been made, be taken to have been exhausted according to the declaration of the award, and in any other case

---

(*t*) Appendix IV., p. 148.

5 A

after the time when any such improvement will in the opinion of the court, after hearing such evidence (if any), as it thinks expedient, have become exhausted.

The instalments and interest shall be charged in favour of the *landlord*, his executors, administrators, and assigns.

The estate or interest of any *landlord* holding for an estate or interest determinable or liable to forfeiture by reason of his creating or suffering any charge thereon shall not be determined or forfeited by reason of his obtaining a charge under this Act, anything in any deed, will, or other instrument to the contrary thereof notwithstanding.

Capital money arising under the Settled Land Act, 1882, may be applied in payment of any moneys expended and costs incurred by a *landlord* under or in pursuance of this Act in or about the execution of any improvement mentioned in the first or second parts of the schedule hereto, as for an improvement authorised by the said Settled Land Act ; and such money may also be applied in discharge of any charge created on a *holding* under or in pursuance of this Act in respect of any such improvement as aforesaid, as in discharge of an incumbrance authorised by the said Settled Land Act to be discharged out of such capital money.

A landlord on paying—See sects. 30, 31 and 56 (*u*). These words exclude the incoming tenant who pays compensation to the outgoing tenant from charging his payments on the holding. He may himself obtain compensation on quitting.

Checks upon limited owners. *The court shall, etc.*—This provision it will be noticed is imperative. It is not very easy to understand to what the "observance in good faith" and so on, refers But it is probably meant to be a check to prevent limited owners from obtaining money from a land company under sect. 32 for compensation which has never been paid. In such case, proof of the consent and notice required by sects. 3 and 4 and of the due execution and unexhausted value of the improvement (if there has been no award), will be necessary before the court will charge the holding.

Powers of sale, &c. *Direction for giving effect to the charge*—Such as a power of sale. In addition to the powers of distress and entry conferred upon it, a land company having a charge for drainage works executed by them upon

(*u*) *Infra*.

glebe lands belonging to a rectory, were held entitled to sell the glebe to pay the arrears of the charge (*x*). This would appear to be the most reasonable course to take when the charge is in arrear, as no tenant would be found to take lands with the liability of distress for the charge in arrear.

46 & 47 Vict. c. 61.

The Act may create a great hardship on those clergy whose sole endowment is glebe lands. If times are bad and rents fall the glebe may be sold by the mortgagee to pay the charges, and thus the endowment will be lost to the incumbency.

Hardship on the clergy.

By sect. 39, however, "the powers by this Act conferred," which it is presumed includes the power of charging the holding with sums paid for compensation, shall not be exercised by an incumbent-landlord except with the previous approval in writing of the Governors of Queen Anne's Bounty. *In every such case*, the Governors may, *if they think fit*, advance the money to pay compensation, and take a charge on the holding themselves.

Where the landlord . . . is not absolute owner—A landowner entitled in fee will obtain no benefit by a charge. A life tenant or other limited owner may obtain a charge in his own favour, in which case if he die his representatives may continue to take the benefit of the charge or he may recoup himself his capital by mortgaging the land under sect. 32 (*y*), and then if he die the remaindermen will bear part of the cost. This part of the section is for the benefit of the remaindermen, as it prevents the life-owner from recouping himself entirely at the expense of the estate, by limiting the number of years over which the instalments are to be spread.

Limited owner.

The executors of a landlord, tenant for life, who have been compelled under the Act to pay compensation for improvements to an outgoing tenant, who had claimed compensation, and whose tenancy had been determined before the death of the landlord, are entitled to a charge upon the holding in respect of the amount which they have so paid. In a recent case (*z*) a petition asked for an order, charging the holding with payment to the petitioners of £35 paid by them to an outgoing tenant, H. The deceased was the tenant for life of a farm, and H. was yearly tenant of the farm under him. H.'s tenancy was determined by him by a notice to quit expiring on March 25, 1890, and before the expiration of his tenancy he claimed compensation under the Act for improvements. Two valuers were appointed, and they, on April 5, agreed upon £35 as the amount of compensation to be paid under sect. 8 of the Act. On April 8, the tenant for life died, having up to that time been in receipt of the rents and profits of the lands in question as tenant for life. The ownership then passed to the remaindermen in fee. On April 24, the executors of the tenant for life paid the £35 to H., and afterwards presented a petition to the county court in order to obtain a charge upon the holding for that amount. Lord Esher, M.R., in the course of his judgment, said : " In my opinion the appellants cannot succeed unless they can bring themselves within the final clause of sect. 61. I agree with Vaughan Williams, J., that *primâ facie* the definition of 'landlord' in that section shuts out the executors of a landlord. The definition says that 'landlord' means (it does not say 'includes')

Executors of landlord who have paid compensation entitled to a charge upon holding.

(*x*) *Scottish Widows' Fund* v. *Craig*, (1882), 20 C.D. 208 ; 51 L.J.Ch. 363 ; 30 W.R. 463.
(*y*) *Infra*.
(*z*) *Gough* v. *Gough*, (1891), 2 Q.B. 665 ; 60 L.J.Q.B. 726 ; 65 L.T. 110 ; 39 W.R. 593 ; 55 J.P. 807.

46 & 47 VICT. c. 61.	'any person for the time being entitled to receive the rents and profits of any holding.' I doubt whether the executors of a landlord would come within that definition. It is a hard and fast definition, and the result is that you cannot give any other meaning to the word 'landlord' in the Act than that which is mentioned in the definition. It is quite different in the case of a tenant. There the draftsman has dropped the word 'means,' and has said that 'tenant' 'includes executors, administrators, etc., of a tenant'—that is, the word as used in the Act includes the ordinary meaning, and adds something to it. In the case of a landlord, on the contrary, the word can have no other meaning than that which is stated in the definition. Then we come to another clause—the final clause—of sect. 61, which would be idle if the words 'landlord' and 'tenant' in it are to be restricted to the meaning given in the prior definitions. The clause provides that the 'designations of landlord and tenant'—that is, the words used in the Act to designate those persons—'shall continue to apply to the parties until the conclusion of any proceedings taken under or in pursuance of this Act in respect of compensation for improvements.' There is, therefore, a time when the terms 'landlord' and 'tenant' are not to be strictly construed according to the prior definitions, but the designations are to continue to apply to the parties although the definitions would not apply. 'To the parties'—the question is whether, in such a case as the present, the phrase will include the executors of a landlord who was tenant for life of the property. The proceedings under the Act were commenced during the life of the tenant for life, and they were to go on till they were concluded. While they were going on the tenant for life died. Were the proceedings concluded by his death? No, they went on. His executors had to pay the sum awarded for compensation, and they became parties to the proceedings. Does the word 'parties' in the final clause of sect. 61 mean the 'parties to the original contract of tenancy' only? . . . Sect. 61 of the Act of 1883 says 'apply to the parties,' omitting the words 'to a contract of tenancy' [which were in the Act of 1875]. The phrase used in the Act of 1875 was a more limited one, and applied to a more limited class. The word 'parties' is now left at large, and we must give effect to the alteration; and we can do that only by saying that the word 'parties' includes a larger number of persons than 'parties to a contract of tenancy.' To whom does the word 'parties' in the later Act apply? It must have some limitation, and I think it must mean parties to the proceedings which are initiated, and are to be carried out under the Act. It will, therefore, include the executors of a landlord when they have become parties to the proceedings. Although the executors of a tenant for life do not come within the definition of 'landlord,' yet, if a question of compensation has arisen, the term 'landlord' is to continue to apply to the parties to the proceedings until the conclusion of the proceedings. According, therefore, to the ordinary rules of construction, this will bring in the executors of a tenant for life who has died during the pending of the proceedings, and in this way justice will be done, and an injustice, which one of my learned brethren has characterised as both monstrous and senseless, will be avoided."
Mortgages.	Charges will of course rank in order of time. Where land is in mortgage, the rights of mortgagees are preserved by sect. 30 (a), limiting the charge to the interest of the landlord and to interests subsequent to that of the landlord.

(a) *Infra*.

By sect. 5 of the Settled Land Act, 1882, it is enacted that, "Where on a sale exchange or partition there is an incumbrance affecting the land sold or given in exchange or on partition, the tenant for life with the consent of the incumbrancer, may charge that incumbrance on any other part of the settled land, whether already charged therewith or not, in exoneration of the part sold or so given, and, by conveyance of the fee simple, or other estate or interest the subject of the settlement, or by creation of a term of years in the settled land, make provision accordingly." *46 & 47 Vict. c. 61. Charge of incumbrance on other part of land.*

30. The sum charged by the order of a *county court* under this Act shall be a charge on the *holding*, or the part thereof charged, for the *landlord's* interest therein, and for all interests therein subsequent to that of the *landlord*; but so that the charge shall not extend beyond the interest of the *landlord*, his executors, administrators, and assigns, in the tenancy where the *landlord* is himself a *tenant* of the *holding*. *Incidence of charge.*

All interest subsequent to that of the landlord—i.e., subsequent in order of time and inferior to the landlord's interest. The Act, by making the charge bind only subsequent interests, saves the rights of mortgagees and other persons having interests superior to the landlord, whilst it will extend to bind the land in the hands of a subsequent mortgagee or purchaser. An intending purchaser or mortgagee of Agricultural Holdings will therefore have to make searches for charges in the county court. *Searches for charges by purchaser.*

Where the landlord is himself a tenant—i.e., where a tenant underleases, and the underlessee obtains compensation from the tenant, who charges it upon his holding. Though the executors or administrators of the deceased tenant and the assignee of his interest will take it burdened with the charge, such a charge will not bind the underlessee's interest. *Underleases.*

Assigns—The word "assigns" is a term of well-known signification, comprehending all those who take either immediately or remotely from or under the assignor, whether by conveyance, devise, descent or act of law (*b*). *Who are assigns.*

A trustee in bankruptcy is probably included in the word "Assigns," as he might disclaim the tenant's interest if the charge was onerous. (By sect. 61 *tenant* includes trustee in bankruptcy of a tenant.) But with this and like exceptions it is presumed that the Act means "voluntary assigns," and not assigns thrust upon him by Act of Parliament, such as a company taking land under compulsory powers (*c*).

31. Where the *landlord* is a *person* entitled to receive the rents and profits of any *holding* as trustee, or in any character otherwise than for his own *Provision in case of trustee.*

(*b*) *Baily* v. *De Crespigny*, (1869), L. R. 4 Q. B. 180; 38 L. J. Q. B. 98; 19 L. T. 681; 17 W. R. 494.
(*c*) *Baily* v. *De Crespigny, supra* (*b*).

46 & 47 Vict. c. 61.

benefit, the amount due from such *landlord* in respect of compensation under this Act, or in respect of compensation authorised by this Act to be substituted for compensation under this Act, shall be charged and recovered as follows and not otherwise; (that is to say,)

(1.) The amount so due shall not be recoverable personally against such *landlord*, nor shall he be under any liability to pay such amount, but the same shall be a charge on and recoverable against the *holding* only.

Form 40 (*d*).

(2.) Such a *landlord* shall, either before or after having paid to the *tenant* the amount due to him, be entitled to obtain from the *county court* a charge on the *holding* to the amount of the sum required to be paid, or which has been paid, as the case may be, to the *tenant*.

(3.) If such *landlord* neglect or fail within one month after the *tenant* has quitted his *holding* to pay to the *tenant* the amount due to him, then after the expiration of such one month the *tenant* shall be entitled to obtain from the *county court* in favour of himself, his executors, administrators, and assigns, a charge on the *holding* to the amount of the sum due to him, and of all costs properly incurred by him in obtaining the charge or in raising the amount due thereunder.

(4.) The court shall, on proof of the *tenant's* title to have a charge made in his favour, make an order charging the *holding* with payment of the amount of the charge, including costs, in like manner and form as in case of a charge which a *landlord* is entitled to obtain.

In any character otherwise than for his own benefit—A mortgagee in possession might be such a person.

Charge before payment.

Either before or after—This section is altogether an exception. The procedure for the recovery of compensation provided by sect. 24 does

---

(*d*) Appendix III., *post* p. 148.

not apply, and the main condition, which by sect. 29 must be satisfied before a charge can be obtained, namely, payment or expenditure of compensation, is here dispensed with. The landlord is to be entitled to obtain the charge, and the court can only require the observance in good faith of the conditions imposed by the Act, proof of the agreement or award. *46 & 47 VICT. c. 61.*

On proof of the tenant's title—i.e., on proof of the agreement or award.

It is provided by sect. 3 of the Tenants' Compensation Act, 1890 (*dd*) that where compensation for improvements comprised in Part I. or Part II. of the First Schedule to this Act, is charged by an order under this section, such charge shall be a land charge within the meaning of the Land Charges Registration and Searches Act, 1888, and shall be registered accordingly.

32. Any company now or hereafter incorporated by Parliament, and having power to advance money for the improvement of land, may take an assignment of any charge made by a *county court* under the provisions of this Act, upon such terms and conditions as may be agreed upon between such company and the *person* entitled to such charge; and such company may assign any charge so acquired by them to any *person* or persons whomsoever. *Advance made by a company.*

Notice to Quit.

33. Where a half-year's notice, expiring with a year of tenancy, is by law necessary and sufficient for *determination of a tenancy from year to year,* in the case of any such tenancy under a *contract of tenancy* made either before or after the commencement of this Act, a year's notice so expiring shall by virtue of this Act be necessary and sufficient for the same, unless the *landlord* and *tenant* of the *holding,* by writing under their hands, agree that this section shall not apply, in which case a half-year's notice shall continue to be sufficient; but nothing in this section shall extend to a case where the *tenant* is adjudged bankrupt, or has filed a petition for a composition or arrangement with his creditors. *Time of notice to quit. Form 1, clause 2 (e). Forms 2, 3 (f).*

(*dd*) 53 & 54 Vict., c. 57. *Post* p. 120.
(*e*) Appendix I., *post* p. 125.
(*f*) Appendix II., *post* p. 135.

46 & 47 VICT.
c. 61.

A half-year's notice expiring with a year of tenancy—*i.e.*, when the tenant enters on March 25th he is now entitled to a half-year's notice, given at such a time that it shall expire on March 25th next after the notice was given. In future he will be entitled to a year's notice so expiring. As to when current tenancies become tenancies under the Act, the reader is referred to sect. 61 (*g*).

The provisions of this section apply to contracts of tenancy "made *either before or after* the commencement of this Act."

Meaning of "by law necessary."

This section does not apply where a half-year's notice or any other notice is expressly stipulated for. This was decided by the Court of Appeal in *Barlow* v. *Teal* (*h*). There was a clause in the tenancy under a written agreement from year to year that the tenancy should continue "until six months' notice shall have been given . . . . in the usual way to determine the tenancy." The Court of Appeal held that the tenancy was not one "where a half-year's notice . . . . is by law necessary" within this section. Brett, M.R., said : " I am of opinion upon the true construction of the Act that the section applies where there is no express stipulation as to the termination of the tenancy, and that it does not apply where there is an express stipulation. Where there is no express stipulation, the mode of determining the contract of demise is governed by the law and not by the contract entered into between the parties. Whenever a tenancy from year to year is created by implication of law, there must be a half-year's notice to quit ; if no stipulation is contained in the demise for the determination of the tenancy, a stipulation would be introduced by law that it should be determined by a half-year's notice. But where the parties to a demise have agreed that a half-year's notice shall be given, that is a stipulation created by the contract entered into between the parties, and it is not a stipulation created by the law. In the present case a six months' notice to quit has been made a term of the demise by the contract and agreement of the parties, and the present case does not fall within the provisions of sect. 33. It follows that the contract of tenancy is without those provisions ; but that is not a fatal objection to the validity of the notice to quit, for where the landlord and the tenant agree in writing that the section shall not apply, the contract as to the notice to quit is nevertheless good. Whenever there is an express contract as to the time of quitting, or as to the mode of giving notice to quit, the enactment does not apply ; the case does not fall within the section." A similar decision was given under the corresponding section of the Agricultural Holdings Act, 1875 (*i*).

Notice to quit—customary half-year.

A six months' notice to determine a yearly tenancy commencing on one of the ordinary Feast-days, means a "customary six months," that is, from one of the usual quarter-days to the quarter-day next but one following, though such six months should exceed or fall short of the number of days which constitute a half-year. Consequently a notice served on March 26 to quit on September 29 then next, is insufficient notice (*k*).

(*g*) *Post* p. 94.
(*h*) (1885), 15 Q.B.D. 501 ; 54 L.J.Q.B. 564 ; 54 L.T. 63 ; 34 W.R. 54 ; 50 J.P. 100. See also *King* v. *Eversfield*, (1897) 2 Q.B. 475 ; 66 L.J.Q.B. 809 ; 77 L.T. 195 ; 46 W.R. 51 ; 51 J.P 740 ; *post* p. 123, where it was held by the Court of Appeal that a tenancy which provided for three calendar months' notice to quit on any day of the year was nevertheless a tenancy from " year to year."
(*i*) *Wilkinson* v. *Calvert*, (1878), 3 C.P.D. 360 ; 47 L.J.C.P. 679 ; 38 L.T. 813 ; 26 W.R. 829.
(*k*) *Morgan* v. *Davies*, (1878), 3 C.P.D. 260 ; 26 W.R. 816.

34. Where, after the commencement of this Act, a *tenant* affixes to his *holding* any engine, machinery, fencing, or other fixture, or erects any building, for which he is not under this Act or otherwise entitled to compensation, and which is not so affixed or erected in pursuance of some obligation in that behalf or instead of some fixture or building belonging to the *landlord*, then such fixture or building shall be the property of and be removable by the *tenant* before or within a reasonable time after the termination of the tenancy. Provided as follows :— 46 & 47 Vict. c. 61.
Tenant's property in fixtures, machinery, &c.

(1.) Before the removal of any fixture or building the *tenant* shall pay all rent owing by him, and shall perform or satisfy all other his obligations to the *landlord* in respect of the *holding* :

(2.) In the removal of any fixture or building the *tenant* shall not do any avoidable damage to any other building or other part of the *holding* :

(3.) Immediately after the removal of any fixture or building the *tenant* shall make good all damage occasioned to any other building or other part of the *holding* by the removal :

(4.) The *tenant* shall not remove any fixture or building without giving one month's previous notice in writing to the *landlord* of the intention of the *tenant* to remove it : Form 15 (*l*).

(5.) At any time before the expiration of the notice of removal, the *landlord*, by notice in writing given by him to the *tenant*, may elect to purchase any fixture or building comprised in the notice of removal, and any fixture or building thus elected to be purchased shall be left by the *tenant*, and shall become the property of the *landlord*, who shall pay the *tenant* the fair value thereof to an incoming Form 16 (*m*).

Forms 17, 31 (*n*).

(*l*) Appendix III., *post* p. 139.
(*m*) Appendix III., *post* p. 139.
(*n*) Appendix III., *post* pp. 139, 143.

46 & 47 VICT.
c. 61.

tenant of the *holding*; and any difference as to the value shall be settled by a reference under this Act, as in case of compensation (but without appeal).

Fixtures :—The word "fixture" is apparently here used in the usual sense of anything annexed to the soil (*o*). It is to be presumed, however, that the Act only applies to what are generally called "landlord's" fixtures, such as engines and machinery, used for the purpose of agriculture, and things *ejusdem generis*, and not to "tenant's" fixtures put up for ornament or domestic use, such as book-cases, chimney-pieces, stoves, grates and so on.

What are fixtures.

In deciding what are fixtures, the questions to consider are, *first*, the mode of annexation to the soil, whether the chattel can be removed without injury to itself or to the freehold; and, *secondly*, the object and purpose of the annexation, whether it was a permanent improvement or merely for a temporary purpose (*p*).

Thus, cotton spinning machines fixed by screws into the wooden floor and into lead poured in a melted state into holes in the floor were held not to be fixtures (*q*). So chattels only resting on the ground by their own weight, though they may have sunk into the ground, or deposited in holes dug in the ground and lined with brickwork are not fixtures (*r*).

It should be remembered that all chattels not fixed to the soil are distrainable for rent.

After the commencement of this Act:—This section only applies to chattels fixed to the soil after the 1st of January, 1884.

Fixtures erected previous to Jan. 1st., 1884.

With respect to chattels fixed prior to that date, the general rule is, that a tenant who has affixed anything to the freehold during his tenancy cannot remove it without his landlord's consent. To this rule there are considerable exceptions in favour of trade governed mainly by the principles laid down in HELLAWELL *v.* EASTWOOD (*s*), but these exceptions do not extend to agriculture.

The Landlord and Tenant Act. 1851 (*t*) contained provisions enabling a tenant of a farm or lands to remove any farm building, either detached or otherwise, or any other building, engine, or machinery, erected either for agricultural purposes, or for the purposes of trade and agriculture, erected with the consent in writing of the landlord, which shall not have been erected or put up in pursuance of some obligation in that behalf.

Under such Act the tenant before removal must give his landlord a month's notice in writing, to enable him to elect to purchase the fixtures; the value to be ascertained by two referees, one chosen by each party, or their umpire.

(*o*) *Elwes* v. *Mawe*, (1802), 2 S.L.C. (10 ed.) 183; 3 East 38; 6 R.R. 523.
(*p*) *Hellawell* v. *Eastwood*, (1851), 6 Ex. 295; 20 L.J. Ex. 154. This case has been since considered and discussed in *Mather* v. *Fraser*, (1856), 2 K. & J. 536; 25 L.J. Ch. 361; 2 Jur. N.S. 900. *Reg.* v. *Lee*, (1866), L.R. 1 Q.B. 241; 35 L.J.M.C. 105; 7 B. & S. 188; 13 L.T. 704; 14 W.R. 311; 12 Jur. N.S. 225. *Longbottom* v. *Berry*, (1869), L.R. 5 Q.B. 123; 39 L.J.Q.B. 37; 22 L.T. 385; 10 B. & S. 852. *Holland* v. *Hodgson*, (1872), L.R. 7 C.P. 328; 41 L.J.C.P. 146; 26 L.T. 709; 20 W.R. 990.
(*q*) *Hellawell* v. *Eastwood*, *supra*, note (*p*).
(*r*) *Ex parte Astbury*, (1869), L.R. 4 Ch. 630; 38 L.J. Bank. 9; 20 L.T. 997.
(*s*) *Supra*, note (*p*).
(*t*) 14 & 15 Vict., c. 25.

The present section is a re-enactment of sect. 53 of the Agricultural Holdings Act, 1875, but is compulsory in its application; and the 1875 Act contained (sect. 53) an additional proviso, that the section should not apply to a steam engine erected by the tenant, if, before erecting it the tenant had not given notice to the landlord, or if the landlord in writing had objected. 46 & 47 Vict. c. 61.

The rights under previous Acts are preserved by sect. 62 of this Act.

Such fixture shall be the property of and be removable by the tenant:— Independently of this Act, the tenant could only remove fixtures during his term, or during a certain time after its expiration, during which he has a right to consider himself in possession *still as tenant* (*u*). When tenant may remove fixtures.

A nice point may arise, whether a trustee in bankruptcy who gives notice to remove the fixtures, and afterwards disclaims the lease, can, after disclaimer remove the chattels. Bankruptcy.

If he disclaim before given notice of removal, it is clear that he cannot remove, since he is after the disclaimer no longer a "tenant" (defined in sect. 61 as the holder of land under a landlord). But when he has paid rent owing and performed his obligations in respect of the holding and given the month's notice of removal, the Act says, the fixtures shall "*be the property of* and be removable by the tenant," and it is submitted, having regard to the last paragraph of section 61 (*x*), that he would clearly have a right to remove them after the tenancy has been put an end to by the disclaimer.

Perform or satisfy all other his obligations to the landlord with respect to his holding:—Besides being obliged to pay up his arrears of rent, the tenant will have to settle with his landlord for all breaches of covenant, waste, and bad farming committed by him before he can remove his fixtures from the soil. Set-off under s. 6 (*y*).

A reference—as in case of compensation (*z*).

Glasshouses are *buildings* within the meaning of this section, and the Market Gardeners' Compensation Act, 1895 (*a*), which provides that sect. 34 of the Agricultural Holdings Act, 1883, shall extend to every fixture and building affixed or erected by the tenant to or upon the holding for the purpose of his trade or business of a market gardener. Glasshouses—buildings—Market Gardeners' Compensation Act, 1895.

Crown and Duchy Lands.

35. This Act shall extend and apply to land belonging to Her Majesty the Queen, her heirs and successors, in right of the Crown. Application of Act to Crown lands.

With respect to such land, for the purposes of this Act, the Commissioners of Her Majesty's Woods,

---

(*u*) *In re Lavies*, (1877), 7 Ch. D. 127; 47 L.J. Bank. 22; 37 L.T. 613; 26 W.R. 136.
(*x*) *Post* p. 94. See also *In re Lavies, supra,* note (*u*). *In re Latham*, (1881), 19 Ch. D. 7; 51 L.J. Ch. 367; 45 L.T. 484; 30 W.R. 144. *Ex parte Hart-Dyke, in re Morrish,* (1882), 22 Ch. D. 410; 52 L.J. Ch. 570; 48 L.T. 303.
(*y*) *Ante* p. 49.
(*z*) *Ante* sections 7-22, pp. 52-61.
(*a*) 58 & 59 Vict., c. 27, s. 3, sub-s. (1), *post* p. 121. *Smith* v. *Richmond*, (1898), 1 Q.B. 683; 67 L.J.Q.B. 439; 78 L.T. 174; 46 W.R. 401. See also *Meux* v. *Cobley,* (1892), 2 Ch. 253; 61 L.J. Ch. 449; 66 L.T. 86.

46 & 47 Vict. c. 61.

Forests, and Land Revenues, or one of them, or other the proper officer or body having charge of such land for the time being, or in case there is no such officer or body, then such *person* as Her Majesty, her heirs or successors, may appoint in writing under the Royal Sign Manual, shall represent Her Majesty, her heirs and successors, and shall be deemed to be the *landlord*.

Any compensation payable under this Act by the Commissioners of Her Majesty's Woods, Forests, and Land Revenues, or either of them, in respect of an improvement mentioned in the first or second part of the First Schedule hereto, shall be deemed to be payable in respect of an improvement of land within sect. 1 of the Crown Lands Act, 1866, and the amount thereof shall be charged and repaid as in that section provided with respect to the costs, charges, and expenses therein mentioned.

29-30 Vict., c. 62, s. 1.

Any compensation payable under this Act by those Commissioners or either of them, in respect of an improvement mentioned in the third part of the First Schedule hereto, shall be deemed to be part of the expenses of the management of the land revenues of the Crown, and shall be payable by those Commissioners out of such money and in such manner as the last-mentioned expenses are by law payable.

Sect. 1 of the Crown Lands Act, 1866.—By this section the cost of improvements is charged upon the capital of the land revenue of the Crown, and repaid out of income. The section does not provide for substituted compensation, unless compensation payable under this Act is intended to mean "compensation under this Act and compensation authorised by this Act to be substituted for compensation under this Act."

Application of Act to land of Duchy of Lancaster.

36. This Act shall extend and apply to land belonging to Her Majesty, her heirs and successors, in right of the Duchy of Lancaster.

With respect to such land for the purposes of this Act, the Chancellor for the time being of the Duchy shall represent Her Majesty, her heirs and successors, and shall be deemed to be the *landlord*.

The amount of any compensation payable under this Act by the Chancellor of the Duchy in respect of an improvement mentioned in the first and second part of the First Schedule to this Act shall be deemed to be an expense incurred in improvement of land belonging to Her Majesty, her heirs or successors, in right of the Duchy, within sect. 25 of the Act of the 57th year of King George the Third, Chapter 97, and shall be raised and paid as in that section provided with respect to the expenses therein mentioned. 46 & 47 Vict. c. 61.
57 Geo. III., c. 97, s. 25.

The amount of any compensation payable under this Act by the Chancellor of the Duchy in respect of an improvement mentioned in the third part of the First Schedule of this Act shall be paid out of the annual revenues of the duchy.

37. This Act shall extend and apply to land belonging to the Duchy of Cornwall. Application of Act to land of Duchy of Cornwall.

With respect to such land, for the purposes of this Act, such *person* as the Duke of Cornwall for the time being, or other the personage for the time being entitled to the revenues and possessions of the Duchy of Cornwall, from time to time, by sign manual, warrant, or otherwise, appoints, shall represent the Duke of Cornwall, or other the personage aforesaid, and be deemed to be the *landlord*, and may do any act or thing under this Act which a *landlord* is authorised or required to do thereunder.

Any compensation payable under this Act by the Duke of Cornwall, or other the personage aforesaid, in respect of an improvement mentioned in the first or second part of the First Schedule to this Act shall be deemed to be payable in respect of an improvement of land within sect. 8 of The Duchy of Cornwall Management Act, 1863, and the amount thereof may be advanced and paid from the money mentioned in that section, subject to the provision therein made for repayment of sums advanced for improvements. 26-27 Vict., c. 49, s. 3.

Ecclesiastical and Charity Lands.

38. Where lands are assigned or secured as the endowment of a see, the powers by this Act conferred Landlord, archbishop or bishop.

80 *Agricultural Holdings (England) Act*, 1883.

46 & 47 Vict. c. 61.

Landlord, incumbent of benefice.

on a *landlord* shall not be exercised by the archbishop or bishop, in respect of those lands, except with the previous approval in writing of the estates committee of the Ecclesiastical Commissioners for England.

39. Where a *landlord* is incumbent of an ecclesiastical benefice, the powers by this Act conferred on a *landlord* shall not be exercised by him in respect of the glebe land or other land belonging to the benefice, except with the previous approval in writing of the patron of the benefice (that is, the *person*, officer, or authority who, in case the benefice were then vacant, would be entitled to present thereto), or of the Governors of the Queen Anne's Bounty (that is, the Governors of the Bounty of Queen Anne for the Augmentation of the Maintenance of the Poor Clergy).

In every such case the Governors of Queen Anne's Bounty may, if they think fit, on behalf of the incumbent, out of any money in their hands, pay to the *tenant* the amount of compensation due to him under this Act; and thereupon they may, instead of the incumbent, obtain from the *county court* a charge on the *holding*, in respect thereof, in favour of themselves.

Every such charge shall be effectual, notwithstanding any change of the incumbent.

See notes to sect. 29.

Landlord, charity trustee, &c.

40. The powers by this Act conferred on a *landlord* in respect of charging the land shall not be exercised by trustees for ecclesiastical or charitable purposes except with the previous approval in writing of the Charity Commissioners for England and Wales.

Resumption for Improvements and Miscellaneous.

Resumption of possession for cottages, &c. Form 4 (b).

41. Where on *tenancy from year to year* a notice to quit is given by the *landlord* with a view to the use of land for any of the following purposes:

The erection of farm labourers' cottages or other houses, with or without gardens;

(b) Appendix II., *post* p. 135.

The providing of gardens for existing farm labourers' cottages or other houses ;

The allotment for labourers of land for gardens or other purposes ;

The planting of trees ;

The opening or working of any coal, ironstone, limestone, or other mineral, or of a stone quarry, clay, sand, or gravel pit, or the construction of any works or buildings to be used in connection therewith ;

The obtaining of brick earth, gravel, or sand ;

The making of a watercourse or reservoir ;

The making of any road, railway, tramroad, siding, canal, or basin, or any wharf, pier, or other work connected therewith ;

and the notice to quit so states, then it shall, by virtue of this Act, be no objection to the notice that it relates to part only of the *holding*.

In every such case the provisions of this Act respecting compensation shall apply as on *determination of a tenancy* in respect of an entire *holding*.

The *tenant* shall also be entitled to a proportionate reduction of rent in respect of the land comprised in the notice to quit, and in respect of any depreciation of the value to him of the residue of the *holding*, caused by the withdrawal of that land from the *holding* or by the use to be made thereof, and the amount of that reduction shall be ascertained by agreement or settled by a reference under this Act, as in case of compensation (but without appeal).

The *tenant* shall further be entitled, at any time within twenty-eight days after service of the notice to quit, to serve on the *landlord* a notice in writing to the effect that he (the *tenant*) accepts the same as a notice to quit the entire *holding*, to take effect at the expiration of the then current year of tenancy ; and the notice to quit shall have effect accordingly.

46 & 47 Vict.
c. 61.

Form 5 (c).

(c) Appendix II., *post* p. 135.

46 & 47 VICT. c. 61.	*Relates to part only of the holding*—Independently of the Act, and of agreement, a notice for part only of the holding is a bad notice (*d*).
Then current year.	*Settled by a reference*—The whole expense of a reference must be undertaken to ascertain some very minute reduction, unless the parties can agree.
	The tenant shall further be entitled—The words "then current year" give the tenant power to determine the tenancy at less than a year's notice ; for instance in a Lady-Day tenancy a landlord might, on March 25, give notice under this section to quit on March 25 year, and the tenant could, within twenty-eight days, accept such notice as notice to quit the entire holding.
Provision as to limited owners.	**42.** Subject to the provisions of this Act in relation to Crown, duchy, ecclesiastical, and charity lands, a *landlord*, whatever may be his estate or interest in his *holding*, may give any consent, make any agreement, or do or have done to him any act in relation to improvements in respect of which compensation is payable under this Act which he might give or make or do or have done to him if he were in the case of an estate of inheritance owner thereof in fee, and in the case of a leasehold possessed of the whole estate in the leasehold.
Settled Land Act, 1882, s. 25-29, scheme to be submitted to trustees.	*Do or have done to him any act*—This section should be considered with the provisions of sects. 25-29 of the Settled Land Act, 1882, referring to the execution of improvements by a tenant for life or trustees. By sects. 25-27 and 29 of that Act, a tenant for life may execute or may "join or concur with any other person interested" in executing the improvements mentioned in sect. 25 of the Act (which include, roughly speaking, all the improvements in Parts 1 and 2 of the schedule to this Act), or in contributing to the cost thereof.
	By sect. 26 of the Settled Land Act the tenant for life must submit the scheme of improvement to the trustees if the money is in their hands, or to the court, if the money is in court, before he can apply the capital money arising by sale or otherwise in payment for the improvement, and he must also obtain a certificate of the land commissioners or of an engineer or able practical surveyor approved by them, or an order of court, certifying that the work has been properly executed, or directing the trustees so to apply the money.
	By sect. 28, the tenant for life and his successors must maintain and repair the improvements made.
	If then the landlord joins with the tenant in executing an improvement, and bears part of the cost, he may charge any compensation paid to the tenant in respect of his share on the land under the present section. If he wish to have his own share of the cost, and the compensation paid to the tenant repaid him out of capital moneys, he must obtain the approval and certificate above mentioned.

(*d*) *Doe v. Archer*, (1811), 14 East 245. See clauses 28 and 10A, Appendix I., *post* pp. 131, 134.

43. When, by any Act of Parliament, deed, or other instrument, a lease of a *holding* is authorised to be made, provided that the best rent, or reservation in the nature of rent, is by such lease reserved, then, whenever any lease of a *holding* is, under such authority, made to the *tenant* of the same, it shall not be necessary, in estimating such rent or reservation, to take into account against the *tenant* the increase (if any) in the value of such *holding* arising from any improvements made or paid for by him on such *holding*.

46 & 47 Vi c. 61.

Provision in case of reservation of rent.

PART II.

Distress.

46 & 47 Vict. c. 61.

Limitation of distress in respect of amount and time.

*Aug. 25th, 1883.

44. After the commencement of this Act it shall not be lawful for any *landlord* entitled to the rent of any *holding* to which this Act applies to distrain for rent, which became due in respect of such *holding* more than one year before the making of such distress, except in the case of arrears of rent in respect of a *holding* to which this Act applies existing at the time of the passing of this Act,* which arrears shall be recoverable by distress up to the 1st day of January, 1885, to the same extent as if this Act had not passed. Provided that where it appears that according to the ordinary course of dealing between the *landlord* and *tenant* of a *holding* the payment of the rent of such *holding* has been allowed to be deferred until the expiration of a quarter of a year or half a year after the date at which such rent legally became due, then for the purpose of this section the rent of such *holding* shall be deemed to have become due at the expiration of such quarter or half year as aforesaid, as the case may be, and not at the date at which it legally became due.

To distrain - Rent may still be recovered by *action* within the six years limited by 3-4 Will. 4, c. 27, sect. 42, though limited by the section as regards the right of distress.

Holding to which this Act applies—Such a holding must come within sect. 54 (*e*).

Rent payable in advance.

The proviso in agreements for payment of the last half year's rent in advance will probably be more commonly resorted to (*f*).

The making of such distress—The distress is made by entry on the land, and by seizure, either actual or formal, of the chattels distrained.

Ordinary course of dealing—Whether rent has fallen into arrear in the ordinary course of dealing will probably be a frequent cause of dispute in cases of alleged wrongful distress. In many districts it is not the custom to call upon a tenant for his rent until nearly six months after it is really due.

(*e*) *Infra*, p. 91.
(*f*) Appendix I., clause 7, *post* p. 126.

In a case within the proviso to this section it was held that the landlord was entitled to distrain for rent then legally due, but not payable according to the course of dealing, and *also* for rent which had become legally due more than a year previously, but had become payable according to the custom of dealing less than a year previously, although the total amount distrained for exceeded one year's rent (*g*). The facts were as follows:—A tenant who had become bankrupt owed to his appellant in September, 1886, £59 4s. 5d., arrears of rent reserved, due by agreement on June 24, 1885, but customarily payable, in half-yearly payments in the months of September and March following, and £80 for one year's rent reserved, due by agreement on June 24, 1886, but customarily payable, as to one-half of the same in the month of September, 1886, and as to the remainder in the month of March, 1887. The landlord distrained on September 16, 1886, for £139 4s. 5d., and the Court (Mathew and Cave, JJ.) held that he was entitled to do so. Mathew, J., said: "I will take the case of a year's rent, payable in advance, becoming due on June 1. Suppose in such a case that a year's rent were then in arrear; on June 2, at common law, the landlord could distrain for both the past and the future rent. It is contended that the Agricultural Holdings Act has the effect of depriving the landlord of the right of distraining for the arrears because the rent has been due for more than a year, but the landlord's answer is that the rent is due by the custom in September. What the County Court Judge has done here is to alter the lease and say in effect that the rent was not payable in advance. It is clear to me that the arrears had not become due more than a year before the distress, and the landlord was entitled to distrain for the rent in advance."

Cave, J., said: "The object of sect. 44 of the Agricultural Holdings Act is to take away the right to distrain for rent which has been due for more than twelve months; but the landlord still has all his other remedies. There was no intention to affect the rent until it had been due for more than a year. In the present case, on June 24, 1885, a year's rent became due; on June 24, 1886, another year's rent became due. On June 23, 1886, the landlord could have distrained for the year's rent which became due on June 24, 1885; on June 25, 1886, he could have distrained for the rent which became due on June 24, 1886. But the landlord was accustomed to allow the tenant three months before he expected payment of any part of the rent, and therefore, by the proviso in the section, he had three months longer to distrain for the rent which became due on June 24, 1885, and the distress in the the middle of September, 1886, was good."

It may often be very difficult to determine the cases in which an "ordinary course of dealing" has been established. The mere deferring of payment of rent for any period will not of itself necessarily bring the case within the proviso to this section.

46 & 47 Vict. c. 61.

Landlord can distrain for rent legally due more than a year previously, but payable less than a year previously.

45. Where *live stock* belonging to another *person* has been taken in by the *tenant* of a *holding* to which this Act applies to be fed at a fair price agreed to be paid for such feeding by the owner of such stock to the *tenant*, such stock shall not be distrained by the

Limitation of distress in respect of things to be distrained.

(*g*) *Ex parte Bull in re Betw*, (1887), 18 Q.B.D. 642; 56 L.J.Q.B. 270; 56 L.T. 571; 35 W.R. 455; 51 J.P. 710.

<small>46 & 47 Vict. c. 61.</small>

landlord for rent where there is other sufficient distress to be found, and if so distrained by reason of other sufficient distress not being found, there shall not be recovered by such distress a sum exceeding the amount of the price so agreed to be paid for the feeding, or if any part of such price has been paid exceeding the amount remaining unpaid, it shall be lawful for the owner of such stock, at any time before it is sold, to redeem such stock by paying to the distrainer a sum equal to such price as aforesaid, and any payment so made to the distrainer shall be in full discharge as against the *tenant* of any sum of the like amount which would be otherwise due from the owner of the stock to the *tenant* in respect of the price of feeding : Provided always, that so long as any portion of such *live stock* shall remain on the said *holding* the right to distrain such portion shall continue to the full extent of the price originally agreed to be paid for the feeding of the whole of such *live stock*, or if part of such price has been *bonâ fide* paid to the *tenant* under the agreement, then to the full extent of the price then remaining unpaid.

<small>Machinery and live stock for breeding purposes.</small>

Agricultural or other machinery which is the *bonâ fide* property of a *person* other than the *tenant*, and is on the premises of the *tenant* under a *bonâ fide* agreement with him for the hire or use thereof in the conduct of his business, and *live stock* of all kinds which is the *bonâ fide* property of a *person* other than the *tenant*, and is on the premises of the *tenant* solely for breeding purposes, shall not be distrained for rent in arrear.

<small>*Live stock*—Includes by sect. 61 "any animal capable of being distrained."</small>

<small>*A fair price*—Some precautions against fraud are necessary to prevent abuse of this section, otherwise it will be found that on a distress being made all the cattle belong to some relation under an agreement for agistment.</small>

<small>"Fair price."</small>
<small>The words "fair price" in this section do not necessarily imply a *money* payment. It was held (*h*) by Lord Coleridge, C.J., and Mathew, J., that cows delivered for agistment on the terms "milk for meat," (*i.e.*, that the cows should feed on the farm, and the farmer</small>

<small>(*h*) *London and Yorkshire Bank v. Belton*, (1885), 15 Q.B.D. 457 ; 54 L.J.Q.B. 568 ; 34 W.R. 31 ; 50 J.P. 86.</small>

should have their milk in return) were exempt from distress. In the course of his judgment, Lord Coleridge, C.J., said : "The simple question is, whether under sect. 45 of 46 & 47 Vict., c. 61, a 'fair price' to be paid for agistment will include an agreement of barter as well as an agreement for payment in cash. The County Court Judge has found (and I quite understand and accept his finding) that agreements of this kind are very common in the part of the country in which he has to administer justice, and it is obvious that if the Act did not apply to them the use and operation of this Act is very considerably narrowed. The conclusion that the Act has failed to that extent is one from which I shrink. The question is, what is the meaning of the words 'fair price'? Putting aside pedantic and scholastic refinements and derivations, 'price' in ordinary colloquial language does not always mean money, and 'fair price' does not always mean 'coin of the realm.' We say that a man got something and paid a 'fair price' for it without meaning that he paid down so many pounds, shillings, and pence, but meaning only that he paid a fair equivalent for what he got. This Act has said that if the agister has paid a 'fair price' certain consequences shall follow—not that he is to escape a fair payment in meal or malt—but that he is not to have his cattle taken from him by the landlord. I think that it was the intention of the Legislature to alter the state of things which previously existed, and these agreements must have been known to the Legislature. If the Legislature has used words which without stretching cover a case of this kind, the inclination of my mind is to put such a construction upon the statute as will give effect to it—not because it is an alleviating statute, but because it is right to give to the words their full meaning. There are expressions in the section, such as the 'amount of the price so agreed to be paid,' 'exceeding the amount remaining unpaid,' and 'equal to such price as aforesaid,' which are, at all events, patient of the interpretation that 'price' is to have a wide meaning, and that if a fair price is paid by the owner his cattle are to be protected to the extent of that fair bargain."

^{46 & 47 Vict.} c. 61.

Where the tenant allowed an owner of cattle "the exclusive right to feed the grass on the land for four weeks" in consideration of £2, the Court (Field and Wills, JJ.) held that the cattle were not "taken in by the tenant to be fed at a fair price," and were therefore not privileged from distress (i). Field, J., said : "At a certain period of the year a tenant farmer wishes to dispose of his aftermath. He may not himself have live stock enough to consume it. Of course under these circumstances he may himself mow it, but he may also render available this part of his interest in the land in one of two ways. He may take some other person's cattle on to the farm and agist them, or, if his holding is on terms such as to enable him to do so he may demise to some other person for a given time the 'herbogium' or 'vestura terræ.' In the latter case Lord Coke says that the person to whom the land is thus demised 'shall have an action of trespass *quare clausum fregit*' (k). The two transactions are therefore essentially different. In the present case I am not concerned to decide whether this agreement by which the tenant gives to another 'the exclusive right to feed the grass on the land for four weeks' amounts to a demise of the surface of the soil. The only question is whether the cattle which are on the land under this agreement are 'taken in by the tenant to be fed at a fair price.' It

"Exclusive right to feed on grass for four weeks."

(i) *Masters v. Green*, (1888), 20 Q.B.D. 807 ; 59 L.T. 476 ; 36 W.R. 591 ; 52 J.P. 597.
(k) Coke upon Littleton, 4 b.

46 & 47 Vict. c. 61.

appears to me that the tenant does not agree either to 'take in' or to 'feed' the cattle, and that the sum which he is to receive is not the 'price' of the feed of the cattle, but a payment in the nature of a rent for use and occupation. The object of the Act, like that of the Lodger's Goods Protection Act, is to prevent the goods of one man being taken to pay the debt of another, and, so far as its policy is concerned, I see no valid distinction between the cases, and no reason why these cattle, just as much as cattle taken on the farm to be agisted, should not be exempt from distress. The duty of the Court is, however, to apply the words of the Act, and in my opinion this transaction is not within them."

Principle of privilege from distress.

Where there is other sufficient distress to be found—Independently of this section, cattle which are upon the land by way of agisting may be distrained for rent (*l*). Mellor, J., in MILES v. FURBER (*m*), remarks— "I cannot help thinking that if it were shown that a person *exercised the trade* of agisting cattle, the same principle would apply as in the case of a pawnbroker," *i.e.*, that the cattle would be absolutely privileged from distress as things delivered to a person exercising a public trade to be managed in the way of his trade.

The amount of the price—See sect. 46 as to procedure for settling the fairness of the price.

Agricultural and other machinery—There is no definition of the word machinery in the Act. It would probably be held to be confined to mills, steam engines, thrashing machines and chattels of a like nature. If it includes ploughs and all kinds of farming implements, it may have the effect of developing a trade in the hire of such implements, and so leaving a farmer's capital free to increase his stock, instead of spending it in expensive implements and machinery.

Remedy for wrongful distress under this Act.

46. Where any dispute arises—

(*a*.) in respect of any distress having been levied contrary to the provisions of this Act; or

(*b*.) as to the ownership of any *live stock* distrained, or as to the price to be paid for the feeding of such stock; or

(*c*.) as to any other matter or thing relating to a distress on a *holding* to which this Act applies:

such dispute may be heard and determined by the *county court* or by a court of summary jurisdiction, and any such *county court* or court of summary jurisdiction may make an order for restoration of any

Form 41 (n).

live stock or things unlawfully distrained, or may

(*l*) 11 Geo. II., c. 19. sect. 8.
(*m*) *Miles v. Furber*, (1873), L.R. 8 Q.B. 77; 42 L.J.Q.B. 41; 27 L.T. 756; 21 W.R. 262; following *Swire v. Leach*, (1865), 18 C.B.N.S. 479; 34 L.J.C.P. 150; 11 L.T. 680; 13 W.R. 385; 11 Jur. N.S. 179.
(*n*) Appendix V., *post* p. 149.

declare the price agreed to be paid in the case where the price of the feeding is required to be ascertained, or may make any other order which justice requires: any such dispute as mentioned in this section shall be deemed to be a matter in which a court of summary jurisdiction has authority by law to make an order on complaint in pursuance of the Summary Jurisdiction Acts; but any person aggrieved by any decision of such court of summary jurisdiction under this section may, on giving such security to the other party as the court may think just, appeal to a court of general or quarter sessions.

46 & 47 VICT. c. 61.

Form 42 (*o*).

Levied contrary to the provisions of this Act—for instance (1) distress for rent due more than a year before the making of the distress, sect. 44; (2) distress of live stock or agricultural machinery contrary to the provisions of sect. 45; (3) distraining for more than the balance, after set-off of compensation under sect. 47.

Any other matter or thing—for instance, Who is the "landlord," "tenant," or "owner" of goods distrained; whether proper notice that the chattels were privileged was given; what is "machinery"; what is the "conduct of his business"; the *bona fides* of the property in machinery, and of the agreement for its hire and use (sect. 45); the amount of security to be given on appeal (sect. 46).

May be heard and determined—the section is voluntary, and does not bar the existing remedy in the High Court for illegal or excessive distress. Clause 29 of Appendix I. (*p*) will generally be found useful.

Court of summary jurisdiction—The procedure before a court of summary jurisdiction is dealt with in the chapter on Procedure (*pp*).

Which justice requires Such as an order for payment of the price declared or damages for the unlawful distress.

Any person aggrieved As the decision of the court of summary jurisdiction, unless appealed from, would be conclusive as to the property in the goods, it would appear reasonable to adopt the construction of the Court of Appeal in *E. p.* LEAROYD *In re* FOULDS (*q*) on the words "person aggrieved," namely, that a third person whose title to property is affected by the decision, such as a bill of sale holder, is entitled to appeal.

Appeal from county court—An appeal lies from the decision of a county court judge in the matter of a dispute heard and determined by him under this section. Smith, J., said: "I do not think that the effect of the latter part of the section is to exclude an appeal from a county court judge" (*r*).

(*o*) Appendix V., *post* p. 150.
(*p*) *Post* p. 132.
(*pp*) *Ante* pp. 37-40.
(*q*) (1878), 10 Ch. D. 3; 48 L.J. Banky. 17; 39 L.T. 525; 27 W.R. 277.
(*r*) *Hanmer* v. *King*, (1887), 57 L.T. 367; 51 J.P. 804.

46 & 47 VICT.
c. 61.

Appeal from quarter sessions—It is in the discretion of the court of quarter sessions to state a case for the High Court. Cases so stated are now deemed to be appeals (*s*).

Set-off of compensation against rent.

47. Where the compensation due under this Act, or under any custom or contract, to a *tenant* has been ascertained before the *landlord* distrains for rent due, the amount of such compensation may be set-off against the rent due, and the *landlord* shall not be entitled to distrain for more than the balance.

Any custom or contract—Valuations for away-going crops, unconsumed produce or tillages, may be set-off against arrears of rent.

Exclusion of certiorari.

48. An order of the *county court* or of a court of summary jurisdiction under this Act shall not be quashed for want of form, or be removed by certiorari or otherwise into any superior court.

49.⎫
50.⎪ Repealed by sect. 9, Law of Distress
51.⎬ Amendment Act, 1888 (*t*), by which Act the
52.⎭ majority of the provisions of these sections have been re-enacted.

(*s*) Judicature Act, 1894 (57 & 58 Vict., c. 16), sect. 2.
(*t*) 51 & 52 Vict., c. 21, *post* p. 107.

PART III.

General Provisions.

53. This Act shall come into force on the 1st day of January, 1884, which day is in this Act referred to as the commencement of this Act.

<small>46 & 47 Vict. c. 61.</small>

<small>Commencement of Act.</small>

54. Nothing in this Act shall apply to a *holding* that is not either wholly agricultural or wholly pastoral, or in part agricultural, and as to the residue pastoral, or in whole or in part cultivated as a market garden, or to any *holding* let to the *tenant* during his continuance in any office, appointment, or employment of the *landlord*.

<small>Exception of non-agricultural and small holdings.</small>

Shall apply to a holding—The referee must decide whether the Act applies. As many nice questions may arise as to the application of the Act this is an additional inducement to exclude it. It will be very difficult to decide under this section whether a tenant requires a year's notice under sect. 33 as being within the Act or not. Holdings on which there is a country house or shooting box or shop are not strictly within the section, but, considering the object and scope of the Act, a court of law would probably try and bring them within it.

Market gardens—Market gardens are brought within the Act by the Market Gardeners' Compensation Act, 1895 (*u*).

Office, appointment, or employment—This would seem to give an opening for an evasion of the Act. This will seriously affect sub-agents and other persons who, in return for their services, hold small amounts of land.

55. Any contract, agreement, or covenant made by a *tenant*, by virtue of which he is deprived of his right to claim compensation under this Act in respect of any improvement mentioned in the First Schedule hereto (except an agreement providing such compensation as is by this Act permitted to be substituted for compensation under this Act), shall, so far as it deprives him of such right, be void both at law and in equity.

<small>Avoidance of agreement inconsistent with Act.</small>

(*u*) 58 & 59 Vict., c. 27, *post* p. 121.

46 & 47 Vict. c. 61.

Whether tenant can contract himself out of the Act.

Deprived of his right to claim compensation —The right to claim compensation does not arise until the tenant has executed the improvements and given the necessary notices. There would appear, therefore, to be nothing in the Act to prevent a tenant contracting not to execute improvements at all, or without leave of his landlord, though if he broke his contract he might claim compensation, and leave his landlord to his action for the breach.

Right of tenant in respect of improvement purchased from outgoing tenant.

56. Where an incoming *tenant* has, with the consent in writing of his *landlord*, paid to an outgoing *tenant* any compensation payable under or in pursuance of this Act in respect of the whole or part of any improvement, such incoming *tenant* shall be entitled on quitting the *holding* to claim compensation in respect of such improvement or part in like manner, if at all, as the outgoing *tenant* would have been entitled if he had remained *tenant* of the *holding*, and quitted the *holding* at the time at which the incoming *tenant* quits the same.

In like manner if at all - Probably the provisions of this section will be largely used, as they will enable landlords to avoid the indebtedness and mortgages to companies contemplated by sects. 29-32. In many cases the improvements will have exhausted themselves before the incoming tenant quits the holding. The landlord, though he may have been taking reduced rent in consequence of the incoming tenant's outlay, will not be paying money out of pocket or charging the holding.

The incoming tenant should be most careful to keep all receipts and vouchers in respect of such payments, and the award made for compensation, so as to be able to prove his claim when the time arises, as otherwise it might be impossible, owing to lapse of time, to obtain evidence of value.

Compensation due by custom -It is customary for incoming tenant to pay outgoing tenant compensation, apart from this Act. There is always, however, an implied contract on the part of the landlord that, if there be no incoming tenant, he will pay the compensation due to the outgoing tenant according to custom (*x*). A custom that the outgoing tenant shall look to incoming tenant for payment, to the exclusion of the landlord, cannot be supported (*y*).

Compensation under this Act to be exclusive.

57. A *tenant* shall not be entitled to claim compensation by custom or otherwise than in manner authorised by this Act in respect of any improvement for which he is entitled to compensation under or in pursuance of this Act, but where he is not entitled to

---

(*x*) *Farell* v. *Gaskoin*, (1852), 7 Ex. 273; 21 L.J.Ex. 85.
(*y*) *Bradburn* v. *Foley*, (1878), 3 C.P.D. 129; 47 L.J.C.P. 331; 38 L.T. 421; 26 W.R. 423.

compensation under or in pursuance of this Act he may recover compensation under any other Act of Parliament, or any agreement or custom, in the same manner as if this Act had not been passed.

46 & 47 Vict. c. 61.

Entitled to compensation—If the tenant neglect to give the proper notices he will not be entitled to compensation.

Any other Act of Parliament—See sect. 62 (*h*.) and (*c*.) (*z*).

Custom—This section does away with the "custom of the country" in respect of improvements to which this Act applies and which have been executed since its commencement. It has no application to special stipulations for compensation under sects. 3, 4, and 5.

58. A *tenant* who has remained in his *holding* during a change or changes of tenancy, shall not thereafter on quitting his *holding* at the *determination of a tenancy* be deprived of his right to claim compensation in respect of improvements by reason only that such improvements were made during a former tenancy or tenancies, and not during the tenancy at the determination of which he is quitting.

Provision as to change of tenancy.

Change or changes of tenancy—This section was introduced, according to Mr. Dodson, to strengthen the words in sect. 1, "on quitting his holding" in the interests of a tenant, who, during the currency of a lease had taken more land.

Object of section.

This section will also apply to a tenant holding over at the expiration of the term; and it would appear to have this effect, that if a tenant have a dispute with his landlord about an increase of rent which he thinks is due to improvements made by himself, and notice to quit is given, but afterwards withdrawn, and the parties come to a compromise, the tenant, on quitting at any future time, can claim for the improvements made before such notice to quit was given.

59. Subject as in this section mentioned, a *tenant* shall not be entitled to compensation in respect of any improvements, other than *manures* as defined by this Act, begun by him, if he holds from year to year, within one year before he quits his *holding*, or at any time after he has given or received final notice to quit, and, if he holds as a lessee, within one year before the expiration of his lease.

Restriction in respect of improvements by tenant about to quit.

A final notice to quit means a notice to quit which has not been waived or withdrawn, but has resulted in the *tenant* quitting his *holding*.

(*z*) *Post* pp. 96, 97.

46 & 47 Vict.
c. 61.

Form 2 (a).

Forms 10, 6 (b).

The foregoing provisions of this section shall not apply in the case of any such improvement as aforesaid—

(1.) Where a *tenant* from year to year has begun such improvement during the last year of his tenancy, and, in pursuance of a notice to quit thereafter given by the *landlord*, has quitted his *holding* at the expiration of that year ; and

(2.) Where a *tenant*, whether a tenant from year to year or a lessee, previously to beginning any such improvement, has served notice on his *landlord* of his intention to begin the same, and the *landlord* has either assented or has failed for a month after the receipt of the notice to object to the making of the improvement.

General saving of rights.

60. Except as in this Act expressed, nothing in this Act shall take away, abridge, or prejudicially affect any power, right, or remedy of a *landlord, tenant*, or other *person* vested in or exercisable by him by virtue of any other Act or law, or under any custom of the country, or otherwise, in respect of a *contract of tenancy* or other contract, or of any improvements, waste, emblements, tillages, away-going crops, fixtures, tax, rate, tithe rent-charge, rent, or other thing.

The right to bring actions for waste and illegal or excessive distress in the High Court are instances of remedies saved by this section. The custom as to valuation between incoming and outgoing tenant is preserved (c).

61. In this Act—

Interpretation.

"Contract of tenancy" means a letting of or agreement for the letting land for a term of years, or for lives, or for lives and years, or from year to year :

A tenancy from year to year under a *contract of tenancy* current at the commencement of the

---

(a) Appendix II., *post* p. 135.
(b) Appendix III., *post* pp. 136, 137.
(c) See note "custom" to sect. 56, *ante* p. 92.

Act shall for the purposes of this Act be deemed to continue to be a tenancy under a *contract of tenancy* current at the commencement of this Act until the first day on which either the *landlord* or *tenant* of such tenancy could, the one by giving notice to the other immediately after the commencement of this Act, cause such tenancy to determine, and on and after such day as aforesaid shall be deemed to be a tenancy under a *contract of tenancy* beginning after the commencement of this Act:

"Determination of tenancy" means the cesser of a *contract of tenancy* by reason of effluxion of time, or from any other cause:

"Landlord" in relation to a *holding* means any *person* for the time being entitled to receive the rents and profits of any *holding*:

"Tenant" means the holder of land under a *landlord* for a term of years, or for lives, or for lives and years, or from year to year:

"Tenant" includes the executors, administrators, assigns, legatee, devisee, or next-of-kin, husband, guardian, committee of the estate or trustees in bankruptcy of a tenant or any *person* deriving title from a tenant; and the right to receive compensation in respect of any improvement made by a *tenant* shall enure to the benefit of such executors, administrators, assigns, and other *persons* as aforesaid:

"Holding" means any parcel of land held by a *tenant*:

"County court," in relation to a *holding*, means the county court within the district whereof the *holding* or the larger part thereof is situate:

"Person" includes a body of persons and a corporation aggregate or sole:

"Live stock" includes any animal capable of being distrained:

"Manures" means any of the improvements numbered twenty-two and twenty-three in the third part of the First Schedule hereto:

46 & 47 VICT.
c. 61.

The designations of *landlord* and *tenant* shall continue to apply to the parties until the conclusion of any proceedings taken under or in pursuance of this Act in respect of compensation for improvements, or under any agreement made in pursuance of this Act.

A tenancy from year to year . . . . *immediately after the commencement of the Act*—i.e., for a Lady Day tenancy, the 25th of March, 1885, and for a Michaelmas tenancy, the 29th of September, 1885.

Tenancy with three months' notice—A tenancy agreement with a clause providing that it may be determined by either party giving to the other three calendar months' notice to quit on any day of the year may be a tenancy from "year to year" where the notice clause is not acted upon until after the expiration of a year. The question whether the agreement creates a tenancy from "year to year" or a quarterly tenancy depends on the construction of the agreement taken as a whole (*d*).

Landlord . . . . *entitled to receive the rents and profits*—It may be a question whether a mortgagor who has attorned tenant to the mortgagee can be said to be entitled to receive the rents and profits. So long as the mortgagee received only his interest, the mortgagor presumably would be so entitled, but if the mortgagee entered into possession of the rents under the attornment clause, he would then be the person entitled to the receipt of the rents and profits.

Executors of landlord—The executors of a landlord, tenant for life, who have been compelled under the Act to pay compensation to an outgoing tenant, who had claimed compensation, and whose tenancy had been determined before the death of the landlord, are entitled to a charge upon the holding in respect of the amount which they have so paid. *Prima facie* the definition of landlord shuts out the executors, but the final clause of the section covers this case (*e*).

Repeal of Acts of 1875 and 1876.

62. On and after the commencement of this Act, the Agricultural Holdings (England) Act, 1875, and the Agricultural Holdings (England) Act, 1875, Amendment Act, 1876, shall be repealed.

Provided that such repeal shall not affect—

(*a.*) Anything duly done or suffered, or any proceedings pending under or in pursuance of any enactment hereby repealed ; or

(*b.*) any right to compensation in respect of improvements to which the Agricultural Holdings (England) Act, 1875, applies, and which were executed before the commencement of this Act ; or

---

(*d*) *King* v. *Eversfield*, (1897), 2 Q.B. 475 ; 66 L.J.Q.B. 809 ; 77 L.T. 195 ; 46 W.R. 51 ; 61 J.P. 740. *Post* p. 123.
(*e*) *Gough* v. *Gough*, (1891), 2 Q.B. 665 ; 60 L.J.Q.B. 726 ; 65 L.T. 110 ; 39 W.R. 593 ; 55 J.P. 807. *Ante* p. 69.

(*c.*) any right to compensation in respect of any improvement to which the Agricultural Holdings (England) Act, 1875, applies, although executed by a *tenant* after the commencement of this Act if made under a *contract of tenancy* current at the commencement of this Act ; or

46 & 47 Vict. c. 61.

(*d.*) any right in respect of fixtures affixed to a *holding* before the commencement of this Act ;

and any right reserved by this Section may be enforced after the commencement of this Act in the same manner in all respects as if no such repeal had taken place.

Compensation under Agricultural Holdings Act, 1875, notice—A notice by a tenant in occupation of a tenancy current at the commencement of this Act, of a claim for compensation for improvements executed after the commencement of the Act is good if given under this Act, though the compensation is to be based upon the principles of the Agricultural Holdings Act, 1875 (*f*).

63. This Act may be cited for all purposes as the Agricultural Holdings (England) Act, 1883.

Short title of Act.

64. This Act shall not apply to Scotland or Ireland.

Limits of Act.

(*f*) *Smith* v. *Acock*, (1885), 53 L.T. 230. *Ante* p. 54.

FIRST SCHEDULE.

PART I.

46 & 47 Vict.
c. 61.
IMPROVEMENTS TO WHICH CONSENT OF LAND-
LORD IS REQUIRED.

(1.) Erection or enlargement of buildings.
(2.) Formation of silos.
(3.) Laying down of permanent pasture.
(4.) Making and planting of osier beds.
(5.) Making of water meadows or works of irrigation.
(6.) Making of gardens.
(7.) Making or improving of roads or bridges.
(8.) Making or improving of watercourses, ponds, wells, or reservoirs, or of works for the application of water power or for supply of water for agricultural or domestic purposes.
(9.) Making of fences.
(10.) Planting of hops.
(11.) Planting of orchards or fruit bushes.
(12.) Reclaiming of waste land.
(13.) Warping of land.
(14.) Embankment and sluices against floods.

Where it is agreed in writing that a holding shall be let or treated as a market garden, improvements (1), (6), and (11), shall cease as regards such holding to be comprised in this Schedule (g).

(g) Market Gardeners' Compensation Act, 1895 (58 & 59 Vict., c. 27), sect. 3, sub-sect. (2), *post* p. 121.

PART II.

IMPROVEMENT IN RESPECT OF WHICH NOTICE TO LANDLORD IS REQUIRED.

46 & 47 VICT.
c. 61.

(15.) Drainage.

PART III.

IMPROVEMENTS TO WHICH CONSENT OF LANDLORD IS NOT REQUIRED.

(16.) Boning of land with undissolved bones.
(17.) Chalking of land.
(18.) Clay-burning.
(19.) Claying of land.
(20.) Liming of land.
(21.) Marling of land.
(22.) Application to land of purchased artificial or other purchased manure.
(23.) Consumption on the holding by cattle, sheep, or pigs of cake or other feeding stuff not produced on the holding.

Where it is agreed in writing that a holding shall be let or treated as a market garden, the improvements mentioned in sect. 3, sub-sect. (3) of the Market Gardeners' Compensation Act, 1895 (*h*), shall be deemed to be comprised in Part III. of this Schedule.

SECOND SCHEDULE.

[This schedule, which depended upon sect. 49 of the Act, must be considered as repealed by sect. 9 of the Law of Distress Amendment Act, 1888 (*i*). It is replaced by Rule 15 (*k*) of the rules made pursuant to sect. 8 of the Law of Distress Amendment Act, 1888 (*l*.)]

(*h*) *Post* p. 122.
(*i*) 51 & 52 Vict., c. 21, *post* p. 107.
(*k*) *Post* p. 114.
(*l*) *Post* p. 110.

THE COUNTY COURT RULES, 1889.
ORDER XL.

AGRICULTURAL HOLDINGS (ENGLAND) ACT, 1883.

Interpretation,
46 & 47 Vict.
c. 61.

1. When an appeal is made to the judge against an award made under the Agricultural Holdings (England) Act, 1883, the party prosecuting the appeal shall be called the appellant, and the party supporting the award the respondent.

Statement of grounds of appeal to be filed.

2. The appellant shall, within seven days after the delivery of the award, file a copy thereof, together with a concise statement in writing of his grounds of appeal, which shall contain the following particulars :—

(1.) If the appeal shall be made on the ground mentioned in sect. 23, sub-sects. 1 and 2, of the said Agricultural Holdings Act, a statement of the several objections to the validity of the award on which he relies :

(2.) If the appeal is on any of the grounds mentioned in sect. 23, sub-sect. 3, of the said Agricultural Holdings Act, a statement showing in respect of what matters compensation is alleged to have been improperly awarded :

(3.) If the appeal is made on any of the grounds mentioned in sect. 23, sub-sect. 4, of the said Agricultural Holdings Act, a statement showing in respect of what matters compensation is alleged to have been improperly withheld :

(4.) No ground of appeal shall be allowed at the trial unless the foregoing provision of this rule shall, in respect of such ground, have been complied with :

(5.) The full names and addresses of the respondent and of the appellant and his solicitor, if the proceedings are commenced through a solicitor.

3. The registrar shall, within twenty-four hours after the filing of the concise statement, transmit a copy thereof by post to every respondent at the address furnished to him, accompanied by a notice requiring the respondent to comply with the provisions of the next following rule, according to the form in the Appendix (*a*). *Copy of statement to be sent to respondent.*

4. The respondent shall, within seven days after the transmission of the grounds of appeal to him, deliver to the registrar a statement in writing, signed by himself or his solicitor, disclosing the following matters :— *Respondent to deliver statement in reply.*

(1.) Whether he disputes the validity in law of all, or any, and which of the grounds of objection to the award :

(2.) Whether he disputes the truth in fact of all, or any, and which of the grounds of appeal :

(3.) Whether he admits the validity in law and and truth in fact of all, or any, and which of the grounds of appeal :

(4.) Whether he prays that the case may be remitted to be re-heard :

(5.) His full name and address, and that of his solicitor, if the statement be delivered through a solicitor.

5. Upon the receipt of the statement in the last preceding rule mentioned, the registrar shall transmit a copy thereof, and of the award and grounds of appeal to the judge, who shall, as soon as conveniently may be, appoint a time and place for the hearing of the appeal, and instruct the registrar to give notice thereof forthwith to the parties. *Copies of both statements to be sent to the judges.*

6. The judge shall hear and determine the appeal, and the order thereupon may be enforced in the same manner as any other judgment of the court (*b*).

(*a*) Form 311A, *post* p. 104.
(*b*) Form 312, *post* p. 104.

Procedure on application for appointment of referee or umpire.
46 & 47 Vict. c. 61.
S. 9 (sub-ss. 6, 9).
S. 10 (sub-s. 2).

7A. (1.) Where a party desires to make application to the court for the appointment of a referee or umpire under sub-sect. 6 or sub-sect. 9 of sect. 9, or sub-sect. 2 of sect. 10 of the said Agricultural Holdings Act, 1883, he shall apply in writing to the registrar to fix a time and place for the hearing of such application.

(2.) If the party so applying produces to the registrar proof that the parties consent to the registrar exercising the powers of the court, the registrar shall fix a time for the hearing of the application before himself. Such time shall be within fourteen days from the date of the application to the registrar, but shall not be less than seven days from the date of such application, unless the parties or their solicitors agree to the application being heard at an earlier date.

(3.) In any other case the registrar shall fix the hearing of the application before the judge for any court appointed to be held within fourteen days from the date of the application to the registrar, but so that the registrar shall not, except by consent of the parties, fix the hearing for a day less than seven days from the date of such application.

(4.) If there is no available court, the registrar shall send notice of the intended application to the judge, who shall, as soon as conveniently may be, fix a time and place for the hearing of the application. Such time shall be within fourteen days from the date of the application to the registrar, but shall not, except by consent of the parties, be less than seven days from such date.

(5.) On the time and place for the hearing of the application being fixed, the registrar shall issue to the applicant a summons under the seal of the court, according to the form 312A in the Appendix, addressed to the other party, and requiring him to attend on the hearing of the application (*c*).

(*c*) Form 312A, *post* p. 105.

(6.) Such summons shall be served by the applicant or his solicitor on the other party in accordance with sect. 28 of the said Act not less than four clear days before the day fixed for the hearing, unless such party, or his solicitor on his behalf, agrees to accept shorter service; and where the other party is acting by a solicitor, a copy of such summons shall be sent to such solicitor by the applicant or his solicitor. 46 & 47 Vict. c. 61, s. 28.

(7.) On the day fixed for the hearing, the judge, or by consent of the parties, the registrar, shall dispose of the application, on hearing the parties, or on hearing the applicant, and on proof of service of the summons on the other party, if such other party does not appear; but where any application is heard by the registrar, he may, if he shall think fit, adjourn the same for hearing by the judge.

(8.) Before appointing any person to serve as referee or umpire, the judge or registrar shall ascertain that such person is willing to serve, if appointed.

(9.) The appointment may be made by indorsement on the summons or by a separate order.

(10.) The costs of the application shall be in the discretion of the judge or registrar, who may order the same to be paid by one party to the other, or to be dealt with as costs attending the reference under sect. 20 of the Act. Such costs, if allowed, shall be taxed on such scale as the judge or registrar shall direct, subject, in the case of any direction by the registrar, to review by the judge. 46 & 47 Vict. c. 61, s. 20.

This rule was substituted for rule 7 after the decision in *In re Griffiths and Morris* (*d*), in which case it was held that the power given to the county court by sect. 9, sub-sect. 6, of the Agricultural Holdings Act, 1883, to appoint a referee or umpire is by sect. 11 to be exercisable by the judge unless the parties consent to its exercise by the registrar.

(*d*) (1895), 1 Q.B. 866; 64 L.J.Q.B. 386; 72 L.T. 290; 43 W.R. 652; 59 J.P. 134; 15 R. 301.

FORMS.

311A.

NOTICE TO A RESPONDENT UNDER THE AGRICULTURAL HOLDINGS (ENGLAND) ACT, 1883.

The Agricultural Holdings (England) Act, 1883.
In the County Court of   holden at
Between *A.B.*, Appellant, and *C.D.*, Respondent.

45 & 47 Vict.
c. 61, order 40,
r. 3.

Take notice, that you are required within seven days of the delivery of this notice to you to file in court a statement, signed by you or your solicitor, in reply to the grounds of appeal sent herewith and that your statement must disclose the following matters:—

(1.) Whether you dispute the validity in law of all or any, and which of the grounds of objection to the award :

(2.) Whether you dispute the truth in fact of all, or any, and which of the grounds of appeal :

(3.) Whether you admit the validity in law and truth in fact of all, or any, and which of the grounds of appeal :

(4.) Whether you pray that the case may be remitted to be re-heard :

(5.) Your name and address, and that of your solicitor, if the statement be delivered through a solicitor.

Dated this   day of   189

Registrar of the Court.

To the above named respondent.

312.

ORDER ON AN APPEAL.

The Agricultural Holdings (England) Act, 1883.

45 & 47 Vict.
c. 61, order 40,
r. 6.

In the County Court of   holden at

In the matter of the County Courts Act, 1888 and

In the matter of the Agricultural Holdings (England) Act, 1883, and
In the matter of an appeal by *A.B.*
The   day of   189

Upon the hearing this day of an appeal by [*name and description of appellant*] against an award dated [*state date*] given under the hand of [*referee's name*], whereby [*state shortly the substance of the award*], and on reading the said award, and on hearing the said *A.B.* and *C.D.*, the respondent,

It is ordered that [*state order, e.g.:*] the said *C.D.*, do within fourteen days of the date of this order pay to the said *A.B.* the sum of £   and £   for costs, and in default of such payments at the time aforesaid, the said *A.B.* may proceed to execution.

312A.

SUMMONS ON APPLICATION FOR APPOINTMENT OF REFEREE OR UMPIRE UNDER THE AGRICULTURAL HOLDINGS (ENGLAND) ACT, 1883.

In the County Court of   holden at
In the matter of the Agricultural Holdings (England) Act, 1883, and
In the matter of a reference for the settlement of a difference between *A.B.* of   , tenant, and *C.D.* of   , landlord.

You are hereby summoned to attend before the judge [*or, where the parties consent*, the Registrar] in chambers at   on   the   day of   at the hour of   in the   noon, on the hearing of an application on the part of   for the appointment by the court of a referee under sub-sect. 6 of sect. 9 of the Agricultural Holdings (England) Act, 1883, by reason of your failure to appoint such referee.

[*or* for the appointment of an umpire under sub-sect. 9 of sect. 9 of the Agricultural Holdings (England) Act, 1883, by reason of the failure of the referees to appoint such umpire.]

[*or* for the appointment of an umpire under sub-sect. 2 of sect. 10 of the Agricultural Holdings (England) Act, 1883.]

And take notice, that in default of your attendance at the time and place above mentioned, the judge [*or, where the parties consent*, the Registrar] will, on proof of service of this summons, proceed to hear and dispose of the said application.

Dated this   day of
To
And to Mr.   , his solicitor.
                              Registrar.

COURT FEES.

	£ s. d.
For every sitting under the Agricultural Holdings (England) Act	1 0 0
Taxing costs under the Agricultural Holdings (England) Act	10 6

COSTS.

DRAWING.	A	B	C
	£ s. d.	£ s. d.	£ s. d.
Item 32. Any statement under the Agricultural Holdings Act, including necessary copies.	0 3 0	0 5 0	0 6 8
Or per folio beyond three.	—	0 1 0	0 1 0

LAW OF DISTRESS AMENDMENT ACT, 1888.

[51 & 52 VICT., c. 21.]

1. This Act may be cited as the Law of Distress Amendment Act, 1888. <small>Short title.</small>

2. This Act shall not apply to Scotland or Ireland. <small>Extent.</small>

3. This Act, except as in this Act otherwise provided, shall come into operation from and immediately after the thirty-first day of October one thousand eight hundred and eighty-eight. <small>Commencement.</small>

4. From and after the passing of this Act the following goods and chattels shall be exempt from distress for rent; namely, any goods or chattels of the tenant or his family which would be protected from seizure in execution under section ninety-six of the County Courts Act, 1846, or any enactment amending or substituted for the same. <small>Certain goods exempted from distress as under 9 & 10 Vict. c. 95, s. 96.</small>

Provided that this enactment shall not extend to any case where the lease, term, or interest of the tenant has expired, and where possession of the premises in respect of which the rent is claimed has been demanded and where the distress is made not earlier than seven days after such demand.

<small>Sect. 96 of the County Courts Act, 1846 is re-enacted by sect. 147 of the County Courts Act, 1888 (51 & 52 Vict., c. 43). By this section wearing apparel and bedding of the tenant or his family, and the tools and implements of his trade to the value of £5 are protected from seizure.</small> <small>What goods are exempt.</small>

5. So much of an Act passed in the second year of the reign of their Majesties King William the Third and Mary, chapter five, as requires appraisement before sale of goods distrained is hereby repealed, except in writing. <small>Repeal of 2 W. & M., c. 5, s. 1, except where appraisement is required in writing.</small>

51 & 52 Vict.
c. 21.

cases where the tenant or owner of the goods and chattels by writing requires such appraisement to be made, and the landlord or other person levying a distress may, except as aforesaid, sell the goods and chattels distrained without causing them to be previously appraised; and for the purposes of sale the goods and chattels distrained shall, at the request in writing of the tenant or owner of such goods and chattels, be removed to a public auction room or to some other fit and proper place specified in such request, and be there sold. The costs and expenses of appraisement when required by the tenant or owner shall be borne and paid by him; and the costs and expenses attending any such removal, and any damage to the goods and chattels arising therefrom, shall be borne and paid by the person requesting the removal.

This section re-enacts sect. 50 of the Agricultural Holdings Act, 1883, with the addition of words empowering the tenant to require appraisement and making him bear the expenses.

Extension of time to replevy at request of tenant.

6. The period of five days provided in the said Act of William and Mary, chapter five, within which the tenant or owner of goods and chattels distrained may replevy the same, shall be extended to a period of not more than fifteen days if the tenant or such owner make a request in writing in that behalf to the landlord or other person levying the distress, and also give security for any additional cost that may be occasioned by such extension of time: Provided that the landlord or person levying the distress may, at the written request, or with the written consent, of the tenant or such owner as aforesaid, sell the goods and chattels distrained, or part of them, at any time before the expiration of such extended period as aforesaid.

This section re-enacts and makes general sect. 51 of the Agricultural Holdings Act, 1883.

Distress to be levied by certified bailiffs.

7. From and after the commencement of this Act no person shall act as a bailiff to levy any distress for rent unless he shall be authorised to act as a bailiff by a certificate in writing under the hand of a county court judge ; and such certificate may be general or apply to a particular distress or distresses, and may be granted at any time after the passing of this Act in such manner as may be prescribed by rules under this Act. [*If any person holding a certificate shall be proved to the satisfaction of the judge of a county court to have been guilty of any extortion or other misconduct in the execution of his duty as a bailiff he shall be liable to have his certificate summarily cancelled by the said judge.*] 51 & 52 VICT. c. 21.

Nothing in this section shall be deemed to exempt such bailiff from any other penalty or proceeding to which he may be liable in respect of such extortion or misconduct.

A county court registrar may exercise the power of granting certificates hereby conferred upon a county court judge in cases in which he may be authorised to do so by rules made under this Act.

If any person not holding a certificate under this section shall levy a distress contrary to the provisions of this Act, the person so levying, and any person who has authorised him so to levy, shall be deemed to have committed a trespass.

This section re-enacts and makes general sect. 52 of the Agricultural Holdings Act, 1883.

In *Hogarth* v. *Jennings* (a) it was held that the managing director of an incorporated company, who distrained in person for rent due to the company, acted as a bailiff within this section, and that, not having a certificate from the county court judge, he was a trespasser. In the course of his judgment, Fry, L.J., said : "The defendant was the managing director of a brewery company, and without any authority other than the general authority which he might derive from his position as managing director, he levied a distress on the plaintiff's goods. The question is whether he was acting as a bailiff within the meaning of the section . . . . I think that a bailiff for making a distress means a person authorised and appointed for that purpose. Assuming that the defendant had authority to distrain from the company, I think that he had it as a bailiff . . . . I think, therefore, that the defendant was not entitled to distrain, as he had no certificate, and consequently he was a trespasser." Director of company acting as bailiff— trespasser.

By sect. 2 of the Law of Distress Amendment Act, 1895 (*b*) if any person not holding a certificate under the Law of Distress Amendment Law of Distress Amendment Act, 1895 (58 & 59 Vict. c. 24).

(*a*) (1892), 1 Q.B. 907; 61 L.J.Q.B. 601; 66 L.T. 821; 40 W.R. 517; 56 J.P. 485.
(*b*) *Post* p. 111.

51 & 52 Vict. c. 21.

General certificate.

Cancellation of certificate.

Act, 1888, levies a distress contrary to the provisions of that Act, he is liable on summary conviction to a fine not exceeding ten pounds. This is without prejudice to any civil liability to which he may be liable.

By rule 4 (*c*) of the rules made pursuant to sect. 8 of this Act, a *general* certificate shall authorise the bailiff named in it to levy at *any* place in England or Wales.

By sect. 1 of the Law of Distress Amendment Act, 1895 (*d*) only a judge of the county court who granted the certificate can cancel it. The portion of the above section in italics is thereby repealed.

Power to make rules.

8. After the passing of this Act the Lord Chancellor may from time to time make, alter, and revoke rules—

(1.) For regulating the security (if any) to be required from bailiffs;

(2.) For regulating the fees, charges, and expenses in and incidental to distresses; and

(3.) For carrying into effect the objects of this Act.

These rules will be found hereafter (*e*).

Repeal, 46 & 47 Vict. c. 61.

9. Sections forty-nine, fifty, fifty-one, and fifty-two of the Agricultural Holdings (England) Act, 1883, are hereby repealed from and after the commencement of this Act, but this repeal shall not affect anything done or suffered before the commencement of this Act under these sections.

(*c*) *Post* p. 113.
(*d*) *Post* p. 111.
(*e*) *Post* p. 113.

LAW OF DISTRESS AMENDMENT ACT, 1895.

[58 & 59 VICT., c. 24.]

1. A certificate granted to a bailiff by the judge of a county court under the Law of Distress Amendment Act, 1888, may at any time be cancelled or declared void by a judge of that county court, and so much of section seven of that Act as refers to the cancellation of certificates is hereby repealed. *Power to cancel bailiff's certificates (51 & 52 Vict. c. 21).*

This section repeals part of sect. 7 of the Law of Distress Amendment Act, 1888 (a).

2. If any person not holding a certificate for the time being in force under the Law of Distress Amendment Act, 1888, levies a distress contrary to the provisions of that Act, he shall without prejudice to any civil liability be liable on summary conviction to a fine not exceeding ten pounds. *Penalty for acting without certificate.*

3. The power to make rules under the Law of Distress Amendment Act, 1888, shall extend to making provision for fixing the duration of certificates granted, or to be hereafter granted, to bailiffs. *Duration of certificates.*

4. A court of summary jurisdiction, on complaint that goods or chattels exempt under section four of the Law of Distress Amendment Act, 1888, from distress for rent, have been taken under such distress, may, by summary order, direct that the goods and chattels so taken, if not sold, be restored; or, if they have been sold, that such sum as the court may *Unlawful distress.*

(a) *Ante* p. 109.

58 & 59 VICT.
C. 24.

determine to be the value thereof shall be paid to the complainant by the person who levied the distress or directed it to be levied.

Evidence by accused.

5. In any proceeding against any person for an offence under this Act such person shall be competent, but not compellable, to give evidence, and the wife of such person may be required to attend to give evidence as an ordinary witness in the case, and shall be competent, but not compellable, to give evidence.

Short title.

6. This Act may be cited as the Law of Distress Amendment Act, 1895.

RULES MADE PURSUANT TO SECTION EIGHT OF THE LAW OF DISTRESS AMENDMENT ACT, 1888.

1. These Rules may be cited as the Distress for Rent Rules, 1888.

2. Certificates granted under the Law of Distress Amendment Act, 1888, herein-after called the Act, may be either general or special. A special certificate shall specify the particular distress or distresses to which it applies. Certificates shall be in the Forms Nos. 1 and 2 in Appendix I. to these Rules, with such variations as circumstances may require.

3. A special certificate may be granted by the judge or registrar, but a general certificate shall only be granted by the judge in person.

4. A general certificate shall authorise the bailiff named in it to levy at any place in England or Wales.

5. Any person (not being an officer of a County Court) holding a certificate under the Agricultural Holdings Act, 1883, shall on application be entitled to obtain, without fee, a general certificate.

6. No certificate shall be granted to any officer of a County Court.

7. Any practising solicitor of the Supreme Court shall, on application, and on payment of the prescribed fee, be entitled to a general or special certificate.

8. A general or special certificate may, on payment of the prescribed fee, be granted to any applicant who satisfies the authority granting the same that he is a fit and proper person to hold the certificate.

9. Where the applicant for a certificate is not a ratepayer, rated on a rateable value of not less than £25 per annum, he may, if the authority applied to thinks fit, be required to give security for the due performance of his duties.

10. The security shall be security to the satisfaction of the registrar. In the case of a general certificate the amount shall be £20, and in the case of a special certificate the amount shall be £5.

11. The security shall be given to the registrar. It may be given by deposit, or by bond, or by guarantee, as the registrar may think fit.

12. On any application to cancel a certificate the judge may, whether he cancels the certificate or not, order that the security shall be forfeited either wholly or in part, and that the amount directed to be forfeited shall be paid to the party aggrieved.

13. Where the judge orders that the security shall be forfeited, either wholly or in part, but does not cancel the certificate, he may direct that the bailiff shall give fresh security as a condition of retaining his certificate.

14. Subject to Rule 12, where a certificate is cancelled by the judge, the security shall also be cancelled, and the deposit (if any) returned.

15. No person shall be entitled to any fees, charges, or expenses for levying a distress, or for doing any act or thing in relation thereto, other than those specified in, and authorised by, the table in Appendix II. to these Rules.

The bailiff and *not* the landlord is entitled to the percentage for levying distress (*a*). The table of fees, charges, and expenses in Appendix II. (*b*), has replaced the charges, etc., under schedule 2 of the Agricultural Holdings Act, 1883.

16. Where the rent due exceeds £20 the fees, charges, and expenses specified in Scale I. shall be allowed, and where the rent due does not exceed £20 the fees, charges, and expenses specified in Scale II. shall be allowed.

17. In case of any difference as to fees, charges, and expenses between the parties, or any of them, the fees, charges, and expenses shall be taxed by the registrar of the district in which the distress is levied.

(*a*) *Philipps* v. *Rees*, (1889), 24 Q.B.D. 17; 59 L.J.Q.B. 1; 38 W.R. 53; overruling *Coode* v. *Johns*, (1886), 17 Q.B.D. 714; 55 L.J.Q.B. 475; 55 L.T. 290; 35 W.R. 47; 51 J.P. 21.
(*b*) *Infra*, p. 116.

The registrar may make such order as he thinks fit as to the costs of such taxation.

18. A copy of the table of fees, charges, and expenses authorised by these Rules shall be posted up by the registrar in a conspicuous place in his office, and every bailiff levying a distress shall, on the request of the tenant, produce to him his certificate and a copy of the table.

19. "Judge" means a judge of County Courts.

"Certificate" means a certificate to act as a bailiff under section seven of the Act.

"Registrar" means registrar of a County Court, and each registrar where there is more than one, and includes a deputy registrar.

APPENDIX I.

FORM 1. GENERAL CERTIFICATE.

[Date.]

In the County Court of , holden at

Pursuant to section seven of the Law of Distress Amendment Act, 1888, I hereby authorise *A.B.*, of , to act as bailiff to levy distresses for rent in England and Wales.

(L.S.) Signed

Judge.

FORM 2. SPECIAL CERTIFICATE.

[Date.]

In the County Court of , holden at

Pursuant to section seven of the Law of Distress Amendment Act, 1888, I hereby authorise *A.B.*, of , to act as a bailiff to levy a distress on the premises of *C.D.*, of , for rent alleged to be due to *E.F.*, of .

(L.S.) Signed

Judge.
or Registrar.

8 A

APPENDIX II.

TABLE OF FEES, CHARGES, AND EXPENSES.

SCALE I.

Distresses for Rent where the Sum demanded and due shall exceed £20 (c).

For levying distress. Three per cent. on any sum exceeding £20 and not exceeding £50. Two and a half per cent. on any sum exceeding £50 and not exceeding £200; and one per cent. on any additional sum.

For man in possession, 5s. per day; to provide his own board in every case.

For advertisements the sum actually and necessarily paid.

For commission to the auctioneer. On sale by auction seven and a half per cent. on the sum realised not exceeding £100, five per cent. on the next £200, four per cent. on the next £200; and on any sum exceeding £500 three per cent. up to £1,000, and two and a half per cent. on any sum exceeding £1,000. A fraction of £1 to be in all cases reckoned £1.

Reasonable fees, charges, and expenses (subject to Rule 17) where distress is withdrawn or where no sale takes place, and for negotiations between landlord and tenant respecting the distress.

For appraisement, on tenant's written request, whether by one broker or more, 6d. in the pound on the value as appraised, in addition to the amount for the stamp.

SCALE II.

Distresses for Rent where the Sum demanded and due shall not exceed £20.

For levying distress, 3s.

For man in possession, 4s. 6d. per day; to provide his own board in every case.

(c) This scale differs materially from that under schedule 2 of the Agricultural Holdings Act, 1883, which is repealed.

For appraisement, on the tenant's written request, whether by one broker or more, 6d. in the pound on the value as appraised, in addition to the amount for the stamp.
For all expenses of advertisements, if any, 10s.
Catalogues, sale and commission, and delivery, 1s. in the pound on the net produce of the sale.
For removal at tenant's request, the reasonable expenses (subject to Rule 17) attending such removal.

RULES, DATED NOVEMBER 29, 1895, UNDER THE LAW OF DISTRESS (AMENDMENT) ACT, 1895.

1. An applicant for a general certificate shall satisfy the judge that he is resident or has his principal place of business in the district of the court, and shall state whether he has ever been refused a certificate or had a former certificate cancelled.

2. A general certificate shall (unless previously determined) have effect until the 1st of February next after the expiration of twelve months from the granting thereof, provided that the judge of the court where the certificate was granted may renew the same from time to time for the like period. This Rule shall apply to every certificate granted before the passing of these Rules as if it had been granted at the date of the commencement of the Act.

3. A certificate shall have effect, notwithstanding cancellation or expiration by non-renewal, for the purpose of any distress where the bailiff has entered into possession before the date of cancellation or expiration.

4. On the renewal of a certificate the registrar shall be satisfied that the security required under Rules 9 and 10 of the Distress Rules, 1888, is subsisting. The fee on the application for renewal shall be two shillings and sixpence.

5. A renewed certificate shall be under the hand of the judge in the Form No. 1 in the Distress Rules, 1888, except that instead of the word "hereby" the words "by this renewed certificate" shall be inserted, and that the date at which the renewed certificate shall become terminable shall be added at the foot thereof.

6. There shall be made and signed by the registrar on the 1st of February in every year, and exhibited in the office of every court a list of the bailiffs holding certificates for the time being; and the fact of the subsequent cancellation of any such certificate shall be notified by the registrar on such list and published by him in some local newspaper.

7. Wherever "cancel" occurs in the Distress Rules, 1888, add "or make void."

8. The following form of cancellation shall be used :—

FORM 3. CANCELLATION OF CERTIFICATE.

Date.

In the County Court of   holden at

In pursuance of sect. 1 of the Law of Distress Amendment Act, 1895. I hereby cancel and make void the certificate granted to *A.B.* of   , to act as bailiff to levy distress for rent in England and Wales, or (terms of special certificate) *save and except as to any distress whereon the said A.B. has distrained and is in possession of the goods.*

(Signed)

Judge.

The 29th of November, 1895.

TENANTS COMPENSATION ACT, 1890.

[53 & 54 VICT. C. 57.]

1. This Act shall be construed as one with the Agricultural Holdings Act, 1883, and the Allotments and Cottage Gardens Compensation for Crops Act, 1887 (in this Act referred to as the principal Acts), and this Act may be cited as the Tenants Compensation Act, 1890. Construction and short title.

2. Where a person occupies land under a contract of tenancy with the mortgagor, whether made before or after the passing of this Act, which is not binding on the mortgagee of such land, then— Compensation to tenants, when mortgagee in possession.

> (1.) The occupier shall, as against the mortgagee who takes possession, be entitled to any compensation which is, or would but for the mortgagee taking possession be due to the occupier from the mortgagor as respects crops, improvements, tillages, or other matters connected with the land, whether under the principal Acts or the custom of the country, or agreements sanctioned by the principal Acts;
>
> Provided that any sum ascertained to be due to the occupier for such compensation or for any costs connected therewith, may be set off against any rent or other sum due from him in respect of the land, and recovered as compensation under the principal Acts, but unless so set off shall, as against the mortgagee, be charged and recovered in accordance

<small>53 & 54 Vict. c. 57.</small>
<small>46 & 47 Vict. c. 61, s. 31 (a).</small>

only with section thirty-one of the Agricultural Holdings Act, 1883, as if the mortgagee were the landlord within the meaning of that section.

(2.) Before the mortgagee deprives the occupier of possession of the land otherwise than in accordance with the said contract, he shall give to the occupier six months' notice in writing of his intention so to deprive him, and if he so deprives him compensation shall be due to the occupier for his crops, and for any expenditure upon the land which he has made in the expectation of holding the land for the full term of his contract of tenancy, in so far as any improvement resulting therefrom is not exhausted at the time of his being so deprived, and such compensation shall be determined in like manner as compensation under the principal Acts, and shall be set off, charged, and recovered in manner before provided in this section. This sub-section shall only apply where the said contract is for a tenancy from year to year, or for a term of years not exceeding twenty-one, at a rack rent.

<small>51 & 52 Vict. c. 51, to apply to compensation under 46 & 47 Vict. c. 61, s. 31 (a).</small>

3. Where compensation for improvements comprised in Part One or Part Two of the First Schedule to the Agricultural Holdings (England) Act, 1883, is charged by an order under section thirty-one of that Act, the charge shall be a land charge within the meaning of the Land Charges Registration and Searches Act, 1888, and shall be registered accordingly.

<small>Exception of tithe rent-charge, 6 & 7 Will. IV. c. 71.</small>

4. This Act shall not apply to provisions for the payment of tithe rent-charge arising under the Tithe Commutation Act, and subsequent Acts relating thereto.

<small>Extent of Act.</small>

5. This Act shall not apply to Scotland or Ireland.

(a) *Ante* p. 71.

MARKET GARDENERS' COMPENSATION ACT, 1895.

[58 & 59 VICT. C. 27.]

1. This Act may be cited as the Market Gardeners' Compensation Act, 1895, and shall be read and construed as part of the Agricultural Holdings (England) Act, 1883, herein-after called the principal Act, as amended by the Tenants Compensation Act, 1890. _{Short title and construction.}

2. This Act shall come into operation on the first day of January one thousand eight hundred and ninety-six, which date is herein-after referred to as the commencement of this Act. _{Commencement of Act.}

3. Where after the commencement of this Act it is agreed in writing that a holding shall be let or treated as a market garden, the following provisions shall have effect:— _{Amendment and extension of 46 & 47 Vict. c. 61, as to improvements executed in or upon market gardens (a).}

(1.) The provisions of section thirty-four of the principal Act shall extend to every fixture or building affixed or erected by the tenant to or upon such holding for the purposes of his trade or business of a market gardener.

(2.) The improvements numbered (1) "erection or enlargement of buildings," (6) "making of gardens," and (11) "planting of orchards or fruit bushes," in Part I. of the First Schedule to the principal Act shall, as far as regards such holding, cease to be comprised in the said schedule.

(a) Agricultural Holdings Act, 1883, sect. 34, *ante* p. 75.

36 & 39 Vict.
c. 27.

(3.) The following improvements shall as far as regards such holding be deemed to be comprised in Part III. of the said schedule :—

(i.) Planting of standard or other fruit trees permanently set out ;
(ii.) Planting of fruit bushes permanently set out ;
(iii.) Planting of strawberry plants ;
(iv.) Planting of asparagus and other vegetable crops ;
(v.) Erection or enlargement of buildings for the purposes of the trade or business of a market gardener.

(4.) Section fifty-six of the principal Act shall be read and construed as if the words "with the consent in writing of his landlord" were not included therein.

(5.) It shall be lawful for the tenant to remove all fruit trees and fruit bushes planted by him on the holding and not permanently set out ; but if the tenant shall not remove such fruit trees and fruit bushes before the termination of his tenancy, such fruit trees and fruit bushes shall remain the property of the landlord, and the tenant shall not be entitled to any compensation in respect thereof.

Waste.

It is not waste for a lessee to convert part of the demised premises into a market garden by erecting glass-houses thereon for the cultivation of hot-house produce (*b*).

Glass-houses— buildings.

Glass-houses are "buildings" (*c*).

Application to current tenancies.

4. Where, under a contract of tenancy current at the commencement of this Act, a holding is at that date in use or cultivation as a market garden with the knowledge of the landlord, and the tenant thereof has then executed thereon, without having received previously to the execution thereof any written notice of dissent by the landlord, any of the improvements

---

(*b*) *Meux* v. *Cobley*, (1892), 2 Ch. 253 ; 61 L.J. Ch. 449 ; 66 L.T. 86.
(*c*) *Smith* v. *Richmond*, (1898), 1 Q.B. 683 ; 67 L.J.Q.B. 439 ; 78 L.T. 174 ; 46 W.R. 401.

in respect of which a right of compensation or removal is given to a tenant by this Act, then the provisions of this Act shall apply in respect of such holding, as if it had been agreed in writing after the commencement of this Act that the holding should be let or treated as a market garden.

58 & 39 Vict.
c. 27.

The parties to an agreement for a letting from year to year may by an agreement stipulate that the tenancy may be determined by a three months' notice at any time. In *King* v. *Eversfield* (*d*) it was held that a tenant of a market garden under such an agreement current at the commencement of the Market Gardeners' Compensation Act, 1895, holds the land under a "contract of tenancy" within the meaning of sect. 4 of the Act, as interpreted by sect. 61 of the Agricultural Holdings Act, 1883, so as to be entitled to compensation for improvements executed before the Act. The facts were as follows: By an agreement dated October 22, 1886, the owner of a piece of land let the same to a tenant from September 29, 1886, at the rent of £19 12s. a year, payable quarterly on the four usual quarter days for payment of rent in every year, and the tenant agreed to pay the said rent at the times aforesaid, and to use the said premises as garden ground only, and to manure, crop, and cultivate the same in a husbandlike manner, and it was agreed that the tenancy might be determined by either party giving to the other three calendar months' notice to quit, or of his intention of quitting, as the case might be, on any day of the year. The land so let was used by the tenant as a market garden. In October, 1896, the landlord gave the tenant notice to quit. The tenant claimed compensation for improvements under sect. 4 of the Market Gardeners' Compensation Act, 1895. The Court of Appeal held that the agreement created a tenancy from year to year, and that the tenant therefore came within sect. 4 of the Market Gardeners' Compensation Act, 1895, as having held under a "contract of tenancy" as defined by sect. 61 of the Agricultural Holdings Act, 1883.

Tenancy from year to year— three months' notice *at any time*.

Lord Esher, M.R., after stating the facts, said: "The tenant, therefore, agreed to pay a yearly rent, though payable quarterly, and, if the agreement stopped there, in my opinion, the appellant would clearly have been a yearly tenant. But then comes the provision for determination of the tenancy by a three months' notice on any day in the year. That was a provision which might not be acted upon, and was not in the present case acted upon, until after the lapse of several years. The case is not at all like the case of a mere letting for three months. I cannot agree with the contention that this provision as to notice entirely alters the nature of a tenancy which upon the construction of the previous part of the agreement would be created by it."

A. L. Smith, L.J., said: "The terms of this agreement so far import a tenancy from year to year. But it is contended that the tenancy is cut down to a quarterly tenancy by the subsequent provision for its determination by a three months' notice to quit on any day of the year. I do not agree with that contention. It is conceded that, if the tenancy had been expressly stated to be from year to year, then,

---

(*d*) (1897), 2 Q.B. 475; 66 L.J.Q.B. 809; 77 L.T. 195; 46 W.R. 51; 61 J.P. 740.

58 & 59 VICT.
c. 27.

Agreement to be construed as a whole.

notwithstanding the provision for a three months' notice, the respondent must fail; but I can see no distinction for this purpose between an agreement which expressly mentions a tenancy from year to year, and one which, like the agreement here, by necessary implication points to such a tenancy. The question is whether, upon the true construction of the agreement taken as a whole, it creates a quarterly tenancy at a rent calculated at the rate of so much a year, with a provision for a three months' notice to quit, or a tenancy from year to year at a yearly rent with a provision for a three months' notice to quit. I think the latter is the true construction."

As to Crown lands and lands belonging to the Duchies of Lancaster and Cornwall.

5. Any compensation payable under this Act shall as regards land belonging to Her Majesty the Queen, Her heirs and successors, in right of the Crown or in right of the Duchy of Lancaster, and as regards land belonging to the Duchy of Cornwall, be paid in the same manner and out of the same funds respectively as if it were payable in respect of an improvement mentioned in the first part of the First Schedule to the principal Act, except that as regards land belonging to Her Majesty the Queen, Her heirs and successors, in right of the Crown, compensation for planting strawberry plants and asparagus and other vegetable crops shall be paid in the same manner and out of the same funds as if it were payable in respect of an improvement mentioned in the third part of the said schedule.

Interpretation.

6. For the purposes of the principal Act and of this Act the expression "market garden" shall mean a holding or that part of a holding which is cultivated wholly or mainly for the purpose of the trade or business of market gardening.

APPENDIX I.

FIRST PRECEDENT.

AGREEMENT FOR A LEASE.

APPLICABLE TO A LADY-DAY TENANCY, OR A MICHAELMAS TENANCY.

(1.)

AN AGREEMENT made the   day of   between *A.B.* of [*or C.D.* agent for *A.B.* of] [who, together with his heirs and assigns and the person or persons for the time being entitled to the premises hereby demised expectant on the term hereby granted is hereinafter called the landlord] of the one part and *C.D.* of   [who, together with his executors, administrators and assigns is hereinafter called the tenant] of the other part. Parties.

1. The landlord agrees to let and the tenant to take the farm and premises situate in the parish of   , in the County of   , and particularly described in the first schedule hereto and hereinafter called the farm, for the term of one year from the   day of   and so on from year to year, determinable at the end of the first or any subsequent year on [*one year's*] six calendar months' notice in writing to quit, at the rents and upon the conditions hereinafter expressed, which the landlord and tenant hereby agree respectively to pay and perform. Parcels.
Term.
Notice to quit. Ss. 33, 59 (*a*).

2. *Section thirty-three* of the Agricultural Holdings (England) Act, 1883, shall not apply to this tenancy. S. 33 excluded (*b*).

Reservations and Rents.

3. The landlord excepts and reserves to himself all trees, saplings, underwood and plantations whatsoever [save such as are comprised in the first schedule] and all mines, minerals, and quarries, with free access for himself and all Reservations.

(*a*) *Ante* pp. 73, 93.
(*b*) *Ante* p. 73.

persons authorised by him to fell, cut, win, work and carry away the same, and also to enter for the purpose of viewing,
S. 41 (c). See Clause 20.
and if necessary, of erecting buildings, making roads, gardens, drains, water courses, plantations and alterations, and of executing repairs, and ascertaining the state and condition of the farm. Also all game, wildfowl and fish [save as provided by the Ground Game Act, 1880] and nests and eggs of game, with the right for himself, his friends and servants at all times to enter the farm for the purpose of sporting and preserving the same.

Rent.

4. The tenant shall pay a rent for the farm of £ per annum, clear of all deductions by four equal quarterly payments on the usual quarter days. The first payment shall be made upon the   day of   .

Rents and penalties.

5. The tenant shall pay a further yearly rent at the rate of £   for every acre of meadow, pasture, or woodlands now let, or of land which may by mutual agreement be laid down to pasture or wood, which shall be pared or broken up without the consent of the landlord and a further yearly rent at the rate of £   for every acre of the arable land which shall not be cultivated in the manner hereinafter mentioned without such consent, and a further yearly rent at the rate of £   for every acre for any land above two acres which shall be sown or set with hemp, flax, or rape grown to seed, or potatoes without such consent, and a further yearly rent of £   for every tree or sapling which the tenant shall wilfully cut down or injure without such consent.

Rents and penalties, how paid.

6. Such further rents shall be paid by equal quarterly payments clear of all deductions in manner above mentioned, and shall be recoverable by distress, and the first payment shall become due on the first quarter-day next after the event on which the same shall become payable. If the tenancy shall be determined under clause 21, the tenant shall pay a proportionate part of all rents, tithe rent charges, rates, taxes, and other outgoings then accruing due for the fraction of the current quarter up to the date of such determination.

Rent, when payable in advance. S. 44 (d).

7. If at any time in any year of the tenancy, the landlord shall give to the tenant or leave at the farm house a notice in writing requiring the tenant immediately to pay all

(c) Ante p. 80.
(d) Ante p. 84.

rents which should become payable from the quarter-day preceding such notice to the Lady-Day [*or* the 29th of September] following, on the delivery of such notice such rent shall become due and payable in advance, and may be recovered by distress or otherwise as rent in arrear.

Landlord's Agreements.

8. *Where tenant does repairs.*—The landlord shall find all materials in the rough for repairs to be done by the tenant. *Where landlord does repairs.*—Except as provided by clause 19 the landlord shall find all materials for repairs, and shall do all such repairs to the farm, including painting, as may from time to time be found necessary. <small>Repairs, s. 6 (*e*).</small>

9. *Where the landlord does drainage.*—The landlord shall do all new draining at his own cost, and shall charge the tenant interest on the cost incurred in respect thereof at the rate of £ per cent. per annum, and the same shall be recoverable by distress, or otherwise, as rent in arrear. This agreement shall be in substitution for the provisions of sect. 4 of the Agricultural Holdings (England) Act, 1883, and all notices under that section shall be dispensed with. <small>Drainage by landlord. s. 4 (*f*).</small>

10. The landlord shall, on the tenant quitting at the determination of his tenancy [provided that the tenant has paid the rents, and performed the conditions of this Agreement], pay the tenant allowances in respect of the matters mentioned in the second schedule hereto at the rates therein mentioned. Such allowances shall be in substitution for any compensation to which the tenant would be entitled under the Agricultural Holdings (England) Act, 1883, in respect of any matters contained in the 3rd part of the 1st schedule to that Act. <small>Agreement as to compensation for improvements in part iii. under s. 5 (*g*).</small>

Tenant's Agreements.

11. The tenant shall pay all rates, taxes, tithes, tithe rent-charges, assessments, and outgoings of every description (except landlord's property tax), now or hereafter payable in respect of the farm. Any of such payments shall, if required by the landlord, be paid to him, and in case the <small>Rates and taxes, &c. s. 6 (*h*).</small>

(*e*) *Ante* p. 49.
(*f*) *Ante* p. 46, clause 18, *infra*.
(*g*) *Ante* p. 48.
(*h*) *Ante* p. 49.

S. 47 (*i*).

tenant shall make default in any of such payments, the landlord may recover the same by distress, or otherwise, as rent in arrear.

Payment of compensation by incoming to outgoing tenant. S. 56 (*k*).

12. In addition to the valuations hereinafter mentioned, the tenant will pay to the outgoing tenant any allowances or compensation which may be due to him in respect of any of the matters in the second schedule hereto.

Cultivation. [NOTE.—*Paras. 13 and 14 are applicable to the four course system. They must be varied according to the rotation of cropping (if any) intended to be enforced.*]

13. The tenant shall farm and manage all parts of the farm in a good husbandlike manner, keeping and leaving it clean, free from weeds, and in good condition. He shall have at least one-fourth of the arable land in clean summer or turnip fallow in every year, and shall also, with the first crop of corn after such fallow, sow good clover or grass seeds.

Rotation of crops.

14. The tenant shall not from any of the lands take more than two white crops under the same course of tillage, nor two successive crops of the same kind of corn, and he shall with one of such white crops lay down the land with clover grass seeds.

[*Here will come any special covenants rendered necessary by the custom of the estate or district in which the farm is situated.*]

To consume hay, straw and manure, &c. S. 6 (b.) (*l*).

15. The tenant shall consume upon the farm all hay, straw, fodder, haulm, chaff, roots, and green crops, grown thereon, and spread thereon all manure (except as hereinafter mentioned) arising thereon. He shall not sell or dispose of any part thereof without the landlord's consent in writing. If the same or any part thereof shall be taken and sold under a distress for rent, or an execution for debt, or otherwise, it may be sold, subject to a condition that it shall be consumed upon the farm, and the manure arising from such consumption shall not be removed from the farm.

Vouchers and samples.

16. Samples taken from the bulk of all the manufactured artificial manures spread upon the farm shall, in each year, be submitted to and sent to the landlord, and the landlord may at any time call for all proper proof and evidence of use and application of such manures, and may call for and inspect all bills, vouchers, and receipts, showing the description of and outlay upon any of the matters mentioned in

---

(*i*) *Ante* p. 90.
(*k*) *Ante* p. 92.
(*l*) *Ante* p. 50.

the 2nd Schedule hereto, [*or if the Schedule is not used* mentioned in the 1st Schedule to the Agricultural Holdings Act, 1883].

17. The tenant shall not mow any meadow or grass land except water meadow more than once in any one year, nor shall he mow the same in two successive years without manuring the same before the second mowing to the satisfaction of the landlord. *To mow grass land.*

18. The tenant shall maintain, keep and leave all ditches, drains, cesspools, watercourses and outfalls properly cleansed and scoured out, and he shall plash and lay the fences in regular succession in the best form and so leave them on quitting. *Drains and outfalls.*

When the tenant is to do all drainage.—The tenant shall do all new draining required upon the farm at his own cost, subject to the approval of the landlord or his agent as to the land to be drained and the method of draining, and shall be paid compensation for the outlay incurred in respect thereof [less the cost of labour and haulage, *or as the case may be*], at the rate of . This Agreement, *etc.* as in *clause 9*. *Drainage by tenant. S. 4 (m).*

19. *Where tenant does all repairs and landlord finds materials.*—The tenant shall keep all buildings and outbuildings on the farm in a good tenantable condition [*or* in as good condition as they were in when he entered or may be put into by the landlord] and shall put and keep all fences, walls, gates, posts, arches, bridges and stiles on the farm in good condition and repair. *Repairs.*

Where landlord does repairs.—The tenant shall paper, glaze, and whitewash such parts of the farm house and buildings as are now or may hereafter be papered, glazed and whitewashed, and shall maintain and leave all the landlord's fixtures and fittings in the farm house and in and about the farm generally in good repair and condition, and shall find straw for thatching, and shall do the haulage gratis within a distance of miles from the farm house of all materials for repairs, or for new erections or drainage, or for any improvements upon the farm.

20. The tenant shall not assign or underlet any part of the farm [except cottages and gardens to labourers] without the previous consent in writing of the landlord, and he shall at all times reside upon the farm. *Not to underlet.*

(*m*) *Ante* p. 46, clause 9, *supra*.

Proviso for re-entry.

21. If and whenever any part of the rents and other payments before reserved shall be in arrear for twenty-one days, whether the same shall have been legally demanded or not, and no sufficient distress can be found upon the farm to satisfy such arrears, or if and whenever there shall be a breach by the tenant of any of the conditions and agreements herein contained, or if and whenever the tenant shall become bankrupt or compound with his creditors, or execute any bill of sale or assignment of his effects, or suffer his effects or any part thereof to be taken in execution then and in any of such cases [save as provided by the Conveyancing and Law of Property Acts, 1881 and 1892], the landlord may re-enter upon any part of the farm in the name of the whole, and thereupon this tenancy shall be absolutely determined, and the tenant shall pay a proportionate part of all rents, tithe rent-charges, rates, taxes, and other outgoings then accruing due for the part of the current quarter up to the date of such determination.

The Last Year of Tenancy and Quitting.

(For a Lady-Day Tenancy only.)

Ploughings for incoming tenant (n).

22. The tenant shall, before the 1st day of preceding the determination of the tenancy, in a husbandlike manner plough the stubbles for the incoming tenant, for which he shall be paid by valuation. If he shall neglect to do so the landlord or incoming tenant may on or at any time after such day enter and do such acts, and in such case shall have accommodation for a servant and for horses on the farm.

Not to turn animals on mowing grass.

23. The tenant shall not, after the 2nd of February next before the end of his tenancy, turn any animal upon any meadow or grass land in rotation or intended for mowing the following harvest, or after the 1st of November upon any land seeded down the preceding spring.

General valuation clause.

24. In addition to any compensation to which the tenant may be entitled under clause 10 of this agreement, or under the Agricultural Holdings (England) Act, 1883, the landlord or incoming tenant shall, upon the termination of the tenancy [unless the tenancy is determined under condition 21], if the tenant pays the rents and performs the stipulations herein contained, but not otherwise, pay to the tenant the amount (if any) of a valuation to be made by two arbitrators or their umpires, under clause 29 of this agreement.

(n) See clause 24, *infra*.

The valuation shall include :—

[*The various payments for clover, seeds, share of wheat, unconsumed hay, straw, haulm, fodder, chaff, manure, ploughings and preparations, and so on, provided for by the customs of the country. Sometimes, instead of a valuation in Lady-Day takes, there is provision for the outgoing tenant having a room in the farmhouse, and boosy pasture on which his stock may consume the hay and fodder ; and in Michaelmas takes, for the outgoing tenant to have barn, granary, and stackyard room in which to stack and thresh his last year's crops.*]

For a Michaelmas Tenancy only.

25. The tenant shall allow the landlord or incoming tenant to enter upon, cultivate and manure, [*here follow the amounts of land to be reserved to an incoming tenant on 3 course, 4 course, and 5 course tillages*]. — Cultivation.

26. The tenant shall sow, or permit the landlord or incoming tenant to sow clover or other proper grass seeds with the summer corn, and shall harrow and roll in the same gratis. The tenant shall give the landlord or incoming tenant notice to supply the seeds   days previous to the time at which such grass seeds should be sown. If the seeds are not supplied within   days, then the tenant shall provide proper seeds, and shall be paid for the same as hereinafter mentioned. The tenant shall not graze or feed young seeds after harvest. — To sow grass seeds.

27. After the   day of   preceding the determination of the tenancy the tenant shall provide for the landlord or incoming tenant accommodation for a servant and for horses on the farm with the joint use of the cartsheds, and stackyard room for corn and hay for such horses, and dry straw for their litter, and room for implements and for storing and preparing artificial manure. — Accommodation for incoming tenant.

[*Here will follow general valuation clause (24) as in Lady-Day tenancy.*] — General valuation clause.

GENERAL CONDITIONS.

28. The landlord may at any time resume possession of any part or parts of the farm (provided any such part shall not exceed   acres) for the purpose of executing thereon any of the improvements mentioned in sect. 41 of the Agricultural Holdings (England) Act, 1883, or in the first Schedule thereto, without any notice whatever to the tenant being necessary. — Resuming possession. S. 41 (*o*).

(*o*) *Ante* p. 80.

9 A

Arbitration clause.

Ss. 7, 10, 23 (*p*).

S. 46 (*q*).

29. All claims or matters in dispute arising under this agreement and all compensation, allowances, payments, and valuations to which either party may claim to be entitled under this agreement, or under the Agricultural Holdings (England) Act, 1883, or otherwise, and all questions as to the construction of this agreement or as to the performance or observance of any of the conditions herein contained shall be ascertained and settled by a referee in manner provided by the Agricultural Holdings (England) Act, 1883, but without any appeal in any case to the county court, and the provisions of sects. 7 and 23 of such Act relating to notices and appeals to the county court, and of sect. 10 relating to the appointment of referees and umpires by the county court or the Land Commissioners, shall not apply to this tenancy. All questions relating to the validity of or arising under any distress made under the provisions of this agreement shall be determined by a court of summary jurisdiction as provided by sect. 46 of the Agricultural Holdings (England) Act, 1883.

1ST SCHEDULE.

(Names of Fields and Acreage.)

2ND SCHEDULE.

Particulars of Outlay.	Application.	Last Year of Tenancy.	Last but one.
Bones ground to ½ in.	To Fallows & Root Crops	*(Amounts of in different tenancy.)*	*compensation years of*
,, ,,	To Pasture . . .		
Lime . . .	{ To Tillage Land and to Pasture . . .		
Peruvian Guano .	To Fallow and Root Crop	[N.B.—Chalk ing, claying, haulage and ances may a similar	ing, clay burning, and marling, other allowbe included in schedule.]
Bone Superphosphate and Turnip Manure .	{ To Fallow and Root Crop		
,, ,,	To Pasture . .		
Good Stable Manure purchased . . .	{ To Tillage Land . .		
,, ,,	To Pasture . .		
Oil Cake, Cotton Cake, or Linseed, &c., &c. . . .	{ Consumed on the Farm		

With such variations as may be advisable.

(*p*) *Ante* pp. 54, 56, 62.
(*q*) *Ante* p. 88.

SECOND PRECEDENT.

AGREEMENT FOR A LEASE.

SHORT FORM.

(1*)

NOTE.—*This precedent is intended for use when the parties desire at once to reduce into writing the terms of a verbal agreement with the intention of executing a more complete agreement at a future date. The references are to the clauses of the first precedent.*

AN AGREEMENT made the   day of   Clause 1.
between *A.B.* of   hereinafter called the landlord of the one part and *C.D.* of   hereinafter called the tenant of the other part.

1a. The landlord shall let to the tenant the   farm for one year from the   day of   and so on from year to year at a rent of £   per annum, payable quarterly, to be determined by six months' [one year's] notice to quit, expiring at the end of any year of the tenancy.

2a. (Here insert clause 2, *supra*, if desired.)   Clause 2.

3a. All trees, plantations, mines, minerals, quarries, and Clause 3. game are reserved to the landlord.

4a. (Here insert clause 7, *supra*, if desired.)   Clause 7.

5a. The tenant shall keep the premises in as good Clauses 8, 18, 19. condition as they were in when he entered, or shall be put into by the landlord, the landlord finding all materials in the rough for repairs (*or as the case may be*), and shall keep all ditches, drains, watercourses and sewers properly cleansed and scoured out.

6a. The tenant shall pay all rates, taxes, and outgoings Clauses 11, 12. of every description, except landlord's property tax now or hereafter payable in respect of the farm, and shall pay to the outgoing tenant any allowances or compensation which may be due to him in respect of any of the matters mentioned in paragraph 12a of this agreement.

7a. The tenant shall farm according to the custom of the Clauses as to country and the rules of good husbandry.   cultivation.

Clauses 15, 16.   8a. The tenant shall not sell off the farm any hay, straw, green crops and manure without the landlord's consent, and he shall produce to the landlord on request, samples taken from the bulk of all manufactured artificial manures spread upon the farm.

Clause 20.   9a. The tenant shall not assign or underlet any part of the farm.

Clause 28.   10a. No notice under clause 41 of the Agricultural Holdings (England) Act shall be necessary for resumption of possession.

Clauses 9, 13.   11a. The landlord shall do all new drainage, and the tenant shall pay a rent of £   per annum on the outlay [*or* the tenant shall do all new drainage subject to the approval of the landlord, and shall be paid for his outlay at the rate of   ]. This agreement shall be in substitution for the provisions of section 4 of the Agricultural Holdings (England) Act, 1883.

Clauses 10, 24, and Schedule.   12a. On the termination of the tenancy the tenant shall be paid by valuation for [*matters set out in clause 24 supra*]. The tenant shall also on quitting be paid allowances in respect of the following matters, namely: [*the matters in the 2nd schedule to form 1 supra p.*   ]. Such allowances shall be in substitution [*etc. as in clause 10 supra*].

Clause 29.   13a. All such allowances and valuations. and all claims and disputes arising under this agreement shall be ascertained and settled by a reference in manner provided by the Agricultural Holdings (England) Act, 1883, but the provisions of sects. 7, 10, and 23 of that Act relating to notices, appointment of referees and umpire and appeals shall not apply to this tenancy. Any questions relating to distress shall be decided by a court of summary jurisdiction as provided by sect. 46 of that Act.

Clause 21.   14a. If any rent is in arrear for twenty-one days, and there is no sufficient distress upon the farm. or if the tenant becomes bankrupt, or compounds with his creditors, or executes a bill of sale, or an assignment of his effects, or suffers his effects to be taken in execution, the landlord may re-enter.

15a. The tenant will at once [*or* when required] execute an agreement embodying the terms of this agreement and all usual covenants and conditions.

APPENDIX II.

Notices to Quit, and Miscellaneous Forms.

(2.)

Sir, the day of 18 *Notice to quit, Ss. 33, 61 (r).*
I hereby [as agent for *A.B.* and on his behalf] give you notice to quit [*or* that I intend to quit] and deliver up possession of the [*particulars of premises*] premises on the day of next, at the end of such year of your [my] tenancy as will expire next after one year [*or* one half year] from the service of this notice.

To *the tenant*, or *landlord*,   Landlord or *tenant*.
  or *his agent*.

(3.)

the day of 18   *Agreement that s. 33 shall not apply (s).*
We [*landlord or his agent*] and [*tenant or his agent*] hereby agree that the provisions of sect. 33 of the Agricultural Holdings (England) Act, 1883, shall not apply to any contract of tenancy now existing [or which may hereafter exist] between us in respect of [*particulars of premises*].

                      Landlord or *agent*.
                       Tenant or *agent*.

(4.)

Sir, the day of 18   *Notice to quit part of premises under s. 41 (t).*
In accordance with sect. 41 of the Agricultural Holdings (England) Act, 1883, I hereby give you notice to quit and deliver up possession of [*particulars of premises such as*, 2 acres 1 rood being that part of a field called Lower Leys which is next to the field called Upper Leys, part of a farm now in your possession called] at the end of such year [*etc.*, *as in No. 2 supra*], as I desire to resume possession thereof for the purpose of executing thereon the following improvements namely [*set them out*].

To *tenant*.   Landlord or *agent*.

(5.)

Sir, the day of 18   *Counter notice under s. 41 by tenant (t).*
I hereby give you notice that I accept your notice to me of the day of , 18 , requiring me to quit

---
(r) *Ante* pp. 73, 94.
(s) *Ante* p. 73.
(t) *Ante* p. 80, clauses 28 and 10a, Appendix I., *supra*.

[*particulars of premises, following landlord's notice to quit*], as notice to quit the entire holding of which such premises form part, to take effect at the expiration of the now current year of my tenancy, and I intend to quit the same accordingly; and I give you notice [*here may follow notice of intention to claim compensation, under Form* 11].
To *landlord* or *agent*. *Tenant*.

APPENDIX III.

Forms under the Compensation Clauses.

(6.)

Consent to tenant executing improvement or to improvement already executed in the first part of the schedule. S. 3 (*u*).

SIR,   the   day of   18
I give my consent to your executing the following improvement [*or*, I consent and approve of the improvement executed by you in the year 18   ] namely [*here specify the improvement*] upon your holding the [*name of the farm*], subject to the following condition, that is to say [*here insert conditions, such as limitation as to cost, compensation, carriage and quality of material, set off to landlord, and so on*].
To *tenant*.   *Landlord* or *agent*.

(7.)

Clause in agreement dispensing with notice under, S. 4 (*x*).

[See *supra*, Appendix I., clauses 9, 18, 11a.]

Notices by tenant of intention to drain holding. S. 4 (*x*).

(8.)

SIR,   the   day of   18
I give you notice that I intend to drain the following parts of my holding the [*name of the farm*] namely [*set out the acreage and situation of the part to be drained, the quality of the soil, the size of the pipes and depth, and distance apart of drain. For instance*—"the lower part of the field called Big Meadow, being about 4 acres 3 roods of clay soil to be drained with $2\frac{1}{2}$ inch pipes; the drains to be eight yards apart, three feet six inches deep, and to be discharged into the ditch at the south boundary by a main drain laid with four inch pipe." *If a rough plan can be added to the notice it would be better.*]
To *landlord* or *agent*.   *Tenant*.

(*u*) *Ante* p. 46.
(*x*) *Ante* p. 46.

(9.)

Sir,   the   day of   18

I give you notice that I intend myself to undertake the execution of any necessary drainage on that part of your holding mentioned in your notice to me of the   day of   , and I shall charge you with £5 per cent. per annum on the outlay incurred in executing the same [*or such a sum as will repay me the outlay in 25 years with interest thereon at £3 per cent.*]

To *tenant*.   *Landlord*.

And see *Appendix I., clauses 9 and 18.*

(10.)

Sir,   the   day of   18

I give you notice that I intend forthwith to execute the following improvements upon my holding the farm. [*Specify them with dates and particulars as in No. 11 infra.*]

To *landlord* or *agent*.   *Tenant*.

(11.)

Sir,   the   day of   18

I hereby give you notice that I intend to claim and do claim [Note.—*Apparently no further claim need be made but the parties go at once to reference*] the sum of £   as compensation in respect of the unexhausted value of the following improvements executed by me upon my holding the   farm [*specify them with the dates, and " as far as possible" the particulars of the intended claim as for instance*—

Laying down the ten acres field (11 acres 3 roods) to permanent pasture in 1884.

Draining 4 acres 3 roods of Big Meadow in 1884.

Five tons of superphosphate applied to Upper Slench Field for turnips, in the year 18   ; *and so on.*]

To *landlord* or *agent*.   *Tenant*.

(12.)

Sir,   the   day of   18

I hereby give you notice that in consequence of your notice of the   day of   18 [*No. 11 supra*] I intend to claim and do claim the sum of £   as

---
(*x*) *Ante* p. 46.
(*y*) *Ante* p. 93.
(*z*) *Ante* p. 52.

compensation in respect of the following matters connected with your contract of tenancy or your holding, namely:—

S. 6 (*a*). [*specify any of the matters under S. 6. as*,

Arrears of rent, due March 25th, 18 .
Cross cropping of a field called Bank field, in the years 1883-4-5.
Damages for breach of covenant to repair.
The amount of a reduction of rent allowed to you in consideration, etc., *with dates and other particulars.*]

To *tenant*. *Landlord*.

(13.)

Agreement as to the amount of compensation. S. 8 (*b*).

AN AGREEMENT made the   day of   18   between [*landlord*] and [*tenant*] [*description of parties*] in pursuance of sect. 8 of the Agricultural Holdings (England) Act, 1883. It is agreed as follows:—

1. The sum payable to the said [*tenant*] by the said [*landlord*] in respect of compensation for the unexhausted value of the improvements mentioned in the schedule hereto, made by the said [*tenant*] upon the   farm shall be £   .

2. The sum payable to the said [*landlord*] by the said [*tenant*] in respect of compensation for [*arrears of rent, rates, taxes, tithe rent-charge, waste, allowances, benefits, breaches of covenant, and so on*] shall be £   .

3. The sum of £   being the balance of the said sums of £   and £   shall be paid by the said [*landlord*] to the said [*tenant*] [*state time and mode for payment, as for instance,* "before the 10th of December next, '*or*' by two instalments, the first on the   "].

In witness whereof the parties hereto have set their hands the day and year above written.

Witness G.H. *Landlord.* *Tenant.*

[SCHEDULE.—*Here set out matters in respect of which compensation is claimed with the sums agreed to be paid in respect of each matter.*]

(14.)

SIR,   the   day of   18

Consent of landlord to incoming tenant paying compensation to outgoing tenant. S. 56 (*c*).

I hereby consent and agree that you shall as incoming tenant of the holding [*name of the farm*] pay to [*outgoing tenant*] as outgoing tenant of the same, the sum of

---

(*a*) *Ante* p. 49.
(*b*) *Ante* p. 54.
(*c*) *Ante* p. 92, see clauses, 11, 12, and 6A., Appendix I., *supra*.

Appendix III.

£ for compensation due to him from from me, under the provisions of the Agricultural Holdings (England) Act, 1883, in respect of the following improvements [*specify them, where an award has been made take the particulars from the award*] executed by him upon the holding.

To *incoming tenant.*　　　　　　　　　　　*Landlord.*

(15.)

SIR,　　　　　　　　the　　　day of　　　18

I hereby give you notice that I intend at the end of one month from the service of this notice, to remove from my holding the [*name of the farm*] the following fixtures and buildings erected by me upon the same, namely, [*specify fixtures, as for instance,* "a wooden barn resting on a brick floor in the farm yard erected by me in the year 18　etc."]

To *landlord.*　　　　　　　　　　　*Tenant.*

(16.)

SIR,　　　　　　　　the　　　day of　　　18

I give you notice that I elect to purchase the [*specify fixtures or buildings shortly*] referred to in your notice of intended removal, dated the　　　day of

To *tenant.*　　　　　　　　　　　*Landlord.*

(17.)

the　　　day of　　　18

We [*landlord* and *tenant*] hereby appoint *A.B.* of [*address and profession*] referee [*or* I (*landlord or tenant*) hereby appoint *A.B.* of etc.] referee on my behalf [*if necessary*, in the place of *C.D.* who is *deceased, unwilling, or incapable of acting*] under the provisions of the Agricultural Holdings (England) Act, 1883. to decide the following matters in respect of a holding [*name and situation of farm*] namely [*here set out the matters in respect of which the reference is required, as for instance* :—"The amount of compensation to be paid by the said *landlord* to the said *tenant* in respect of the following improvements made by him upon the holding," *naming them, with dates and particulars, or* "the value of the following fixtures," *naming them, with date of erection and particulars,* "and the amount of compensation to be paid by the said *tenant* to the said *landlord* in respect of the following *acts of waste, etc.*" *with dates and particulars.*]

　　　　　　　　　　　　Landlord and *tenant.*
　　　　　　　　　　　　Or *landlord* or *tenant.*

(*d*) *Ante* p. 75.
(*e*) *Ante* p. 55.

(18.)

Notice of appointment of a referee.
Notice requiring the other party to appoint a referee.
S. 9.
Sub-s. 5 (f).

S. 10 (g).

SIR,   the   day of   18
I give you notice that I have appointed *E.F.* of etc., to act as referee on my behalf [*if appointed in place of another*, in the place of *C.D.* who is deceased, etc., *according to facts*] to assess compensation under the Agricultural Holdings (England) Act, 1883. in respect of the holding named [*etc.. or* to assess the value of a steam engine, *or according to facts*] and [*if necessary*] I require you to appoint a referee in the same manner. And I further require that [*see form 24 infra*].

To *landlord* or *tenant*.   *Landlord* or *tenant*.

Notice to referee requiring him to act within seven days.
S. 9.
Sub-s. 2 (h).

(19.)

SIR,   the   day of   18
I require you as referee [*on behalf of*   ] within seven days from the receipt of this notice to act in the reference between myself and *A.B.* in the matter of [the compensation claimed by me and by the said *A.B.* respectively in respect of a holding named, *etc.*, *or* in the matter of the value of a steam engine, *etc.*, *or according to facts;* state shortly the name of the holding and what the claim was for].

To *referee*.   *C.D.*

Consent to revocation of submission to reference.
S. 12 (i).

(20.)

SIR,   the   day of   18
I consent to you revoking your submission to reference and appointment in writing of *C.D.* as referee appointed to assess the compensation claimed by us respectively in respect of [*etc.*, *as in form 18*, *or according to facts*].

To   *Signed*

Revocation of submission to reference.
S. 12 (i).

(21.)

SIR,   the   day of   18
I hereby revoke my submission to reference and appointment in writing of you as referee in the matter of [*etc.*, *as in form 19*].

                                                 Signed

(f) *Ante* p. 55.
(g) *Ante* p. 56.
(h) *Ante* p. 55.
(i) *Ante* p. 57.

Appendix III.

(22.)

               the   day of   18   *Extension of time by referees. S. 16 (k).*

We extend the time for making our award in the matters referred to us respecting the compensation claimed by *C.D.* and by [*etc., as in form 19*] until the   day of 18.

                               Signed by both referees.

(23.)

SIR,   the   day of   18   *Request to referee to appoint an umpire. S. 9. Sub-s. o (l).*

I require you to appoint an umpire [in the place of *C.D.*, deceased, *etc., as in form 17*] within seven days from the receipt of this notice to act in the reference between myself and *A.B.* in the matter of [*etc., as in form 19*].

To *referee.*   *Signed*

(24.)

SIR,   the   day of   18   *Notice requiring the appointment of umpire by Land Commissioners or by the County Court. S. 10. Sub-s. 1 (m).*

I require that the umpire in the reference between myself and *A.B.* in the matter of [*etc., as in form 19*] shall be appointed by the Land Commissioners [*or* by the County Court].

To *landlord* or *tenant.*   *Signed*

(25.)

SIRS   the   day of   18   *Application to Land Commissioners to appoint an umpire. S. 10. Sub-s. 1 (m).*

I require you to appoint an umpire [in the place of *C.D.* deceased. *etc., as in form 17*] to act in a reference now pending between myself and *A.B.* in the matter of [*etc., as in form 19*].

                               Signed

(26.)

SIR,   the   day of   18   *Notice of dissent from appointment of umpire by the County Court. S. 10. Sub-s. 2 (n).*

I give you notice that I dissent from the appointment of the umpire by the County Court in the reference now pending between myself and *A.B.* in the matter of [*etc., as in form 19*].

To *landlord* or *tenant.*   *Signed*

(k) *Ante* p. 58.
(l) *Ante* p. 56.
(m) *Ante* p. 56.
(n) *Ante* p. 57.

(27.)

Appointment of umpire or fresh umpire by referees.
S. 9.
Sub-s. 7 (o).

the day of 18

We *E.F.* of [*address and occupation*] and *G.H.* of [*address and occupation*] referees on behalf of *A.B.* and *C.D.* respectively appointed to assess [*etc.*, *as in form 18*], do hereby appoint *L.M.* umpire [in the place of *C.D.* etc., as in *form 17*], in respect of the matters so referred to us.

Signed by both referees.

(28.)

Notice to umpire of the reference to him.
S. 18 (p).

Sir, the day of 18

I [*or* we] hereby give you notice that I [*or* we, *or* *A.B.* and *C.D.*, referees duly appointed] cannot agree in making an award in the matter of [*etc.*, *as in form 19*], and you as umpire can proceed to consider the matters referred to them.

To *umpire*.

Signed by either, or both parties, or either, or both referees.

(29.)

Notice to proceed with reference in absence of parties.
S. 14 (q).

Sir, the day of 18

[In the matter of the Agricultural Holdings (England) Act, 1883, and of a reference between yourself and *A.B.* relative to a holding named] I [we] shall consider [*or* shall continue to consider] the matters referred to me [us] at o'clock in the noon. on the day of 18 , at [*specify place*], and if either party be absent I [we] shall proceed with the same in their absence.

To *either party*. *Signed*

(30.)

Notice to produce by referees or umpire.
S. 13 (r).

Sir, the day of 18

[In the matter of the Agricultural Holdings (England) Act, 1883, and of a reference between yourself and *A.B.*, relative to a holding named]. Take notice, that I [we] require you to produce at o'clock in the noon, on the day of 18 , at [*specify place*], for my [our] inspection the following documents. vouchers, and samples namely [*set them out as*:— all receipts, vouchers, letters, and other documents in your possession relating to the holding, *or* a letter from *C.D.* to *E.F.*, dated the 7th day of February, 1884, *or* a memorandum of agreement, *etc.*, *with date and*

(*o*) *Ante* p. 56.
(*p*) *Ante* p. 59.
(*q*) *Ante* p. 58.
(*r*) *Ante* p. 57.

parties, or the plans and specifications for *the erection of buildings, or drainage, or* a receipt for, *or* a sample from the bulk of 40 tons of Peruvian guano put by you upon the fields in the year 18 *and so on*].

To *Referee, or referees, or umpire.*

(31.)

To all to whom these presents shall come we *A.B.* of [*address and description*] and *C.D.* of [*or if made by a single referee or umpire*, I *A.B.* of send greeting.

Form of award. Ss. 15, 17, 19, 20, 21 (s).

Whereas *E.F.* of claims compensation from *G.H.* of under the provisions of the Agricultural Holdings (England) Act, 1883, in respect of the following matters and things, namely:—[*set out the matters referred to in the words of the appointment of the referee, form 17*]. And whereas the said *G.H.* claims from the said *E.F.* like compensation in respect of the following matters and things, namely:—[set out items of counterclaim, as above] [*or* Whereas the said *E.F.* and *G.H.* are unable to agree as to the value of a [*fixture or building*] which the said *E.F.* has erected upon his holding the farm]. And whereas [*here set out all the circumstances relating to the appointment of a referee or umpire; if award made by single referee* the said *E.F.* and *G.H.* have jointly appointed me sole referee, and have referred all the said matters and things to my decision and award, *if award made by two referees* the said *E.F.* and *G.H.* have respectively appointed us the said *A.B.* and *C.D.* referees on their behalf, and have referred, *etc.*; *if award made by an umpire or by referees or umpire appointed by the county court or Land Commissioners or in the place of a deceased or incapable referee or of one failing to act, or if time has been extended, etc., state the facts*]. Now these presents witness that we [I] the said do hereby order and award as follows:—

The said *E.F.* is entitled to compensation from the said *G.H.* in the sums and in respect of the matters following [*set them out as for instance*:—

S. 10 (*t*).

The unexhausted value of a barn built by the said *E.F.*, *giving particulars of size, material, and so on*, in August, 18 . £

(*s*) *Ante* pp. 58 61.
(*t*) *Ante* p. 60.

The unexhausted value of the drainage done by the said
E.F. in the Bank Field, *giving particulars*, in March, 18   .
£

The unexhausted value of forty tons of lime laid upon
the Home Field, containing   acres, in February, 18   .
£   —*and so on.*]

The said *E.F.* is not entitled to any compensation from
the said *G.H.* in respect of the matters following [*set them
out as above*].

The said *G.H.* is entitled to compensation from the said
E.F. in the sums and in respect of the matters following
[*set them out, as for instance* :—

Seventeen acres of arable land called the Lower Slench
and the Lark Leys left in foul condition from twitch and
other noxious weeds contrary to covenant. £
     chains of ditches, watercourses and drains, in the
fields called, *naming them*, silted up and blocked. £

Dilapidations in respect of a cow-house and two barns
left wholly out of repair, *particulars*, £   —*and so on.*]

Value of fixture.   [*Or* the value of the said engine erected by the said *E.F.*
in October, 18   , is £   .]

And we [I] further award that the value of the said
improvements will be exhausted as follows :—

[*Set them out, as for instance*—The barn built by the said
E.F. as aforesaid in the year 18   , etc., etc.]

Ss. 20, 21 (*n*).   And we [I] further award and direct that all costs of and
attending this reference and award shall be paid by the said
    to the said   .

And we [I] further award that the said   pay to the
said   the sum of £   being the balance due from him
in respect of such claims for compensation and costs within
six weeks from the date of this award, namely, on the
    day of   18   .

In witness whereof we [I] have set our [my] hand[s] this
    day of   18   .

Referee, referees or umpire.

(*n*) *Ante* p. 61.

APPENDIX IV.

COUNTY COURT FORMS.

(32.)

[*For forms of summons on application for appointment of referee or umpire, see County Court Rules, 1889, Order XL., Form 312A (x).*] — County Court summons on application for appointment of referee or umpire.

(33.)

I appoint *E.F.* referee on behalf of *C.D.* in the above matters, *or* I appoint *E.F.* umpire to decide the above matters in question between *A.B.* and *C.D.* [*state if by consent*].

The   day of   18   *Judge or Registrar.*

— Appointment [by endorsement on summons] of a referee or umpire. S. 9, sub-s. 6. Ss. 10, 11 (y).

(34.)

Heading as in Form 312A (*x*), *and proceed as in that form with the variations* "for an order to appoint a guardian [*or* a next friend] for the purposes of the Act to *A.B.* an infant [*or* a person of unsound mind not so found, *or* a married woman].

Dated, etc., *as in Form 312A (x).*   *Registrar.*

— Summons to County Court to appoint a guardian of party who is an infant or of unsound mind, or next friend of a married woman. Ss. 25, 26 (z).

(35.)

Heading as in Form 312A (x), and proceed as in that form with the variations, "an application on the part of *E.F.* [*the umpire or as the case may be*] for an order to enlarge the time limited for the said *E.F.* to make his award until the   day of   18 .

Dated, etc., *as in Form 312A (x).*   *Registrar.*

— Summons to County Court to extend time for making award. S. 18 (a).

(*x*) *Ante* p. 105.
(*y*) *Ante* pp. 55, 57. See also County Court Rules, 1889, Order XL... rule 7A (9) *ante* p. 102.
(*z*) *Ante* pp. 65, 66.
(*a*) *Ante* p. 59.

(36.)

Heading as in Form 312A (aa).

Order by registrar of County Court (1) appointing guardian, or next friend, or (2) extending time for making award.
Ss. 18, 25, 26 (b).

Upon hearing the parties concerned [*or* the solicitors for the parties concerned] I appoint *E.F.* guardian [*or* next friend] of the said *C.D.*, *or*, I order that the time limited for the said *E.F.* to make his award be enlarged until the   day of   18 .

Dated the   day of   18 .   *Registrar.*

(37.)

Concise statement in writing of grounds of appeal.
S. 23(c).

In the County Court of   holden at

The Agricultural Holdings (England) Act, 1883.

Between *A.B.* Appellant,
and
C.D. Respondent.

I *A.B.* desire to appeal from the award made by *E.F.* dated the   day of   18 sent herewith, and the grounds of my appeal are as follows, viz. :—

[Set them out, *e.g.*—

[*Here set out particulars to comply with Order XL., Rule 2, of the County Court Rules, 1889 (d).*]

Dated the   day of   18 . *The appellant or his solicitor.*

(38.)

Heading as in Form 37.

[*The Registrar shall send a copy of the particulars in form 37, supra, to every respondent.*]

Notice to a respondent to comply with Order XL., Rules 3, 4, and Form 311A (e).

Take notice, that you are required within eight days of the delivery of this notice to you, to file in court a statement, signed by you or your solicitor, in reply to the grounds of appeal sent herewith, and that your statement must disclose the following matters :

(1.) Whether you dispute the validity in law of all or any, and which of the grounds of objection to the award :

(2.) Whether you dispute the truth in fact of all or any, and which of the grounds of appeal :

(aa) *Ante* p. 105.
(b) *Ante* pp. 59, 65, 66.
(c) *Ante* p. 62.
(d) *Ante* p. 100.
(e) *Ante* pp. 101, 104.

(3.) Whether you admit the validity in law and truth in fact of all or any, and which of the grounds of appeal:

(4.) Whether you pray that the case may be remitted to be re-heard:

(5) Your name and address, and that of your solicitor, if the statement be delivered through a solicitor.

Dated this   day of   18 . *Registrar of the Court.*
To the above-named respondent.

(38*b*.)

Heading as in Form 37.

1. I dispute the validity in law of the first ground of objection to the award. Statement of respondent on appeal to comply with Order XI., Rule 4 (*f*).

2. I dispute the truth in fact of the second ground of appeal.

3. I do not admit the validity in law and truth in fact, etc.

4. I do not pray that the case may be remitted to be re-heard, *and so on.*

5. My name and address is   , and the name of my solicitor is

The day of   18 .   *Signed*
To *the Registrar of the Court.*

(39.)

In the County Court of   holden at

In the matter of "The County Courts Act, 1888," and Order on appeal in County Court.
In the matter of "The Agricultural Holdings s. 23 (*g*).
(England) Act, 1883," and
In the matter of an appeal by *A.B.*

the   day of   18 .

Upon the hearing this day of an appeal by [*name and description of appellant*], against an award dated [*state date*], given under the hand of [*referee's name*], whereby [*state shortly the substance of the award*], and on reading the said award, and on hearing the said *A.B.* and *C.D.* the respondent.

It is ordered that [*state order, e.g.*, the said *C.D.* do, within fourteen days of the date of this order, pay to the

---

(*f*) *Ante* p. 103.
(*g*) *Ante* p. 62. See also County Court Rules, 1889, Order XL., Form 312, *ante* p.104.

148   Appendix IV.

said *A.B.* the sum of £   , and £   for costs, and in default of such payments, at the time aforesaid, the said *A.B.* may proceed to execution].

(40.)
*Heading as in Form 312*A (*gg*).

<small>Petition for charge of holding with moneys paid for compensation.
Ss. 29-32 (*h*).</small>

The Humble Petition of the said *A.B.*
Sheweth—

1. *Where landlord is petitioner*—Your petitioner is entitled [for his life, *etc.*, *or state whether as trustee of settlement, charity trustee, mortgagee in possession, incumbent, owner in fee, or as the case may be*] to the rents and profits of a certain agricultural holding called   situate at   in the county of   and containing   acres, or thereabouts [*state whether agricultural or pastoral, etc.*], as landlord thereof, and *C.D.* occupied the same up to the   day of   last past, as tenant thereof, from year to year [*or as the case may be*].

Where tenant is petitioner—Your petititioner occupied a certain agricultural holding [*etc., leaving out the words* "as landlord thereof, and *C.D.* occupied the same"]. *C.D.* is the landlord of the said holding.

2. On [the said *C.D.* quitting the said holding, at the determination of his tenancy, the said *C.D.* [your petitioner] claimed to receive from your petitioner [the said *C.D.* the sum of £   in respect of [*state claim*].

3. Your petitioner [the said *C.D.*] claimed to receive from the said *C.D.* [your petitioner] the sum of £   in respect of [*state counterclaim*].

4. All proper notices were given and proceedings taken under the provisions of the Agricultural Holdings (England) Act, 1883, and *E.F.* was duly appointed sole referee [*or state agreement between parties or as the case may be*] to decide and award upon the matters in difference between your petitioner and the said *C.D.*

5. The said *E.F.*, by his award given under his hand the   day of   18 , awarded and ordered [*set out so much of the award as is necessary*].

6. *Where landlord is petitioner*—In accordance with the said award your petitioner has paid to the said *C.D.* the sum of £   for compensation [or for balance of compensation *or* for costs *or otherwise*].

(*gg*) *Ante* p. 105.
(*h*) *Ante* pp. 67-73.

Where trustee is petitioner omit this clause. Where tenant is petitioner and landlord is trustee omit the clause and insert the following:—The said *C.D.* has neglected and failed to pay your petitioner the amount due to him under the said award [*or order or agreement*].
Your petititioner therefore prays:

    1. *Where landlord is petitioner*—For an order that the said holding [*specify premises*] do stand charged with the repayment to your petitioner, his executors, administrators and assigns of the sum of £   paid by him to the said *C.D.* as aforesaid, in such instalments and with such interest and with such power of sale and other directions for giving effect to the charge as the court may think fit.

    Where trustee is petitioner omit the words—paid by him to the said *C.D.* as aforesaid. *Where tenant is petitioner omit these words and insert after the words* "the sum of £   "—and all costs properly incurred in obtaining the charge, or in raising the amount due thereunder.

    2. Such further or other relief as the nature of the case may require.

NOTE.—It is intended that this petition shall be served on [*necessary parties*].

APPENDIX V.

FORMS UNDER DISTRESS CLAUSES.

(41.)

In the [*county of   . Petty Sessional Division of*   ]. Order for the restoration of a chattel, &c. S. 46 (*i*).
Before the Court of Summary Jurisdiction sitting at
        The   day of   18 .

A.B. having made a complaint that *C.D.* (hereinafter (Summ. Jurisd. called the defendant) on the   day of   at   [*state the* Act, 1879, s. 34.) *facts entitling the complainant to the order*], and the defendant having appeared [*or* the defendant not having appeared,

---

(*i*) *Ante* p. 88.

but proof having been given that the defendant was duly summoned to appear], and on hearing the matter of the complaint, it is this day adjudged and ordered by this court that the defendant do [*state the matter required to be done with conditions as to time or mode of action imposed by the court*].

And if on a copy of a minute of this order being served on the defendant, either personally or by leaving it for him at his last or usual abode, he neglects or refuses to obey this order, then it is adjudged that the defendant for such his disobedience be imprisoned in Her Majesty's prison at   for the space of [*not exceeding two months*] or until he has remedied his default.

[*Or* forfeit and pay to the clerk of this court (*or other the person to whom payment is to be made*) at   the sum of (*amount of fine not exceeding £1 for every day, and not exceeding in the aggregate £20*) for every day in which he shall be in default in obeying the said order.]

And it is also adjudged and ordered that the defendant pay to the complainant the sum of   for costs forthwith [*or* on the   day of   *or* by instalments, etc.].

And if default is made in payment according to this adjudication and order, it is ordered that the sum due thereunder be levied by distress and sale of the defendant's goods.

(*Signed*)
of Her Majesty's Justices of the Peace
for the [county] of

L.S.

(42.)

Notice of appeal to Quarter Sessions against order of justices under s. 46 (*k*).

To *A.B* of [*address and description*].

I *C.D.* of [*address and description*] hereby give you notice that I intend to appeal to the next general [*or* quarter] sessions of the peace to be holden at   in and for the [county *or* borough] of   against an order made upon or about the   day of   , by *G.H.* and *L.M.* of Her Majesty's justices of the peace for the said [county *or* borough] of   whereby it was ordered [*set out order*]. And I give you notice that my grounds of appeal are [*set out grounds for appeal*].

The   day of   .   (*Signed*)

(*k*) *Ante* p. 88.

INDEX.

A

AGREEMENT,
compensation due under, 2, 8, 11, 12, 13. 25, 46, 47, 54, 55. 138.
for "fair and reasonable compensation," 8, 11, 12, 48, 49.
referee to award compensation under, 12, 59.
depriving tenant of compensation, avoidance of, 13, 91.
inconsistent with Agricultural Holdings Act, avoidance of, 91, 92.
to do drainage, 20, 127, 129.
as to amount of compensation or value of fixture, 27, 54.
for a lease, form of, 125 134.
that sect. 33 shall not apply, 73, 135.
clause in, dispensing with notice under sect. 4, 136.

AGRICULTURAL HOLDING,
to which Act applies, 1, 91.
when treated as market garden, 1, 121.
when Act does not apply to, 1, 91.
what notice to quit necessary, 2, 3. 42, 73, 74. 81, 135.
writing necessary to exclude notice to quit, 3, 73. 135.
resumption of possession by landlord for improvements, 3, 80, 81.
reduction in rent in case of resumption of possession by landlord, 4. 81.
compensation in case of resumption of possession by landlord, 3, 81.
removal by tenant of fixtures, 4, 75, 139.
limit to right of distress by landlord, 5, 6, 84.
set-off by landlord of rent in arrear, 6, 49, 50, 54.
to what improvements Agricultural Holdings Act applies, 7, 8, 41.
when right to compensation arises, 8, 9, 41.
compensation on change of tenancy, 9, 93.
cost of drainage a charge on, 10, 20, 67.
improvements requiring consent of landlord, 9, 46, 98.
improvements not requiring consent of landlord, 10. 11, 99.
improvements of, when let as market garden, 11, 121, 122.
agreement for compensation. 8, 11, 12, 13, 25, 46-49, 54. 55, 56. 138.
avoidance of agreement depriving tenant of compensation, 13, 91, 92.
when yearly tenant not entitled to compensation. 14, 15. 93.
when lessee is not entitled to compensation, 14, 15, 93.
notice to be given by tenant of claim for compensation, 15, 16, 25, 26, 49, 52, 137.
addition to claim for compensation by tenant, 15, 50.
when compensation charge on, 17. 18, 35, 36. 67-72.
notice by landlord of set-off to compensation, 20, 50, 52, 137.
inherent capabilities of soil of, 41, 44.
tenant of, holding over by custom, 52, 53.
when executor of landlord entitled to charge on, 69, 70.

AGRICULTURAL HOLDING—(*continued*).
    assignment of charge upon, to land company, 73.
    notice to quit, 2, 3, 42, 73, 74.
    when improvement need not be taken into account in estimating rent of, 83.
    live-stock on, when privileged from distress, 85, 86.
    remedy in case of wrongful distress on, 37–40, 88–90.
    set-off by tenant of compensation against rent, 90.
    compensation payable to tenant of, when not entitled under Agricultural Holdings Act, 92, 93.
    defined, 91, 95.
    fixtures affixed to, before commencement of Act, 97.
    consumption on, by cattle of feeding stuff not produced on, 99.
    form of agreement for lease of, 129–132.
    short form of agreement for lease of, 133, 134.
    petition for charge on, 67–72, 148.

AGRICULTURAL HOLDINGS ACT, 1875.
    notice where compensation based on, 53, 54, 97.
    repeal of, 96.

APPEAL,
    no, from referee as to value of fixtures, 4, 75, 76.
    to County Court from referee, 13, 34, 62.
    procedure on, to County Court, 35, 100.
    to Quarter Sessions from justices, 38, 40, 150.
    from County Court on disputes as to distress, 89.
    from Quarter Sessions, 90.
    statement of grounds of, to County Court, 100, 146.
    respondent to, to deliver statement in reply, 101, 147.
    enforcement of order on, 101.
    form of notice of, to respondent, 104.
    order on, 104, 105, 147, 148.

APPELLANT,
    to file grounds of appeal, 100, 146.

APPRAISEMENT,
    in case of distress, 6, 7, 107, 108.

ARBITRATION,
    as to value of fixtures, 4, 27, 75, 76.
    compensation to be settled by, 54, 55.
    as to compensation under agreement, 12, 13, 59.
    parties to, 24, 100.
    costs of, 24, 32, 33, 61.
    revocation of submission to, 28, 57, 140.
    appointment of referees, 27–30, 55, 56, 102, 139, 140.
              umpire, 28–30, 55–57, 102, 141.
    time for delivery of award, 32, 33, 58, 59.
    appeal from, 34, 62, 100.
    procedure on appeal, 35, 100.
    recovery of compensation awarded, 35, 63, 64.
    power of referee or umpire to call for evidence, etc., 31, 57, 58.
    when referee or umpire may proceed in absence of parties, 58, 142.
    common law reference may include matters within Agricultural Holdings Act, 60.

INDEX. 153

ASSIGNMENT,
    of charge upon holding to land company, 73.

AWARD,
    must distinguish compensation under agreement and under Act, 12, 59.
    death of referee or umpire before, 28, 55, 56.
    time for delivery of, 32, 33, 58, 141.
    must be in writing, 33, 58.
    must give particulars of compensation, 33, 60.
    must state by whom costs to be paid, 33, 61.
    to fix time for payment of compensation, 34, 61.
    appeal from, 34, 62.
    cannot be removed into any Court, 34, 61.
    to landlord in excess of award to tenant, 51, 64, 65.
    must be signed by referee or umpire, 58.
    County Court judge cannot order execution in respect of, if outside Agricultural Holdings Act, 65.
    form of, 143.
    summons and order in County Court to extend time for award, 145, 146.

B

BAILIFF,
    certificate to, to levy distress, 7, 108, 109, 113, 117, 118.
    form of certificate of, 115.
    cancellation of certificate of, 111, 118.
    penalty for acting without certificate, 111.
    duration of certificate of, 111.
    when security required from, 113, 114.
    forfeiture of security of, 114.

BANKRUPT,
    notice to quit where tenant, 3, 73.
    no right of set-off by creditor who is debtor of estate of, 43.

BANKRUPTCY,
    of lessee, 43.

BONING,
    of land, 99.

BRIDGES,
    making of, 98.

BUILDINGS,
    erection or enlargement of, on holding, 98.

C

CHALKING,
    of land, 99.

CHARGE,
cost of drainage a, on holding. 10, 20, 67.
on holding for compensation paid by landlord. 17, 18, 35, 36, 67-72.
on glebe lands by incumbent, 37, 80.
assignment of, by landlord. 37, 73.
procedure to obtain, 37, 148.
when executor of landlord entitled to, on holding, 69, 70.
land company may take assignment of, 73.
petition for, on holding, 67 73, 148, 149.

CHARITY LANDS,
leases of, 9, 83.
powers of landlord, when consent of Charity Commissioners necessary, 80.

CLAYING,
of land. 99.

COMPENSATION,
for unexhausted improvements 2, 20, 41.
agreement for. 2, 11, 12, 13, 25, 27, 46, 47, 54, 59, 138.
agreement not to claim, avoidance of, 91.
in case of resumption of possession by landlord for improvements, 80, 81.
set-off by landlord of rent in arrear against, 6, 49, 50, 54.
due under custom, 8, 26, 48, 92.
"fair and reasonable," 8, 11, 44, 48, 49.
when right to, arises, 8, 9, 41, 92, 93.
on change of tenancy, 9, 93.
to tenant for drainage, 10, 46, 47.
under agreement to be awarded by referee, 12, 59.
avoidance of agreement depriving tenant of, 13, 91.
for improvement, basis of, 14, 15, 44.
not payable for improvements after certain times, 14, 15, 92, 93.
notice to be given by tenant of claim for, 15, 16, 25, 49, 52, 137.
addition to claim for, by tenant, 15, 50.
when charge on holding, 17, 18, 35, 36, 67-72, 148.
payable by incoming tenant, 20, 92, 138.
right of incoming tenant to, 92, 138.
notice by landlord of set-off to compensation, 26, 52, 137, 138.
award to fix time for payment of, 34, 61.
how recovered, 35, 63, 64.
trustee in bankruptcy cannot claim, 43.
to tenant when mortgagee in possession, 44, 119, 120.
for improvements executed before January 1, 1884, 45.
in case of tenancy current on January 1, 1884, 48.
deductions from, 49.
failure to give notice of claim for, 52.
based on Agricultural Holdings Act, 1875, notice of, 53, 54.
to be settled by reference, 54, 55.
set-off by tenant against rent, 90.
how recovered when not payable under Agricultural Holdings Act, 92, 93.

COMPOSITION WITH CREDITORS.
notice to quit where tenant has petitioned for, 3, 73.

INDEX. 155

CONSENT,
  of landlord to improvement, when required, 9, 46, 98, 136.
              when not required, 10, 11, 99.
  of landlord to incoming tenant paying compensation, 52, 138
  to revocation of submission, 140.

CONTRACT. *See* AGREEMENT.

CORNWALL,
  Duchy of, application of Act to, 79.
              application of Market Gardeners' Compensation Act to, 124.
COSTS,
  of reference, 24, 32, 33, 61.
  of County Court proceedings, 24, 31, 66, 103.
  taxation of, of reference, 32, 61.
  award to fix time for payment of, of reference, 34, 61.
  recovery of, 35, 63.
  between solicitor and client cannot be awarded by referee or umpire, 61.
  of distress, 114-117.

COUNTERCLAIM. *See* SET-OFF.

COUNTY COURT,
  appeal to, from referee, 13, 34, 62.
  may grant charge on holding, 17, 18, 67-72.
  costs of proceedings in, 24, 31, 66.
  appointment of guardian or next friend by, 24, 65, 66, 145.
              referee by, 27-30, 55, 56, 102, 145.
              umpire by, 29, 30, 56, 57, 102, 141, 145.
  recovery of compensation and costs in, 35, 63, 64.
  may decide disputes arising out of distress, 38, 88, 89
  appeal from, in case of disputes arising out of distress, 89.
  appellant to file grounds of appeal to, 100
  enforcement of order of, 101.
  order of, on appeal, 104, 105, 147, 148.
  fees, 106.
  notice of dissent from appointment of umpire by, 141.
  extension of time for award by, 59, 65, 66, 145, 146.

COUNTY COURT JUDGE,
  bailiffs appointed by certificate of, 7, 108, 109, 113.
  power to cancel certificate of bailiff, 111.
  referee or umpire appointed by, 30, 57.
  case stated by, for High Court, 34, 62.
  cannot order execution if award outside Act, 65.
  copies of statement of appellant and respondent to be sent to, 101.
  may order forfeiture of bailiff's security, 114.

COVENANT,
  set-off by landlord of damages for breach of, 14, 17, 52.

CREDITORS. *See* COMPOSITION WITH CREDITORS.

CROWN LANDS,
  application of Agricultural Holdings Act to, 77.
              Market Gardeners' Compensation Act to, 124.

CULTIVATION,
  clauses in agreement for lease as to, 20, 128, 133.

CUSTOM,
  distress for rent payable according to, 6, 84, 85.
  compensation payable under. 8. 26, 48, 92.
  holding over by. 52, 53.

D

DEDUCTION,
  from compensation for improvement 49, 50.

DETERMINATION,
  of tenancy, right to compensation on, 41.
    by surrender, 42.
    by notice to quit, 42.
    by forfeiture, 43.
    defined, 95.

DISTRESS,
  procedure for settlement of disputes in case of wrongful, 5, 37-40, 88-90.
  remedy for wrongful, 111, 112.
  limit to right of, by landlord. 5, 6, 84-86.
  things privileged from distress, 6, 85, 86, 107.
  tenant may require appraisement, 6, 7, 107.
  time for replevy in case of, 7, 108.
  certified bailiffs to levy, 7, 108, 113.
  for rent due more than a year before, but payable less than a year before, 85.
  live stock and machinery, when privileged from, 85, 86.
  penalty for acting without certificate, 111.
  evidence in case of wrongful, 112.
  fee on application for certificate of bailiff for, 113.
  fees payable in case of, 114-117.

DRAINAGE,
  improvement, notice to landlord, 10, 46, 47, 99, 136.
  landlord may do, 10, 46, 47, 137.
  cost of, a charge on holding, 10, 20, 36, 67.
  when tenant may do, 10, 46, 47.
  agreement to do, 20, 127, 129.

E

ECCLESIASTICAL LAND,
  approval of Ecclesiastical Commissioners necessary to exercise of powers under Act, 80.

EMBANKMENT,
  making of, 98.

EVADE,
  manner in which to, Agricultural Holdings Act, 18.

INDEX. 157

EVIDENCE,
    power of referee or umpire to call for, 31, 57, 58.
    required by Court before charging holding, 36, 67.
    in case of wrongful distress, 112.
    notice to produce, by referees or umpire, 57, 142.

EXECUTION,
    cannot be ordered of award outside Agricultural Holdings Act, 65.

EXECUTOR,
    of landlord, when entitled to charge on holding, 69, 70, 96.

EXEMPT,
    things, from distress, 6, 7, 107.

F

"FAIR AND REASONABLE,"
    compensation, 8, 11, 44, 48, 49.

"FAIR PRICE,"
    meaning of, 86-88.

FEES,
    Court, on appeal to County Court, 106.
    payable in case of distress, 114, 116, 117.

FENCES,
    making of, 98.

FIXTURE,
    removal by tenant, 4, 5, 75-77, 139.
    landlord may purchase, after notice to remove, 4, 5, 75.
    arbitration as to value of, 4, 75, 76.
    provisions as to, apply to market gardens, 4, 5. 121, 122.
    tenant's notice of removal of, 26, 27, 75, 139.
    landlord's notice to purchase, 27, 75, 139.
    landlord and tenant may agree value of, 27, 75.
    what are, 76, 77.
    affixed to holding before commencement of Act, 97.
    in market garden, 121, 122.

FORFEITURE,
    determination of tenancy by, 43.

FORM,
    of summons on application for appointment of referee or umpire, 105.
    of certificate of bailiff, 115.
    of agreement for a lease. 125-132.
    short, of agreement for lease, 133, 134.
    of notice to quit, 135.
    of agreement that sect. 33 shall not apply, 135.
    of notice to quit part of premises under sect. 41, 135.
    of counter-notice under sect. 41, 135, 136
    of consent by landlord to improvement, 136.
    of notice by tenant of intention to drain, 136.

FORM—*(continued)*.
　　of notice by landlord that he intends to do drainage, 137.
　　of notice by tenant of intention to execute improvement, 137.
　　of notice by tenant of claim for compensation, 137.
　　of counter-notice by landlord of claim for compensation, 137, 138.
　　of agreement as to amount of compensation, 138.
　　of consent of landlord to incoming tenant paying compensation to outgoing tenant, 138.
　　of notice by tenant of intention to remove fixtures, 139.
　　of notice by landlord that he intends to purchase fixtures, 139.
　　of appointment of a referee or fresh referee, 139, 145.
　　of notice of appointment of referee, 140.
　　of notice to referee requiring him to act within seven days, 140.
　　of consent to revocation of submission to reference, 140.
　　of revocation of submission to reference, 140.
　　of notice of extension of time for award by referees, 141.
　　of request to referee to appoint an umpire, 141.
　　of notice requiring appointment of umpire by Land Commissioners or County Court, 141.
　　of application to Land Commissioners to appoint umpire, 141.
　　of notice of dissent from appointment of umpire by County Court, 141.
　　of appointment of umpire or fresh umpire, 142, 145.
　　of notice to umpire of the reference to him, 142.
　　of notice to proceed with reference in absence of parties, 142.
　　of notice to produce by referees or umpire, 142.
　　of award, 143.
　　of County Court summons on application for appointment of referee or umpire, 105, 145.
　　of summons to County Court to appoint a guardian or next friend, 145.
　　of summons to County Court to extend time for making award, 145.
　　of order of County Court appointing guardian or next friend, 146.
　　of statement of grounds of appeal, 146.
　　of notice to a respondent of appeal to furnish statement, 104, 146, 147.
　　of statement of respondent to appeal, 147.
　　of order of County Court on appeal, 104, 105, 147, 148.
　　of petition for charging holding with moneys paid for compensation, 148, 149.
　　of order for restoration of a chattel under Summary Jurisdiction Act, 149, 150.
　　of notice of appeal to Quarter Sessions against order of justices, 150.

FRUIT,
　　bushes, planting of, 98.

G

GARDENS,
　　making of, 98.

GLASSHOUSE,
　　a building, 77.

GLEBE,
　　charge by incumbent on, 37, 80.

GUARDIAN,
    appointment of, to infant or person of unsound mind, 24, 65, 66, 145, 146.

H

HIGH COURT,
    case stated by County Court judge for, 34, 62.

HOLDING. *See* AGRICULTURAL HOLDING.

HOLDING OVER,
    by custom, 52, 53.

HOPS,
    planting of, 98.

I

IMPROVEMENT,
    general right of tenant to compensation for, 41.
    Act compulsory with regard to unexhausted, 2, 41. 91.
    resumption of possession of holding by landlord for, 3. 80, 81.
    to which Agricultural Holdings Act applies, 7, 8, 41, 98, 99.
    executed after Jan. 1st, 1884, under then existing tenancy, 8, 48.
        tenancies beginning after that date, 8, 48.
    executed before Jan. 1st, 1884, 45.
    in case of trust and charity lands, 9, 77-80, 83.
    when consent of landlord required to, 9, 46, 98, 136.
    notice required for drainage, 10, 46, 47, 99, 136.
    landlord may do drainage, 10, 46. 47, 137.
    when consent of landlord not required to, 10, 11, 99.
    what constitutes, when holding let as market garden, 11, 121, 122.
    agreement for compensation for, 11, 12, 13, 46, 48, 49.
    avoidance of agreement depriving tenant of compensation for, 13, 91
    basis of compensation for, 14, 44.
    restrictions on compensation for, 14, 15, 93.
    after what dates compensation not payable, 14, 15, 93.
    notice to be given by tenant of claim for compensation, 15, 16, 25, 52, 137.
    addition to claim for compensation by tenant, 15. 50.
    after notice to quit, 16, 93.
    on glebe lands, charge for, 37, 80.
    notice by tenant of intended, to landlord, 46, 47, 137.
    when landlord may do, 47.
    in case of tenancy current on Jan. 1st, 1884, 48.
    compensation for, due under custom, 8, 26, 48.
    deductions from compensation for, 49, 50.
    need not be taken into account in estimating rent of holding, 83.
    form of consent of landlord to, 136.

INCUMBENT
    of benefice, charge by, of compensation on glebe, 37, 80.

INFANT,
: appointment of guardian, 24, 65, 66.

INHERENT
: capabilities of soil. 41, 44.

INTERPRETATION,
: of terms in Agricultural Holdings Act, 94-96.

IRRIGATION,
: making works of, 98.

J

JUDGE. *See* COUNTY COURT JUDGE.

JUSTICES,
: costs of proceedings before, 24.
: summary proceedings before, in case of distress, 37-40, 149.
: appeal from, 38, 150.
: power of, of Court of Summary Jurisdiction, 39, 40, 149.

L

LANCASTER,
: duchy of, application of Agricultural Holdings Act to, 78, 79.
: Market Gardeners' Compensation Act to, 124.

LAND,
: re-claiming of waste, 98.
: boning of, 99.
: chalking of, 99.
: claying of, 99.
: liming of, 99.
: marling of, 99.
: application of purchased artificial manure, 99.

LAND COMMISSIONERS,
: appointment of umpire by, 29, 30, 56, 57, 141.

LAND COMPANY,
: may take assignment of charge on holding, 73.

LANDLORD,
: Act does not apply to tenant in employment of, 1, 91.
: power to exclude statutory notice to quit, 3, 73.
: resumption of possession by, for improvement, 3, 4, 80, 81, 135.
: may purchase fixtures after notice by tenant of intention to remove, 4, 5, 27, 75, 76, 139.
: limit to right of distress by, 5, 6, 84-86, 107.
: set-off by, against claim by tenant. 6, 14, 17, 26, 49, 50, 54.
: consent of, to improvement, when required, 9, 46, 98. 136.
: notice to, in case of drainage improvement, 10, 46. 47, 99, 136.
: may do drainage, 10, 46, 47, 137.
: consent of, to improvement, when not required, 10, 11, 99.

INDEX.

LANDLORD—(continued).
    may agree with tenant for "fair and reasonable" compensation, 11, 48, 49.
    appeal by, to County Court, 13, 62.
    charge on holding for compensation paid by, 17, 18, 35, 36, 67-71.
    notice by tenant to, of claim for compensation, 15, 16, 25, 26, 52, 137.
    extent of charge on holding when under-lessee, 36, 71.
                      limited owner, 36, 37, 67-71, 82.
                      when trustee, 71, 72.
    assignment of charge by, 37, 73.
    consent of, to improvement executed before Jan. 1st, 1884, 45.
    agreement with tenant for compensation, 8, 11, 12, 13, 25, 46, 47, 48, 49, 54, 55, 138.
    notice by tenant to, of intended improvement, when necessary, 46, 47, 137.
    when improvement may be done by, 47.
    award to, in excess of award to tenant, 51, 64, 65.
    notice by, to tenant, of counterclaim, 52, 137, 138.
    executors of, when entitled to charge on holding, 69, 70, 96.
    when consent of Ecclesiastical Commissioners necessary to exercise of powers by, 79, 80.
    consent necessary when, incumbent of ecclesiastical benefice, 80.
    when consent of Charity Commissioners necessary to exercise of powers by, 80.
    set-off by tenant of compensation against rent due to, 90.
    consent of, to incoming tenant paying compensation to outgoing, 92, 138.
    defined, 95, 96.
    form of consent of, to improvement, 136.

LEASE,
    Agricultural Holdings applies to, 1, 94.
    of trust and charity lands, 9, 83.
    form of agreement for, 125-132.
    short form of agreement for, 133, 134.

LESSEE,
    when not entitled to compensation, 14, 15, 93.
    bankruptcy of, 43.

LIMING,
    of land, 99.

LIVE STOCK,
    when privileged from distress, 6, 85, 86.
    dispute as to ownership of, how settled, 37-40, 88, 89.
    defined, 95.

M

MACHINERY,
    when privileged from distress, 6, 85-87.

MANURE,
    clauses in agreement relating to, 21, 128, 134.
    deduction from compensation for, 50.
    defined, 95.
    application to land of purchased, 99.

MARKET GARDEN,
    when holding treated as, 1, 121.
    provisions of Agricultural Holdings Act, as to fixtures apply
        to, 4, 5, 121, 122.
    improvements to holding treated as, 11, 121-123.
    application of Market Gardeners' Compensation Act, 1895, to
        current tenancies, 122, 123.
    definition of, 124.

MARLING,
    of land, 99.

MARRIED WOMAN,
    appointment of next friend of, 24, 66.
    when concurrence of husband necessary, 66.

MORTGAGEE,
    rights of, where holding charged, 70, 71.
    in possession, compensation to tenant when, 44, 119, 120.

N

NEXT FRIEND,
    appointment of, of married woman, 24, 66, 145, 146.

NOTICE,
    to quit, what necessary, 2, 3, 42, 73, 74, 81.
        writing necessary to exclude statutory, 3, 73, 135.
        three months', may be yearly tenancy, 3, 74, 123.
        Act does not apply where tenant bankrupt, etc., 3, 73.
        where landlord resumes possession for improvements, 3 4,
            81, 135.
        improvements after, 16, 93.
        form of, 135.
    by tenant of intention to remove fixtures, 4, 5, 26, 27, 175, 139.
        of intention to do drainage, 10, 46, 47, 136.
        of claim for compensation, 15, 16, 25, 26, 49, 52, 137.
        of intention to do improvements, 46, 47, 137.
        under section 41, 135.
    by landlord, of set-off, 17, 26, 52, 137, 138.
        of intention to purchase fixture, 27, 75, 139.
        that he intends to do drainage, 10, 46, 47, 137.
    service of, under Agricultural Holdings Act, 24, 25, 66, 67.
    when must be in writing, under Agricultural Holdings Act, 25.
    failure to give, of compensation, 52.
    of claim for compensation where two or more terms, 53.
    where compensation based on Agricultural Holdings Act, 1875,
        53, 54, 97.
    of appointment of referee or umpire must be in writing, 56, 139, 140.
    form of, to a respondent to appeal, 104.
    to referee requiring him to act within seven days, 140.
    to umpire of reference to him, 59, 142.
    by referee or umpire to proceed in absence of parties, 58, 142.
    to produce by referee or umpire, 57, 142.
    of appeal to Quarter Sessions from justices, 150.
    to respondent to appeal to comply with Order XL., rules 3 and 4,
        146, 147.

O

ORCHARDS,
    planting of, 98.

ORDER,
    enforcement of, of County Court on appeal, 101.
    on appeal, 104, 105, 147, 148.
    for restoration of chattels by Court of Summary Jurisdiction, 149.
    by registrar of County Court appointing guardian or next friend, 146.

OSIER,
    beds, making and planting of, 98.

OWNER,
    when landlord limited, 36, 37, 67-71, 82.

OWNERSHIP,
    of live stock, dispute as to, how settled, 37-40, 88, 89.

P

PARTIES,
    to reference, 24.
    appointment of referee by, 27, 55, 56.
    revocation of submission by, 28, 57.
    failure of, to appoint referees or umpire, 29, 55.
    when referee or umpire may proceed in absence of, 58, 142.

PASTORAL,
    holdings within Act, 1, 91.

PASTURE,
    laying down permanent, 98.

PERMISSIVE,
    Agricultural Holdings Act when, 2.

PETITION,
    for charge on holding, 37, 67-72, 148.

POSSESSION,
    resumption of, by landlord for improvement, 3, 80, 81, 135.

PROCEDURE,
    for appointment of referee or umpire, by County Court, 30, 102.
    on appeal from reference, 35, 100, 145-149.
    to obtain charge, 37, 88, 148.
    before justices in case of wrongful distress, 37-40, 88, 89, 149, 150.

PROHIBITION,
    where execution is ordered in respect of award outside Agricultural Holdings Act, 65.

Q

QUARTER SESSIONS,
    appeal to, from justices, 38, 40, 150.
    appeal from, 90,

QUIT. *See* NOTICE TO QUIT.

R

RATES,
    set-off by landlord of, against claim for compensation, 14, 50.

RECOGNISANCE,
    in case of appeal to Quarter Sessions, 40.

REFEREE,
    may award compensation under agreement, 12, 59.
    appeal to County Court from, 13, 34, 62.
    appointment of, 27–30, 55, 56, 102, 105, 139, 145.
    death of, or failure to act, before award, 28, 55.
    failure of parties to appoint, 29, 30, 55, 56.
    power to call for evidence, 31, 57, 58, 142.
    remuneration of, 32, 61.
    time for delivery of award by, 32, 33, 58, 141.
    extension of time for delivery of award by, 32, 141.
    must sign award, 33, 58.
    when, may proceed in absence of party, 58, 142.
    cannot award costs between solicitor and client, 61.
    form of notice of appointment of, 139, 140.
    notice to, requiring him to act within seven days, 140.
    request to appoint umpire, 56, 141.
    appointment of umpire by, 56, 142.

REFERENCE. *See* ARBITRATION.

REGISTRAR,
    when, may appoint referee or umpire, 30, 57, 103.
    to tax costs of reference, 32, 61.
    extension of time for award by, 33, 58, 141.
    to send copy of grounds of appeal to respondent, 101.

RENT,
    reduction in, when landlord resumes possession for improvements, 4, 81.
    distress for, limits of, 5, 6, 84-86.
    in arrear, set-off by landlord, 6, 14, 49, 50.
    when improvement not to be taken into account in estimating, 83.
    due more than year previous to distress, when it can be distrained for, 85.
    in arrear, set-off by tenant of compensation against, 90.
    fees and charges in case of distress for, 114-117.

REPEAL,
    of Acts by Agricultural Holdings Act, 1883, 96.

INDEX.

REPLEVY,
>   time for, 6, 7, 108.

RESPONDENT,
>   registrar to send copy of grounds of appeal to, 101.
>   to deliver statement in reply, 101, 147.
>   notice to, on appeal, 104, 146, 147.

REVOCATION,
>   of submission to reference, 28, 57. 140.

ROADS,
>   making of, 98.

RULES,
>   for regulating distress, 110, 113-118.

S

SERVICE,
>   of notices under Agricultural Holdings Act, 24, 25, 66, 67.

SET-OFF,
>   by landlord against claim by tenant, 6, 14, 17, 26, 49, 50, 52, 54.
>   no right to, where creditor becomes debtor to bankrupt's estate, 43.
>   by tenant of compensation against rent due, 90.

SILOS,
>   formation of, 98.

SLUICES,
>   making of, 98.

SOLICITOR,
>   costs as between, and client cannot be awarded by referee or umpire, 61.

SUBMISSION,
>   revocation of, 28, 57, 140.

SUMMARY JURISDICTION,
>   disputes under distress clauses may be settled by, 37-40, 88, 89.
>   power of justices of Court of, 39, 40.
>   disobedience to order of Court of, 39, 40.
>   order for restoration of a chattel by Court of. 149.

SUMMONS,
>   form of, on application for appointment of referee or umpire by County Court, 105, 145.
>   form of, to County Court to appoint guardian or next friend, 145, 146.
>   to County Court to extend time for making award, 145 146.

SURRENDER,
>   determination of tenancy by, 42.
>   rights of under-lessee on, 42, 43.

T

TAXATION,
of costs, 32, 61.

TAXES,
set-off by landlord against claim for compensation, 14, 50.

TENANCY,
Agricultural Holdings Act applies to yearly, 1, 91.
with three months' notice to quit may be a yearly, 3, 123.
compensation on change of, 9. 93.
right of tenant to compensation on determination of, 41.
how determined, 42. 43.
current at commencement of Agricultural Holdings Act, 1883, 48.
contract of, meaning of, 94
determination of, defined, 95.
Market Gardeners' Compensation Act applies to current, 122, 123.

TENANT,
general right to compensation, 8, 9, 41.
Act does not apply when in office or employment of landlord, 1. 91.
power to exclude statutory notice to quit, 3, 73.
notice to quit where bankrupt, etc., 3, 73.
 where landlord resumes possession for improvements, 3, 4, 81, 135.
compensation to, where landlord resumes possession for improvements, 4, 80, 81.
removal of fixtures by, 4, 5, 75, 76.
notice by, of intention to remove fixtures, 4, 26, 27, 75, 139.
may require appraisement in case of distress, 6, 7, 107.
time for replevy by, 6, 7, 108.
must give notice to landlord of intention to do drainage, 10, 46, 47, 136
when, may do drainage, 10, 46, 47.
may agree with landlord for compensation, 8, 11, 46, 48, 49, 54, 55, 138.
appeal by, to County Court, 13, 34, 62.
avoidance of agreement depriving, of compensation, 13, 91, 92.
set-off by landlord against claim for compensation by, 14, 17, 26, 52, 54.
yearly, when not entitled to compensation, 14, 15. 93.
notices to be given by, of claim for compensation, 15, 16, 25, 26, 49, 52, 137.
addition to claim for compensation by, 15, 50.
when charge on holding may be obtained by, 18, 35, 71, 72.
improvements by, after notice to quit, 16, 93.
compensation payable by incoming, 20, 92.
notice to, by landlord of intention to purchase fixture, 27, 75, 76.
compensation to, when mortgagee in possession, 44, 119, 120.
notice to landlord of intended improvement, when necessary, 46, 47, 137.
award to landlord in excess of award to, 51, 64, 65.
holding over by custom, 52, 53.
reduction of rent payable by, when landlord resumes possession for improvements, 81.
live-stock on holding of, when privileged from distress, 85, 86.
remedy of, in case of wrongful distress, 37-40, 88-90.

TENANT —(continued).
    set-off by, of compensation against rent due, 90.
    right of incoming, to compensation paid by him with consent of landlord, 92, 138.
    compensation payable to, when not entitled under Agricultural Holdings Act, 92, 93.
    defined, 95.
    improvements by, to market garden, 121-124.

TIME,
    for delivery of award by referee or umpire, 32, 33, 58, 59, 141.
                    extended by registrar, 33, 59, 145, 146.
    to appeal from award, 34, 62.
    length of notice to quit, 73, 74

TITHES,
    set-off by landlord against claim for compensation, 14, 50, 51.

TRUST
    lands, leases of, 9, 83.

TRUSTEE,
    charge on holding when landlord, 35, 36, 71, 72.
    in bankruptcy cannot claim compensation, 43.

U

UMPIRE,
    appointment of, 28-30, 55-57, 102, 105, 141, 142, 145.
    death of, or failure to act, 29, 56.
    failure of parties to appoint, 29, 30, 55, 56.
    power to call for evidence, 31, 57, 58, 142.
    remuneration of, 32, 61.
    time for delivery of award by, 32, 33, 59.
    must sign award, 33, 58.
    when may proceed in absence of party, 58.
    may award compensation under agreement, 59.
    cannot award costs between solicitor and client, 61.
    appeal from, 13, 34, 62.
    request to referee to appoint, 56, 141.
    notice of dissent from appointment of, by County Court, 56, 141.
    notice to, of reference to him, 59, 142.

UNDER-LESSEE,
    where landlord, extent of charge on holding, 36, 71.
    rights of, on surrender, 42, 43.

UNSOUND MIND,
    appointment of guardian to person of, 24, 65, 66, 145, 146.

W

WASTE,
    set-off by landlord against claim for compensation, 14, 17, 49, 50, 52.
    what is, 51.
    land, reclaiming of, 98.

WATER,
  making supply for agricultural or domestic purposes, 98.

WRITING,
  necessary if holding to be treated as market garden, 1, 121.
  necessary to exclude notice to quit required by Act, 3. 73.
  when notices under Agricultural Holdings Act must be in, 25.
  award must be in, 33. 58.
  notice of appointment of referee or umpire must be in, 56.

WRONGFUL,
  distress, remedy for, 88-90, 111, 112.
  evidence in case of, distress, 112.

Y

YEARLY,
  tenancy, Act applies to, 1, 94.
    with three months' notice to quit, 3, 96.
  tenant, when not entitled to compensation, 14, 15, 93.

LIST

OF

LEGAL AND GENERAL BOOKS

PRINTED AND PUBLISHED

BY

WATERLOW & SONS LIMITED,

LAW, PARLIAMENTARY AND GENERAL
STATIONERS, PRINTERS, &c.,

85 & 86, LONDON WALL;

FINSBURY STATIONERY WORKS, E.C.;

AND

49, PARLIAMENT STREET, S.W.,

ETC., ETC.,

LONDON.

BRANCH OFFICE: TEMPLE ROW, BIRMINGHAM.

WATERLOW & SONS LIMITED, LAW PUBLISHERS.

LIST OF PUBLICATIONS.

AGRICULTURAL HOLDINGS (ENGLAND) ACT, 1883, with Notes and Forms, and a Summary of the Procedure. By J. W. JEUDWINE, of Lincoln's Inn, Barrister-at-Law.
[*New Edition in preparation.*]

BANKERS', INSURANCE MANAGERS' AND AGENTS' MAGAZINE.—A First Class Monthly Financial Publication, and the recognized organ of communication for the Banking interest. 1s. 6d. per number, or 21s. per annum, including two double numbers.

BANKING ALMANAC, DIRECTORY, AND DIARY.—A Year Book of Statistics and complete Banking Directory. The Edition for 1898 is the 54th year of publication of this invaluable book, which has long been patronized by the Bank of England and the Private and Joint Stock Banks throughout the Kingdom. In cloth, 12s. 6d. net.

BANKRUPTCY ACTS, 1883 TO 1890, with the General Rules, Forms, Scales of Costs, Fees and Percentages, Board of Trade and Court Orders, Debtors Act, 1869, Deeds of Arrangement Act, 1887, Rules as to Administration Orders, &c., and a Commentary thereon. By His Honour Judge CHALMERS and E. HOUGH, Inspector in Bankruptcy, Board of Trade. Fourth Edition, revised to October, 1896. By M. MUIR MACKENZIE, Barrister-at-Law, and E. HOUGH. In cloth, 25s.

BILLS OF EXCHANGE ACT, 1882.—An Act to Codify the Law relating to Bills of Exchange, Cheques, and Promissory Notes. With Comments and Explanatory Notes. By His Honour Judge CHALMERS. Eighth Edition. In cloth, 3s. 6d.

CODE OF CONTRACT LAW, relating to Sales of Goods of the value of £10 and upwards. A Handbook for the use of professional and business men. By HENRY J. PARRINGTON, of Middlesbrough, Solicitor. In cloth, 3s. 6d.

CODE OF THE LAW OF RATING AND PROCEDURE ON APPEAL, with an Appendix containing all the Statutes (including the Agricultural Rates Act, 1896), fully annotated, and Specimens of Valuations made for the Purposes of Rating. By SYLVAIN MAYER, B.A., PH.D., of the Middle Temple and Northern Circuit, Barrister-at-Law; Author of "The French Code of Commerce," etc. In 1 vol., Royal 8vo., about 600 pages, 25s.

COMPUTATOR.—A Treatise and Ready-Help for the young Banker's or Accountant's Clerk. With tables, &c. By A. WALKER. In cloth, 1s.

COUNTRY BANKERS' HANDBOOK to the Rules and Practices of (I.) the Bank of England, (II.) London Bankers' Clearing House, (III.) the Stock Exchange. With useful Miscellaneous Notes. By J. GEORGE KIDDY. Second Edition. In cloth, 2s. 6d.

CRIMINAL LAW AMENDMENT ACT, 1885, with Preface and Commentary. By R. W. BURNIE, of the Middle Temple, Barrister-at-Law. In boards, 2s. 6d.

85 & 86, LONDON WALL, LONDON.

WATERLOW & SONS LIMITED, LAW PUBLISHERS.

LIST OF PUBLICATIONS—CONTINUED.

COUNTY COUNCIL COMPENDIUM; OR DIGEST OF THE MUNICIPAL CORPO-RATIONS ACT, 1882; THE COUNTY ELECTORS AND LOCAL GOVERNMENT ACTS, 1888.—Being a Treatise on the above Statutes and others re-enacted therein. With Copious Notes and Appendices, &c. Second Edition. By HENRY STEPHEN and HORACE E. MILLER, LL.B., Barristers-at-Law. In cloth, 21s.

COUNTY COUNCILLOR'S VADE-MECUM.—A Handbook for County Councillors and Aldermen. By HENRY STEPHEN and HORACE MILLER, LL.B., Authors of "The County Council Compendium." Crown 8vo. In cloth, 2s. 6d.

COUNTY COURTS ACT, 1888.—Queen's Printers' Copy, with an introduction indicating the leading alterations made by the Act, a Comprehensive Index, &c., &c., and the County Courts Admiralty Jurisdiction Acts, 1868 and 1869, with a separate Index, by R. T. HUNTER, Chief Clerk, County Court, Stockton-on-Tees. Second Edition. In boards, cloth backs, 5s. The same may be had with the Act Interleaved for Notes. In boards, 6s.

COUNTY COURT RULES, 1889, with an Index to the Pages, Orders, Rules, Forms and Fees, an Alphabetical List of Forms (referring to page, order, and rule), and Tables showing the Fees and Costs on any given sum. By R. T. HUNTER, Chief Clerk, County Court, Stockton-on-Tees. In boards, 7s., or in roan, 10s. 6d. The same Index in separate form, in boards, 3s. 6d.

COSTS IN THE COUNTY COURTS under the County Courts Act, 1888, and Rules of 1889 and 1892, with the Sections and Rules relating thereto and Precedents. By R. T. HUNTER, Chief Clerk, County Court, Stockton-on-Tees. Price 6s.

DEBTORS AND CREDITORS.—A Guide to the Proceedings for Recovery of Debt by Action in the County Courts or in the High Court, and the Administration of Insolvent Estates, showing the position of Debtors and Creditors under the various proceedings. By ERNEST SAVILLE, of the Bankruptcy Department, Board of Trade. In cloth, 3s. 6d.

DEEDS OF ARRANGEMENT ACT, 1887, AND THE BANKRUPTCY (DISCHARGE AND CLOSURE) ACT, 1887, with Rules, Forms, and Scales of Fees prescribed thereunder; also with Notes and Index. By His Honour Judge CHALMERS and E. HOUGH, Inspector in Bankruptcy, Board of Trade. In cloth, 3s. 6d.

DUE DATE TABLES FOR ACCEPTING BILLS OF EXCHANGE.—Compiled by HENRY BELL and JOHN MONTGOMERY, JR. These Tables are most useful to Bankers, Merchants, Manufacturers and others, are perpetually serviceable, and suffer no alteration from year to year. In cloth, 7s. 6d.

DUTIES OF EXECUTORS.—By F. W. DENDY, Solicitor and Notary. Seventh Edition. Revised in accordance with the Finance Acts, 1894 and 1896. Post free, 1s. 8d.

ELECTORAL BOUNDARIES OF THE UNITED KINGDOM, being Schedules 5, 6, and 7 of the Parliamentary Elections (Redistribution) Act, 1885. With Index. In boards, 2s. 6d.

85 & 86, LONDON WALL, LONDON.

WATERLOW & SONS LIMITED, LAW PUBLISHERS.

LIST OF PUBLICATIONS—CONTINUED.

ENGLISH MUNICIPAL CODE, or the MUNICIPAL CORPORATIONS (Consolidation) ACT, 1882, with Statutes and Cases from 1882 to 1888, Notes, Comments, References, Statistical Appendix, and Voluminous Index, by Sir J. R. SOMERS VINE, C.M.G., F.R.G.S., F.S.S. Third Edition. In cloth, 7s. 6d.

ENGLISH MUNICIPAL INSTITUTIONS: THEIR GROWTH AND DEVELOPMENT STATISTICALLY ILLUSTRATED.—"A most useful and valuable work."—*Vide* Public Press. By Sir J. R. SOMERS VINE, C.M.G., F.R.G.S., F.S.S. Royal 8vo, cloth, 10s. 6d.

FORM OF BILLS OF SALE UNDER THE BILLS OF SALE ACT (1878) AMENDMENT ACT, 1882.—By STANLEY BUCKMASTER, M.A., of the Inner Temple, Barrister-at-Law. In cloth, 2s. 6d.

FRANCHISE ACTS, 1884-5, being the Representation of the People Act, 1884; Registration Act, 1885; Parliamentary Elections (Redistribution) Act, 1885, and Medical Relief Disqualification Removal Act, 1885, with Introduction and Notes. By MILES WALKER MATTINSON, Barrister-at-Law. In boards, 2s. 6d.

GENERAL RAILWAY ACTS, 1830-1884.—A Collection of the Public General Acts for the Regulation of Railways, including the Companies, Lands, and Railways Clauses Consolidation Acts.
[*New Edition in preparation.*]

GUIDE TO THE LAW AND PRACTICE OF PETTY SESSIONS, with the Summary Jurisdiction Act, 1879. By EDWARD T. AYERS, Solicitor and late Assistant Clerk to Justices, Great Yarmouth. In cloth, 5s.

GUIDE TO THE LAW OF DISTRESS FOR RENT.—A Handbook for Landlords, Land Agents, Certified Bailiffs, and others. By R. T. HUNTER, Chief Clerk, County Court, Stockton-on-Tees. Eighth Edition. In cloth, 3s. 6d. net.

GUIDE TO THE PREPARATION OF BILLS OF COSTS (PRIDMORE'S), containing Practical Directions for Taxing Costs, and complete Precedents of Bills of Costs in all the Divisions, in conformity with the present Practice. Ninth Edition. By CHAS. W. SCOTT, one of the principal Clerks in the Chancery Taxing Office, Royal Courts of Justice. In cloth, 25s.

HANDBOOK OF THE LAW RELATING TO THE MANAGEMENT OF PARLIAMENTARY, COUNTY COUNCIL AND MUNICIPAL ELECTIONS.—A statement of the Law relating to the machinery of Elections. Second Edition. By H. STEPHEN, Barrister-at-Law. In cloth, 1s.

HANDBOOK TO THE ESTATE DUTY, comprising the Finance Acts, 1894 and 1896, with a comment thereon, an Appendix of Forms, Duties, &c., and an Index. By ALFRED W. SOWARD, of the Legacy and Succession Duty Office, Somerset House. Second Edition. In cloth, 5s. net.

SUPPLEMENT TO DITTO, comprising the matter of a Third Edition, 2s. 6d. net.

85 & 86, LONDON WALL, LONDON.

WATERLOW & SONS LIMITED, LAW PUBLISHERS.

LIST OF PUBLICATIONS—CONTINUED.

HANDBOOK FOR JUSTICES AT QUARTER SESSIONS.—A reliable Handbook for use of Justices on points of Procedure and Practice. In cloth 5s. nett; by post, 5s. 3d.

HANDBOOK TO THE SMALL HOLDINGS ACT, 1892, AND THE STATUTORY PROVISIONS INCORPORATED THEREIN.—By HORACE E. MILLER, LL.B., Barrister-at-Law. In cloth, 2s. 6d.

HANDBOOK TO THE STAMP DUTIES, containing the Text of the Stamp Act, 1891, and subsequent Revenue Acts affecting the Stamp Duties, with a complete Alphabetical Table of all documents liable to Stamp Duty. Tenth Edition. Post free, 2s. 6d.

HIRE-PURCHASE SYSTEM.—An Epitome of the Law relating to all matters connected with Hire-Purchase Agreements, and having special reference to the decision of the House of Lords in "Helby v. Matthews." By WILLIAM H. RUSSELL, Solicitor, Cheltenham. Second Edition, revised and enlarged, 3s. net.

INDIAN EXCHANGE TABLES.—By J. I. BERRY. In cloth, 21s., or with Supplement 25s.

INTEREST TABLES at the rate of two and three-quarters per cent. per annum on sums varying from £1 to £10,000 for all periods from 1 to 364 days, and from 1 to 12 months. Compiled by F. ALBAN BARRAUD, Solicitor. In cloth. 2s. 6d.

JOINT-STOCK COMPANIES' PRACTICAL GUIDE. — By HENRY HURRELL and CLARENDON G. HYDE, Barristers-at-Law. Invaluable to the Legal Profession, and to Secretaries, Directors, Promoters, and all other persons engaged in the formation or management of Joint-Stock Companies. Sixth Edition. In cloth, 5s.

LAW AND PROCEDURE OF SUMMARY JUDGMENT ON SPECIALLY INDORSED WRIT, under Order XIV. By C. CAVANAGH, of the Middle Temple, Barrister-at-Law. In cloth, 5s. net.

LAW AND PRACTICE OF REGISTRATION OF DEEDS IN THE COUNTY OF MIDDLESEX under the Middlesex Deeds Acts, containing the full texts of the Acts, Rules and Fee Order with Notes, Instructions, Precedents of Memorials, &c. By C. FORTESCUE-BRICKDALE, of Lincoln's Inn, Barrister-at-Law. In cloth, 3s. 6d.

THE LAW AND PRACTICE RELATING TO WORKMEN'S COMPENSATION AND EMPLOYERS' LIABILITY, being a Treatise on, and Practical Guide to the Workmen's Compensation Act, 1897, the Employers' Liability Act, 1880, Lord Campbell's Act, and the material sections of the Factory and Workshop Acts 1878 to 1895. By WILLIAM ELLIS HILL, M.A., Oxon, of the Inner Temple and Northern Circuit, Barrister-at-Law. In cloth, 6s. net.

LAW OF BUILDING, ENGINEERING, AND SHIP BUILDING CONTRACTS.—By ALFRED A. HUDSON, of the Inner Temple, Barrister-at-Law. Second Edition, in 2 vols., 50s.

85 & 86, LONDON WALL, LONDON.

WATERLOW & SONS LIMITED, LAW PUBLISHERS.

LIST OF PUBLICATIONS—CONTINUED.

LAW OF DIRECTORS AND OFFICERS OF JOINT STOCK COMPANIES, their Powers, Duties, and Liabilities. By HENRY HURRELL, of the Middle Temple, and CLARENDON G. HYDE, of the Middle Temple, Barristers-at-Law. Third Edition. In cloth, 6s.

LAW OF MERCANTILE AGENTS; OR, THE FACTORS ACT, 1889.—By M. MOLONEY, Barrister-at-Law. In cloth boards, post free, 1s. 7d.

LAW OF MERCHANT SHIPPING AND FREIGHT, with Tables of Cases, Forms, and Complete Index. By J. T. FOARD, of the Inner Temple, Barrister-at-Law. Royal 8vo. In half-calf, 21s.

LAW OF RATES AND CHARGES ON RAILWAYS AND CANALS.—Synopsis of the Railway and Canal Traffic Act, 1888. By PERCY GYE and THOS. WAGHORN, of the Inner Temple, Barristers-at-Law. In boards, 2s. In cloth, 3s.

LAW RELATING TO BETTING, TIME BARGAINS AND GAMING, including the Law relating to Stakeholders, Stewards, the Winners of Races; Stock Exchange Transactions; Lotteries, Gaming Houses, Betting Houses, &c. By GEORGE HERBERT STUTFIELD and HENRY S. CAUTLEY, Barristers-at-Law. Third Edition, revised and enlarged. In boards, 2s. 6d.

LAW RELATING TO CORRUPT PRACTICES AT PARLIAMENTARY, MUNICIPAL AND OTHER ELECTIONS, AND THE PRACTICE ON ELECTION PETITIONS, with an Appendix of Statutes, Rules and Forms. By MILES WALKER MATTINSON and STUART CUNNINGHAM MACASKIE, of Gray's Inn, Barristers-at-Law. Third Edition. In cloth, 10s.

LEGAL ADVICE to Engineers, Architects, Surveyors, Contractors, and Employers. By A. A. HUDSON, Barrister-at-Law. Post free, 1s. 7d.

LOCAL GOVERNMENT ACT, 1894.—Queen's Printers' Copy, with an exhaustive Index. By HORACE E. MILLER, LL.B., Barrister-at-Law. Post free, 2s. 3d.

MANUAL OF HYDROLOGY.—By N. BEARDMORE, C.E. In cloth, 24s.

MANUAL OF THEATRICAL LAW, containing Instructions for Licensing Theatres and Music Halls, and Chapters on the Law of Contracts between Actors and Managers, &c., &c. By CLARENCE HAMLYN, of the Middle Temple, Barrister-at-Law. In cloth, 5s.

MERCATOR'S BUSINESS AND SOCIAL TELEGRAPHIC POCKET CODE.—Compiled by a Practical Telegraphist. In cloth, 5s. net.

MERCHANDISE MARKS ACTS, 1887 and 1891, with Commentaries, Decided Cases, and references to Expert Evidence before Select Committees. By FRANK SAFFORD, of the Middle Temple, Barrister-at-Law. In cloth, 7s. 6d.

ORGANIZATION OF A SOLICITOR'S OFFICE, being a reprint (with revisions) of a Series of Articles contributed to the "Solicitors' Journal." By EDWARD F. TURNER, Solicitor. Third Edition. In cloth, 7s. 6d.

WATERLOW & SONS LIMITED, LAW PUBLISHERS.

LIST OF PUBLICATIONS—CONTINUED.

PARISH AND DISTRICT COUNCILS.—A Treatise on the Local Government Act, 1894, with the incorporated Provisions of other Acts, and the Orders and Circulars issued by the Local Government Board. By HORACE E. MILLER, LL.B., Barrister-at-Law. In cloth, 7s. 6d.

POSITION IN LAW OF WOMEN.—Showing how it differs from that of Men, and the effect of the Married Women's Property Act, 1882. By THOMAS BARRETT-LENNARD, of the Middle Temple, Barrister-at Law. In cloth, 6s.

PRACTICAL HINTS ON THE PREPARATION AND REGISTRATION of Joint-Stock Companies' Forms, with Precedents, Tables of Fees and Stamp Duties and an Index. Third Edition. Post free, 1s. 8d.

PRACTICAL SUGGESTIONS ON THE PREPARATION AND REGISTRATION OF DEEDS and other Documents at the various Public Offices, with Tables of Fees and an Index. Second Edition. Post free, 1s. 8d.

PRACTICE OF THE LAND REGISTRY UNDER THE TRANSFER OF LAND ACT, 1862, with such portions of the Rules as are now in force, General Instructions, Notes, Forms, and Precedents. By CHARLES FORTESCUE-BRICKDALE, B.A., of Lincoln's Inn, Barrister, Assisting Barrister to the Land Registry. In cloth, 3s. 6d.

PRACTITIONER'S PROBATE MANUAL.—Containing Instructions as to Procedure in obtaining Grants of Probate and Administration, with numerous Precedents of Forms, and full particulars as to Duties, Fees, &c., with a copious Index. Seventh Edition; with a Supplement showing the changes effected by the Land Transfer Act, 1897. In cloth, 6s. net.

RAILWAYS IN SCOTLAND, 1845-1873.—The General Acts for the Regulation of Railways in Scotland, including the Companies, Lands and Railways Clauses (Scotland) Acts, complete to the close of 1873, and a copious Index. A Supplement to the General Railway Acts. 12mo. In cloth 5s.

RELATIONSHIP OF LANDLORD AND TENANT.—By EDGAR FOA, Barrister-at-Law. Second Edition. In cloth, 25s.

RIGHTS AND DUTIES OF TRUSTEES IN BANKRUPTCY AND UNDER DEEDS OF ARRANGEMENT, containing Information as to Appointment and Security, Realizing and Distributing the Property of Estates. Administration of Estates and Rendering of Accounts to the Board of Trade by Trustees under Deeds of Arrangement; and a Time Table showing the time at which the principal Duties of Trustees are to be performed. By H. F. WREFORD. In cloth, 3s. 6d.

SCALES OF CONVEYANCING COSTS under the Solicitors' Remuneration Act, 1881, with a table of reported cases decided thereunder. In paper covers, 6d.

SHORT AND CONCISE PRECEDENTS OF THE CLAUSES MOST GENERALLY IN USE IN FARMING AGREEMENTS, with complete Forms of Agreements, Dissertations, and Full Notes, and a Table of Contents. By J. W. JEUDWINE, of Lincoln's Inn, Barrister-at-Law. In boards, 2s.

85 & 86, LONDON WALL, LONDON.

WATERLOW & SONS LIMITED, LAW PUBLISHERS.

LIST OF PUBLICATIONS—CONTINUED.

SOLICITORS' DIARY, ALMANAC, LEGAL DIGEST, AND DIRECTORY.—The Edition for 1898 is the 54th year of publication of this important Annual, which is now universally recognized as the most useful Legal Diary published. Prices— 3s. 6d., 5s., 6s., and 8s. 6d., according to diary space and binding.

SOLICITORS' POCKET BOOK.—In leather tuck, 2s. 6d.; roan wallet, 4s. 6d.; and Russia wallet, 7s. 6d.

STANDING ORDERS.—The Standing Orders of the Lords and Commons relative to Private Bills, with Appendix. Published at the close of each Session. In cloth, 5s.

SUMMARY JURISDICTION ACT, 1884, with Notes. A Supplement to Ayers' "Guide to the Law and Practice of Petty Sessions." By EDWARD T. AYERS, Solicitor. In boards, 2s.

SUMMARY JURISDICTION ACTS.—Tabular View of the Summary Jurisdiction of Justices as to Indictable Offences. By E. T. AYERS, Solicitor, Great Yarmouth. Printed on indestructible paper, 2s. net.

STOCK EXCHANGE ACCOUNTS, with an Appendix of Forms. By STEPHEN H. M. KILLIK. In cloth, 3s. 6d. net.

TABLE OF CORRUPT AND ILLEGAL PRACTICES WHICH VITIATE THE ELECTION. By M. W. MATTINSON and S. C. MACASKIE, Barristers-at-Law. On linen-lined card. Prices: 1 copy, 2d.; 50 copies, 6s.; 100 copies, 10s. May also be had printed on stout cardboard, 11 × 17, suitable for affixing to the walls of Committee Rooms. Price 6d. each.

TABLE OF FEES, CHARGES AND EXPENSES, AND COURT FEES, UNDER THE LAW OF DISTRESS AMENDMENT ACT, 1888.—Stamp Duty on Appraisement. Fees Chargeable by High Bailiffs, &c. By R. T. HUNTER, Chief Clerk, County Court, Stockton-on-Tees. Mounted on linen and folded in cloth case. 1s. 6d.

TABLES FOR THE IMMEDIATE CONVERSION OF PRODUCTS INTO INTEREST AT TWENTY-NINE RATES, viz.:—from one to eight per cent. inclusive, &c., &c. By A. CROSBIE and W. C. LAW. Second Edition. Improved and enlarged. In roan, 12s. 6d.

TRUSTEE ACT, 1893, including a Guide for Trustees to Investments. By ARTHUR LEE ELLIS, of Lincoln's Inn, Barrister-at-Law. Fifth Edition. In cloth, 6s.

WATERLOW'S BIJOU AND CONDENSED DIARIES.—Published in October. These elegant and useful Pocket Diaries are issued in two sizes, series Y, $3\frac{3}{4}$ × $2\frac{1}{2}$, series Z, $4\frac{1}{4}$ × $2\frac{3}{4}$, artistically printed in two colours on metallic paper, and can be had in paper covers at 1s. 6d. and 1s. 9d. each, and covered in silk at 2s. and 2s. 6d. each, or in roan, morocco, Russian or crocodile wallets, from 5s. each.

WATERLOW'S SCRIBBLING DIARY. Foolscap folio, 6 days on a page, interleaved, strong paper cover. 1s.; 3 days, 1s. 6d.; 2 days, $\frac{1}{2}$ bound cloth, 3s.; 1 day, 5s.

85 & 86, LONDON WALL, LONDON.

WATERLOW & SONS LIMITED, LAW PUBLISHERS.

PRACTICAL SUGGESTIONS
ON THE
PREPARATION
AND
REGISTRATION OF DEEDS
AND OTHER DOCUMENTS,
AT THE VARIOUS PUBLIC OFFICES,
WITH
TABLES OF FEES
AND AN
INDEX.

Second Edition.

POST FREE, ONE SHILLING AND EIGHT PENCE.

PRACTICAL HINTS
ON THE
PREPARATION AND REGISTRATION
OF
Joint Stock Companies' Forms,
WITH
Precedents, Table of Fees and Stamp Duties, and an Index.

Third Edition.

POST FREE, ONE SHILLING AND EIGHT PENCE.

---

85 & 86, LONDON WALL, LONDON.

WATERLOW & SONS LIMITED, LAW PUBLISHERS.

Handbook

TO THE

ESTATE DUTY

COMPRISING

The Finance Acts, 1894 and 1896,

WITH

A LENGTHY COMMENT THEREON,

An Appendix of Forms, Duties, and Fees on taking out Grants,

AND AN

INDEX.

SECOND EDITION.

BY

ALFRED W SOWARD,

Of the Legacy and Succession Duty Office, Somerset House.

In cloth. 5s. nett.

ALSO SUPPLEMENT TO THE ABOVE, comprising the matter of a THIRD EDITION.

Price 2s. 6d. nett.

Since the issue of the Second Edition of the Handbook, several important cases upon the Estate Duty, involving leading questions of principle, have been decided by the Courts, and a considerable number of changes of practice, consequent upon a better understanding of the Finance Acts, 1894 and 1896, have been made.

The arrangement of the Supplement is identical with that of the Second Edition of the Handbook, and a complete system of references enables the two books to be read together as one, with perfect ease.

Subscribers who already possess the Second Edition will, by purchasing the Supplement, have a COMPLETE TREATISE on the Law and Practice of the Estate Duty brought up to date.

New subscribers will kindly observe that the Second Edition and the Supplement together form the Third edition of the Handbook, and can be had bound in One Volume, Cloth, 7s. 6d. nett.

85 & 86, LONDON WALL, LONDON.

THE PRACTITIONER'S
PROBATE MANUAL,

CONTAINING

INSTRUCTIONS AS TO PROCEDURE IN OBTAINING GRANTS OF PROBATE AND ADMINISTRATION,

WITH

NUMEROUS PRECEDENTS OF FORMS,

AND

Full Particulars

As to the preparation of the Affidavits for Inland Revenue, required by the Finance Acts, 1894 and 1896,

WITH

SCALES OF DUTIES, FEES, COSTS, &c.

AND

A COPIOUS INDEX.

SEVENTH EDITION,
with a Supplement showing the changes effected by the Land Transfer Act, 1897.

In Cloth, 6s. net.

85 & 86, LONDON WALL, LONDON.

WATERLOW & SONS LIMITED, PARCHMENT DEALERS.

PRICE LIST OF PARCHMENT.

PLAIN.

When ordering, the full size of Skin should always be given.		ORDINARY QUALITY.		BEST SELECTED.	
		Each.	Per doz.	Each.	Per doz.
Depth. Width.		s. d.	s. d.	s. d.	s. d.
8½ × 13	. . .	0 4	3 6	0 5	4 6
10½ × 17	. . .	0 9	8 0	0 10	9 0
12 × 16	. . .	0 9	8 0	0 10	9 0
10½ × 21	. . .	0 10	9 6	1 0	11 0
13 × 17	. . .	0 10	9 6	1 0	11 0
15 × 20	. . .	1 0	11 6	1 2	12 6
16 × 21	. . .	1 2	13 0	1 4	14 6
17 × 22	. . .	1 4	15 0	1 6	16 6
18 × 24	. . .	1 6	17 6	1 8	19 0
19 × 25	. . .	1 10	20 0	2 0	22 0
22 × 27	. . .	2 0	22 0	2 3	25 0
23 × 28	. . .	2 3	25 0	2 6	28 0
26 × 29	. . .	2 6	28 6	2 9	31 0
27 × 30	. . .	2 9	31 6	3 0	34 0
28 × 32	. . .	3 3	35 0	3 6	37 0

Larger sizes can be supplied.

INDENTURES AND FOLLOWERS.

RED LINED AND RULED OR RED LINED ONLY.

When ordering, the full size of Skin should always be given.			ORDINARY QUALITY.		BEST SELECTED.	
			Each.	Per doz.	Each.	Per doz.
			s. d.	s. d.	s. d.	s. d.
OPEN INDENTURES AND FOLLOWERS		15 × 20	1 6	15 0	1 9	18 0
		19 × 25	2 6	26 0	2 9	28 0
		22 × 27	2 9	28 0	3 0	30 0
		26 × 29	3 0	30 0	3 6	36 0
		27 × 30	3 6	35 0	4 0	40 0
		23 × 28	2 6	26 0	3 0	30 0
		24 × 29	3 0	30 0	3 6	36 0
BOOKWAY INDENTURES AND FOLLOWERS	Sizes before folding.	10½ × 17	1 0	10 6	1 2	12 0
		11½ × 18	1 2	12 0	1 4	13 6
		13 × 17	1 3	14 0	1 6	16 0
		16 × 21	1 9	18 0	2 0	21 0
		18 × 24	2 3	22 0	2 6	25 0
		19 × 25	2 6	26 0	2 9	28 0
		22 × 27	2 9	28 0	3 0	30 0

85 & 86, LONDON WALL, LONDON.

WATERLOW & SONS LIMITED, PARCHMENT DEALERS.

PRICE LIST OF PARCHMENT—continued.

PROBATES,
WITH OR WITHOUT HEADING, BLACK LINED AND RULED.

When ordering, the full size of Skin should always be given.	ORDINARY QUALITY.		BEST SELECTED.	
	Each.	Per doz.	Each.	Per doz.
	s. d.	s. d.	s. d.	s. d.
12 × 16 .	1 0	10 6	1 2	12 0
15 × 20 .	1 6	15 0	1 9	18 0
18 × 24 .	2 0	22 0	2 3	25 0
22 × 27 .	2 9	28 0	3 0	30 0
26 × 29 .	3 0	30 0	3 6	36 0
28 × 32 .	3 9	40 0	4 0	45 0

BOOKWAY PROBATES,
HEADED, RULED AND ENDORSED.

	ORDINARY QUALITY.		BEST SELECTED.	
	Each.	Per doz.	Each.	Per doz.
	s. d.	s. d.	s. d.	s. d.
Fronts (headed and ruled) 10 × 12	0 10	9 0	1 0	10 6
Insides (ruled only) . 10 × 12	0 10	9 0	1 0	10 6
Backs (ruled and endorsed) 12 × 12	0 10	9 0	1 0	10 6
Do. (ruled only) 12 × 12	0 10	9 0	1 0	10 6
Fronts (headed and ruled) 10½ × 13½	1 0	10 6	1 2	12 0
Insides (ruled only) 10½ × 13½	1 0	10 6	1 2	12 0
Backs (ruled and endorsed) 10½ × 15	1 0	10 6	1 2	12 0
Do. (ruled only) 10½ × 15	1 0	10 6	1 2	12 0

For Paper Indentures, see next page.

85 & 86, LONDON WALL, LONDON.

WATERLOW & SONS LIMITED, PARCHMENT DEALERS.

PAPER INDENTURES, AGREEMENTS, &c.,

PRINTED, RULED AND RED-LINED, WHEN NOT OTHERWISE DESCRIBED.

	Large Post 4to.	Medium 4to.	F'cap.	Demy.	Royal.
	Per Quire.	Per Quire.	Per Quire.	Per Quire.	Per Quire.
	s. d.	s. d.	s. d.	s. d.	s. d.
This Indenture	2 6	3 0	3 6	4 6	6 6
Ditto (ruled grey feint only)	—	—	—	4 0	6 0
Memorandum of Agreement	2 6	3 0	3 6	4 6	6 6
Ditto (ruled grey feint only)	—	—	3 0	4 0	—
An Agreement	2 6	3 0	3 6	4 6	—
Ditto (ruled grey feint only)	—	—	—	4 0	—
Inventory and Valuation	—	—	3 6	4 6	—
Ditto (ruled grey feint only)	—	—	3 0	—	—
Inventory (ditto)	—	—	3 0	—	—
Valuation (ditto)	—	—	3 0	—	—
Know all Men	2 6	—	3 6	4 6	—
This is the Last Will and Testament (not red lined)	2 6	3 0	3 6	4 6	—
Followers	2 6	3 0	3 6	4 6	6 6

		s. d.
This is the Last Will and Testament, on Lined Brief . per quire		2 6
This Indenture, on ditto	„	2 6
Followers .	„	1 4
Specification, on F'cap ½ sheets, ruled grey feint	„	1 6
Followers on F'cap ½ sheets, ruled grey feint .	„	1 6

85 & 86, LONDON WALL, LONDON.

WATERLOW & SONS LIMITED, LAW STATIONERS.

LAW WRITING AND ENGROSSING.

WATERLOW & SONS LIMITED desire to call the attention of Solicitors to the facilities which they are enabled to offer for the execution of all classes of Legal Work.

A competent staff of law writers and clerks is constantly engaged at 85 and 86, London Wall, and at 49, Parliament Street, Westminster, and W. & S. Ld. are therefore enabled to execute any work entrusted to them with the utmost care and despatch.

DEEDS, etc., carefully and correctly engrossed.

STAMP DUTIES assessed and paid.

Charges for copying at per folio of 72 words   *s. d.*

Engrossments in Round-hand 0 2
Attested Copies and Fair Copies 0 1½
Wills, Abstracts, Parliamentary Briefs and Minutes of Evidence 0 2
Abstracting Titles and Fair Copy 0 6

Drafts, etc., received from the country can be engrossed or copied and sent by return post when required.

A Large Stock of STAMPED PARCHMENT AND PAPER of every description being kept ready for immediate use, any order can be executed without the slightest delay.

LAW LITHOGRAPHY.

The facilities afforded by WATERLOW & SONS LIMITED in this department having led to so great an increase of their business, they are enabled to retain a staff of hands capable of completing, in a few hours, any amount of work however large.

Briefs, Abstracts, Minutes of Evidence, Reports and Legal Documents, Builders' Quantities, Contracts, Specifications, etc., lithographed in good plain round-hand, with the greatest accuracy.

A Brief of 100 sheets can, if necessary, be lithographed in three or four hours. The evidence taken daily on Private Bills or Arbitration Cases may be neatly and correctly lithographed or printed *during the night*, and delivered to Counsel *before* 9 o'clock the *following morning.*

The following prices are intended as a guide to the charges for the ordinary description of Law Lithography; where a great number of copies of any document are required, special estimates will be given.

Abstracts copied Briefwise, 5 to 8 folios, per sheet on Superfine Paper :—
8 Copies . . . 6d. per sheet.
12 „ . . . 4½d. „
20 „ . . . 3½d. „
30 „ . . . 3d. „
50 „ . . . 2d. „
100 „ . . . 1½d. „
Per 100, after the first 100, 10s. 6d.

Drafts, 4 to 5 folios per page, on Superfine Laid Copy :—
10 Copies . . . 4d. per page.
20 „ . . . 2¼d. „
50 „ . . . 1½d. „
100 „ . . . 7s. 6d.
Per 100, after the first 100, 5s. 6d.
Deeds, Law Letters, and Forms Lithographed.

Where preferred, the charge will be made by the folio, in proportion to the above scale.

Minutes of Evidence and Parliamentary Documents are charged at 2d. per folio.

85 & 86, LONDON WALL, LONDON.

WATERLOW & SONS LIMITED, LAW STATIONERS.

LAW AGENCY DEPARTMENT.

WATERLOW & SONS LIMITED devote special attention to this department, and are in daily attendance at Somerset House and the various Public Offices.

PAPERS LODGED FOR PROBATE AND ADMINISTRATION.

ESTATE DUTY, LEGACY, SUCCESSION AND RESIDUARY ACCOUNTS PASSED, AND DUTIES PAID.

PROBATES AND LETTERS OF ADMINISTRATION LODGED FOR REGISTRATION AT COMPANIES' OFFICES.

BILLS OF SALE AND DEEDS OF ARRANGEMENT STAMPED AND FILED,

JOINT-STOCK COMPANIES REGISTERED, AND ANNUAL SUMMARIES, SPECIAL RESOLUTIONS, etc., FILED.

DEEDS LODGED FOR ENROLMENT AT THE CENTRAL OFFICE AND FOR REGISTRATION AT THE MIDDLESEX REGISTRY.

DEEDS LODGED FOR ADJUDICATION OF STAMP DUTY.

ADVERTISEMENTS INSERTED IN THE "LONDON GAZETTE" AND OTHER LONDON PAPERS.

SEARCHES MADE AT ANY OF THE PUBLIC OFFICES WITH THE GREATEST CARE AND EXPEDITION.

DEEDS AND OTHER INSTRUMENTS STAMPED,

a small charge being made for attendance and postage. The greatest care is exercised in the assessment of Stamp Duty payable on any document entrusted to the Company for stamping, but they incur no responsibility in the event of an improper assessment being made.

SOLICITORS AND PARLIAMENTARY COSTS SKILFULLY DRAWN FOR TAXATION, &c., AND ARREARS CAREFULLY WORKED UP FROM ANY AVAILABLE MATERIAL BY PRACTICAL AND EXPERIENCED COSTS DRAFTSMEN.

REGISTRATION OF COPYRIGHT BOOKS AND DRAWINGS.

REGISTRATION OF TRADE-MARKS AND OF DESIGNS.

APPLICATIONS FOR PATENTS CONDUCTED UNDER THE PERSONAL SUPERVISION OF A FELLOW OF THE INSTITUTE OF PATENT AGENTS.

85 & 86, LONDON WALL, LONDON.

www.ingramcontent.com/pod-product-compliance
Lightning Source LLC
Chambersburg PA
CBHW020840160426
43192CB00007B/728